The Value of Literature

The Value of Literature

Rafe McGregor

ROWMAN &
LITTLEFIELD
INTERNATIONAL
London • New York

Published by Rowman & Littlefield International, Ltd.
Unit A, Whitacre Mews, 26-34 Stannary Street, London SE11 4AB
www.rowmaninternational.com

Rowman & Littlefield International, Ltd. is an affiliate of Rowman & Littlefield
4501 Forbes Boulevard, Suite 200, Lanham, Maryland 20706, USA
With additional offices in Boulder, New York, Toronto (Canada), and London (UK)
www.rowman.com

British Library Cataloguing in Publication Information Available
A catalogue record for this book is available from the British Library

ISBN: HB 978-1-78348-923-7
ISBN: PB 978-1-78348-924-4

Library of Congress Cataloging-in-Publication Data

Names: McGregor, Rafe, author.
Title: The value of literature / Rafe McGregor.
Description: Lanham, Maryland : Rowman & Littlefield International, Ltd., [2016] | Includes biblio-
     graphical references and index.
Identifiers: LCCN 2016013455 (print) | LCCN 2016026367 (ebook) | ISBN 9781783489237 (cloth :
     alk. paper) | ISBN 9781783489251 (Electronic) | ISBN 9781783489244 (paperback)
Subjects: LCSH: Literature--Philosophy. | Values in literature. | Authors and readers. | Literature--
     Appreciation. | Literature--History and criticism.
Classification: LCC PN56.V28 .M44 2016 (print) | LCC PN56.V28 (ebook) | DDC 801/.3--dc23
LC record available at https://lccn.loc.gov/2016013455

♾ ™ The paper used in this publication meets the minimum requirements of American
National Standard for Information Sciences Permanence of Paper for Printed Library
Materials, ANSI/NISO Z39.48-1992.

Printed in the United States of America

Table of Contents

Preface   vii

Acknowledgements   xi

1   Literary Representation   1
    1. Carey's Kelly: Fact or Fiction?   1
    2. Types of Value   6
    3. Literature, Fiction, and Art   11
    4. Values of Literature   13
    5. Autonomy versus Heteronomy   20
    Notes   25

2   Literary Education   29
    6. Art in Three Dimensions   29
    7. Clarificationism and Literary Realism   33
    8. Literature as Moral Philosophy   37
    9. Ethical Criticism and Moral Improvement   41
    Notes   44

3   Poetic Thickness   47
    10. Form and Content   47
    11. Resonant Meaning   50
    12. Poetic Thickness   53
    13. Objections   58
    Notes   65

4   Narrative Thickness   69
    14. Literary Narratives   69
    15. Narrative Thickness   72
    16. Work Identity   78

  17. Didactic Thinness?   82
  Notes   89

5   Literary Thickness   93
  18. Literary Thickness (I)   93
  19. Reference and Truth   95
  20. Aboutness   104
  Notes   108

6   Literary Value   111
  21. Literary Thickness (II)   111
  22. Experiential Value   117
  23. Thickness and Value   126
  24. The Argument from Literary Thickness   129
  Notes   130

7   Literary Autonomy   133
  25. Vice and Mimesis   133
  26. Literature in Two Dimensions   140
  27. Moral Merits and Empirical Evidence   142
  28. Literary Humanism   147
  Notes   149

Bibliography   151

Index   157

About the Author   161

Preface

This book is a defence of the value of literature. I shall argue that literature has value for art, for culture, and for humanity—in short, that it matters. Unlike most contemporary defenders of literary value, my strategy does not involve arguing that literature is good as a means to one of the various ends that matter to human beings. I do not think that literature necessarily makes us cleverer, more sensitive, more virtuous, more creative, or just generally better people. Nor do I think that there is a necessary relation between literature and edification, clarification, cultural critique, catharsis, or therapy. The oral and written traditions of literature that developed across the globe in the last three thousand years have clearly provided all these goods and been good for human beings in all of these ways, but the relations are contingent rather than necessary. As such, rather than offer an argument that forges a tenuous link between literature and truth, or literature and virtue, or literature and the sacred, I shall analyse the non-derivative, *sui generic* value characteristic of literature and attempt to show why that matters as an end in itself.

The claim that there is a distinctively literary value—like the claim that there is a distinctly artistic value—is not controversial. What is controversial is the nature of the distinctively literary value, which seems to resist quantification, definition, and even articulation. In other words, most people agree that literature is valuable in some special way, but most people cannot delineate that way with any certainty. James Joyce captures the puzzling nature of this apparent paradox perfectly in a delightful passage in the "Ithaca" episode of *Ulysses*. Sitting in his kitchen with Stephen Dedalus in the early hours of the morning, Leopold Bloom reflects on the value of Shakespeare's oeuvre. He knows that Shakespeare matters, that his works belong to the category of literary rather than popular fiction, and conceives—in his prosaic and eminently sensible manner—of this significance in terms of instruction. Yet

Bloom finds that despite his best efforts, he has failed to apply any of the alleged lessons to his own life. Shakespeare has, in practical terms, proved entirely useless. I described this passage as "delightful", which it is, and this delight—albeit revealed as a peculiarly and particularly intellectual type of delight—is indeed all that I shall have to offer for literary value. I shall maintain that the pleasure which characterises the literary experience is the source of literature's *sui generic* value and that literature therefore does not serve much of a purpose at all. The only practical consequence of reading about Bloom's attempts to solve the puzzle of literary value—to which, in typically literary fashion, no explicit answer is offered—is the likelihood that one will persevere through all 309 questions of "Ithaca". All *Ulysses* seems to do is make us want to read more—more of the novel, more Joyce, more literature. *Ulysses* achieves this modest result by providing a distinctive kind of pleasure and I shall argue that this pleasure alone accounts for why literature matters.

My argument for the *sui generic* value of literature will draw on the ancient distinction between literary form and literary content and will offer a fresh perspective on the relationship between the two, which I call *literary thickness*. I shall argue that the satisfaction afforded by a literary work is realised by means of literary thickness, understood as a demand the reader makes of that work rather than a property he or she discovers therein. The demand for literary thickness reconciles two conflicting axes of reader interest in literary works—the formal interest in the mode of representation and the substantive interest in the subject of representation—and is characteristic of literary appreciation, the evaluation of literature *qua* literature. I shall then argue for a necessary relation between literary thickness and non-derivative or final value and thus for the claim that literature is autonomous. Chapter 1 delineates the different types of value—derivative, non-derivative, relational, and non-relational—and the way in which the different types of value have been associated with literature. In chapter 2, I present the two most compelling objections to my argument, from Noël Carroll and Martha Nussbaum respectively.

My argument then proceeds as follows:

1. In literary works both the substantive and formal axes are salient.
2. If both the substantive and formal axes are salient, then literary appreciation is characterised by literary thickness—the demand for form-content inseparability.
3. Therefore the appreciation of literary works is characterised by literary thickness.
4. Literary value is the value of the experience of literary appreciation.
5. If the experience of literary appreciation is characterised by literary thickness, then literary value is final.

6. Therefore literary value is final.

Number (1) is based on the arguments for poetic thickness in chapter 3, narrative thickness in chapter 4, and literary thickness in chapter 5. Drawing on chapter 5, I argue for (2) and (3) by recourse to the principle of functionality in the first part of chapter 6. I demonstrate (4) in the second part of chapter 6. The third part of chapter 6 establishes the relations between instrumental value and the substantive axis on the one hand and final value and the formal axis/literary thickness on the other—that is, (5). Drawing on chapter 5 once again, I show that the formal axis is not characteristic of literary appreciation and conclude with (6) in the fourth and final part of chapter 6. In the terms set out in chapter 1, the argument establishes the autonomy of literature: *The value of a work of literature* qua *literature is the value of the experience afforded by the work. And the experience afforded by the work is valuable to the degree that this experience is finally valuable—that is, produces literary satisfaction.* I respond to the objections from both Carroll and Nussbaum in chapter 7, demonstrating why my account of literary value is rationally more justifiable than either of theirs. In this way, I hope to complete the project that A. C. Bradley began in 1901, in his "Poetry for Poetry's Sake" lecture, which made an original but unsuccessful attempt to link the intimate relation between form and content in poetry to the *sui generic* value of poetry. I aim, first, to succeed where Bradley failed, and second, to extend his thesis beyond poetic literature to the art form of literature. In so doing, I shall show why literature matters despite being useless and why the formal salience of the literary use of language does not run counter to the humanist intuition that literature is firmly rooted in the real.

Acknowledgements

It would be impossible to spend as long at the University of York as I did, with the interests I have, without being influenced by Peter Lamarque and Derek Attridge. I was fortunate enough to work with the former for the better part of five years and unfortunate enough never to have met the latter, but I make no apologies for my intellectual debt to both. I am also grateful to two people without whose encouragement I would not have finished this book and who had no reason to assist me aside from their generosity of spirit, Tzachi Zamir and John Gibson.

Two chapters (3 and 4) and two sections (§1 and §21) draw on three previously published papers. I am grateful to the publishers for permission to reproduce them here.

1. "Poetic Thickness," *British Journal of Aesthetics 54*, no. 1 (2014), 49–64.
2. "Literary Thickness," *British Journal of Aesthetics 55*, no. 3 (2015), 343–60.
3. "Narrative Thickness," *Estetika: The Central European Journal of Aesthetics 52*, no. 1 (2015), 3–22.

Finally, I am grateful to Sarah Campbell and two anonymous referees at Rowman & Littlefield International for their invaluable assistance.

Chapter One

Literary Representation

The purpose of this chapter is to classify my humanist theory of literary value in two respects: as occupying the space between literary aesthetics and literary theory with regard to academic discipline and within the tradition of autonomy rather than heteronomy with regard to the history of art criticism and appreciation. I present an example of literary appreciation in §1, answering the question of whether Peter Carey's *True History of the Kelly Gang* should be read as fact or fiction. Section §2 discusses philosophical value theory, distinguishing between intrinsic and extrinsic value on the one hand and final and instrumental value on the other. In §3 I explain the assumptions I shall make concerning the relations between fiction and literature, and literature and art. Section §4 draws the previous two sections together, distinguishing the characteristically literary value from the various other values associated with literature. I locate my position with respect to the various autonomous and heteronomous approaches to literary value in §5.

1. CAREY'S KELLY: FACT OR FICTION?

Peter Carey's *True History of the Kelly Gang* is a book about Ned Kelly, Australia's most famous outlaw. Notwithstanding the local subject matter, it is an international bestseller and won Carey his second Booker Prize. The popular and critical success appears to be—at least partly—attributable to the peculiar relation between fact and fiction charted by the work, a relation that prompts the question of how one should read it. Is *True History of the Kelly Gang* valuable as fact, as fiction, as both fact and fiction, or in some other way altogether? Carey was apparently dismayed at the early responses to the book, noting that they were "as much as history as literature. But there have

1

been some more sophisticated readings of it".[1] Paul Eggert explains this initial mismatch between authorial intention and reader response:

> Unsophisticated readers are liable to believe that Carey's novel is a real auto-biography, printed from a manuscript actually written by Ned Kelly. The first edition bears many factitious markers of historical authenticity: imitation quar-ter-bound leather with the spine untitled as if it were an individually bound manuscript; sections individually guillotined rather than as a whole quire, creating something like a rough, deckled-edge finish; and speckled endpapers and textured paper-stock gesturing at the handmade. The novel itself is di-vided, not into chapters, but into what purports to be a series of numbered manuscript parcels.[2]

The most informed reason for confusing literature with autobiography is not the form of Carey's work, however, but its content. Aside from present-ing numerous historical events, and weaving history into literature, Carey has selected in Kelly precisely the man who might have written the autobiogra-phy the reader appears to hold. Despite his lack of education—or perhaps because of it—Kelly was very much aware of the power of the press, and visited the office of the *Ovens and Murray Advertiser* to complain about his portrayal in the newspaper prior to being outlawed. He dictated the *Cameron Letter*, a seventeen-page, three-and-a-half-thousand-word letter vindicating his actions to Joe Byrne (the most literate member of his gang) before the Euroa bank robbery in December 1878. This was sent to Donald Cameron, a member of the Australian Legislative Assembly who had publicly criticised the police handling of the hunt for Kelly. Prior to the raid on Jerilderie in February 1879, Kelly dictated a fifty-six-page, seven-and-a-half-thousand-word letter to Byrne, and attempted to have the *Jerilderie Letter* printed and published at gunpoint. Neither of the letters reached the public due to con-cerns that they might result in popular support for Kelly's cause—and an insurrection may indeed have been his intention. Finally, Kelly dictated a letter to the Governor of Victoria six days before his execution, expressing his regret that he had been unable to make a fuller statement of his life and cause. Carey has seized the opportunity missed by Kelly and produced a manuscript written under the premise of Kelly justifying his life to the daughter he has never met.

The daughter and her mother, Mary Hearn, are both fictional, but the history that emerges is an imaginative reconstruction of the life of a compas-sionate man doomed by social, economic—and possibly biological—influ-ences to lead a life of violence, a course which he appears to have made every attempt to avoid. I cannot offer a précis of the narrative, or a detailed account of Kelly as a character in *True History of the Kelly Gang*, but the portrayal of his personality is essential to understanding the work—*qua* auto-biography or *qua* literature—and the following extract is representative:

I'm sure you know that I have spilled human blood when there were no other choice at that time I were no more guilty than a soldier in a war. But if there was a law against the murder of a beast I would plead guilty and you would be correct to put the black cap on your head for I killed my little heifer badly and am sorry for it still. By the time she fell her neck was a sea of laceration I will never forget the terror in her eyes.[3]

Kelly's sensitivity to suffering and sense of responsibility are both conspicuous, extending even to an animal he is required to slaughter for food, and stand in stark contrast to his persona as a homicidal maniac following the murders at Stringybark Creek in October 1878. The treatment of his life in the narrative is stated succinctly and accurately by Mary in her comment on Kelly's *Cameron Letter*: "she said there were not a soul alive who could read these words and blame me as the papers did".[4]

Bringing a historical rather than literary interest to *True History of the Kelly Gang* is an easy error to make, but it remains an error because *qua* autobiography, the work is unsatisfying. In fact, it fails at the first hurdle: the premise of the work, the thread that links the parcels together, is Kelly's relationship with Mary and his desire to communicate with their daughter— but both Mary and the daughter are Carey's inventions. The novel takes the real Kelly as its subject, but even if the narrative in the first seven parcels is entirely accurate, the appearance of Mary in the eighth marks an unambiguous parting with history. Yet Kelly's meeting with Mary, their conception of a child, and the addressing of the parcels as a letter to that child are crucial to both the understanding and the appreciation of the novel. I imagine that those *unsophisticated* readers who took a historical interest in the work and were inspired to research Kelly further would have been disappointed to discover that it contained such serious flaws *qua* autobiography.

I mentioned that Carey binds fact and fiction together in his work, and the method is employed to the extent that he actually appropriates sentences from the *Jerilderie Letter*. The following two passages describe the same incident; the first is written by Kelly, the second by Carey:

1. Mrs McCormack, "turned on me . . . I did not say much to the woman as my Mother was present but that same day me and my uncle was cutting calves Gould wrapped up a note and a pair of the calves testicles and gave them to me to give them to Mrs Mc Cormack. . . . consequently Mc Cormack said he would summons me . . . . He said I was a liar & he could welt me or any of my breed I was about 14 years of age but accepted the challenge And dismounting when Mrs Mc Cormack struck my horse in the flank with a bullock's shin it jumped forward And my fist came in collision with McCormack's nose And caused him to loose [*sic*] his equilibrium and fall postrate". (McDermott 2001, 3–6)[5]

2. Then Mrs McCormick came rushing down the steps wielding a bullock's shinbone she must of picked up on the way. Mr McCormick
   followed behind her shouting out I were despised everyone in the
   district he said I were a coward and were hiding behind my mother's
   skirts. At this insult I dismounted. Mrs McCormick then struck my
   horse on the flank with her impertinent weapon and the horse jumped
   forward and as I were holding the rein it caused my fist to come into
   collision with McCormick's nose and he lost his equilibrium and fell
   prostrate. Tying up my horse to finish the battle I seen Cons Hall
   descend from the pub like a glistening old spider gliding down from
   the centre of its web.[6]

The first point to note is that although Carey writes in a vernacular similar
to that which Kelly used, he does not replicate Kelly's diction exactly. The
narrator of the parcels in *True History of the Kelly Gang* writes in a manner
that is close enough to Kelly's actual style to maintain verisimilitude while
making effective use of tropes and an understated expression of emotion. The
idiosyncratic morphology and poor syntax are initially quite jarring: single-
sentence paragraphs are composed of staccato phrases and clauses and there
are no quotation marks to indicate direct speech. The mode of presentation
engenders the experience of all thirteen parcels as something of an extended
interior monologue, in spite of the numerous conversations that occur. Once
one is attuned to the unruly grammar, however, the loss of clarity becomes a
small price to pay for the lyrical quality of the prose, which at times resem-
bles the finest stream of consciousness writing and creates the desire for
recital rather than reading. As a literary device, the narration of the novel is
an essential part of the invitation to regard Kelly with sympathy as well as
the force behind the forward motion of the plot.

The second point to note is the implausibility of this incident in both
accounts. Despite Kelly's claim about his age, he was probably sixteen when
the clash with McCormick occurred—already physically capable and no
stranger to violence. McCormick's insult is a dire one as the opinion of many
of Kelly's associates is that he has erotic feelings for his mother.[7] There is no
question that he intends to administer a beating to McCormick and the description of Kelly's fist "accidentally" hitting McCormick's nose so hard that
he knocks him down is unconvincing to the extent that—assuming this defence—the consequent custodial sentence comes as no surprise.

Even if this particular incident did occur exactly as recorded in both of the
above accounts, Carey casts doubt as to the reliability of Kelly's narration
throughout the novel: his first shooting involves an unlikely suicidal charge
by Bill Frost which leaves Kelly no choice but to shoot him; Mary is so
certain of Kelly's homicidal temper that she drugs him to prevent him from
murdering the father of her son; at Stringybark Creek, a reluctant and regret-

ful Kelly single-handedly kills three policemen while his three compatriots kill none. When Kelly is outlawed the conflict escalates, and Carey establishes a subtle distance between reader and narrator such that one realises that one is no longer privy to Kelly's innermost thoughts, which in turn calls into question whether one ever was. His letter threatening to kill any resident of Victoria who assists the police in any way is shocking in both its violence and its hubris. Kelly concludes: "I DO NOT WISH TO GIVE THE ORDER FULL FORCE WITHOUT GIVING TIMELY WARNING BUT I AM A WIDOW'S SON OUTLAWED AND MUST BE OBEYED".[8] This is no longer the voice of the courageous but doomed victim of circumstances with whom one thinks one is familiar. The whole insurrection, which is such an important part of Kelly's life, is described in very little detail, except for the motive, to force the authorities to release his mother from prison. Again, there is a darkness and an arrogance that has not previously been disclosed— which is, of course, precisely what one would expect in a man who is attempting to justify his actions to a daughter whom he is likely never to meet.

True History of the Kelly Gang is thus not a straightforward sympathetic account, a history told from Kelly's point of view. Carey's work is instead Kelly's story: it is history in a literal sense; *his story*, told by him. The first clue to the complexity of the novel is in the title, the missing definite article before "true". This could reflect a grammatical error on the part of the uneducated narrator, but has a deeper significance in drawing attention to the first two words of the title. On a popular understanding, *true history* is redundant because if a history is not factual, then it is fictional and fails to qualify as history. On the other hand, Eggert quotes Carey's claim to have deliberately selected the title for the purpose of signalling that the work is *not* a history— the idea being that contemporary professional historians are sceptical about the transparency of history.[9] Whichever understanding one has of *true history*, that it protests too much or that it is oxymoronic, the title serves to direct attention to the history-in-the-novel and the function the history-in-the-novel serves.

The form selected by Carey—the parcels, with their detailed notes, sandwiched between historical writing and the curious description of Kelly's death—interrupts the flow of Kelly's vernacular and disrupts the imaginative engagement with the novel, drawing attention in an explicit and overt manner to the purported historical character of the work. This effect is exacerbated at further points in the narrative: Kelly slips into the third person when he describes his apprenticeship to Harry Power and the related discovery of his mother's betrayal; he also describes events where he acknowledges his absence. Most telling, however, are the reproduction of newspaper articles with annotations, first by Mary and then by Kelly himself. One reads the newspaper articles with notes about their inaccuracy and is at the same time aware that the novel itself simultaneously represents and misrepresents historical events. The introduction to the eighth parcel casts a further doubt as to narrative veracity: "*Pages describing the shooting of Constable Fitzpatrick are much revised by a second hand reliably presumed to be that of Joe Byrne.*"[10] Finally, there is Kelly's own commentary on the relation between history and truth, which includes passages such as the following: "In the hut at Faithfull's Creek I seen proof that if a man could tell his true history to Australians he might be believed it is the clearest sight I ever seen and soon Joe seen it too".[11]

I am not suggesting that *True History of the Kelly Gang* is not a sympathetic account of Kelly's life. It is, and despite the suggestions that he is not above omission or deception, there is no doubt that one comes to understand the situation in which Kelly and other poor immigrants—many of whom were either deported from the United Kingdom or the descendants of deportees—found themselves. For many Irish immigrants, like the Kellys, the one-sided conflict between landlords and peasants at home was simply relocated and reproduced in the colonial conflict between squatters and selectors. Carey's novel achieves something more than showing Kelly's side of the story, however: it presents *his story*, suggests that while a great deal of that story is probably true, some of it is probably not, and leaves the reader to pass his or her own judgement. To read the work *qua* literature is to accept Carey's explicit invitation to attend to the history-in-the-novel and the function the combination of formal devices and historical content serves within this telling of Kelly's story as his story. This is to make what I shall call a demand for *literary thickness* of the novel, to appreciate the value of not only the historical people, places, and events represented, but also how they are portrayed, why they are portrayed in that way, and their significance beyond the immediate context of Victorian Australia.

2. TYPES OF VALUE

To attribute value to an entity is to judge that the entity counts in some way, that it is worth something. The most basic distinction in value is between *instrumental values* and *non-instrumental values*. Money is typically valued for its purchasing power rather than for the values of the metal coins or paper notes themselves and is therefore instrumentally valuable—that is, valuable as an instrument for purchasing goods and services. Analgesic pills are similarly typically valued as an instrument for relieving pain rather than for their taste. Instrumental value is often called *extrinsic value* because the value attributed to the entity (currency note, pill) is attributed in virtue of something (purchasing power, pain relief) to which the entity is related, as opposed to the entity itself. Another way to characterise instrumental value is that it is derivative, because the values of currency notes and analgesic pills to which I have alluded are derived from their value in purchasing and pain-relieving respectively. For obvious reasons, instrumental value is further characterised as the entity having value "for the sake of" (something else) and being valuable as a means (rather than an end).

If the above values are derivative, then it seems that there is a category of values—or perhaps just one value—which is not derivative. In the case of money, the chain between the currency note and non-derivative value may be long and complex, but in the case of the analgesic pill it might be short: a derivative value of the pill is its value in removing pain and if the reduction of pain is considered pleasurable, then the pleasure produced by the pill could be considered non-derivatively valuable. One does not appear to have to seek something else from which pleasure derives its value, to ask why pleasure is good or desirable; the goodness and desirability are self-evident—part of the meaning of the concept itself. Non-derivative, non-instrumental value is also called *intrinsic value* because the value of, for example, pleasure with which I am concerned is not related to something outside it, but to the pleasure itself, the experience of pleasure by an individual. The view that the most obvious intrinsic good is pleasure (and the most obvious intrinsic evil, pain) is widely held. Pleasure is also characterised as having value *for its own sake* or being valuable (as an end) in itself.

I shall therefore accept that there are at least two categories of value:

1. instrumental, derivative, or extrinsic value; value for the sake of (something else) or as a means (to an end); and
2. non-instrumental, non-derivative, or intrinsic value; value for its own sake or (as an end) in itself.

Despite this dual categorisation, an entity can be valuable both instrumentally and non-instrumentally simultaneously and instrumental values are both numerous and difficult—if not impossible—to catalogue comprehensively. A pound coin is valuable as a pound sterling in the United Kingdom (instrumentally), but it could also be valued as a piece of nickel brass alloy (either instrumentally or non-instrumentally, dependent upon the reason the alloy is valued) or as a prop to stop a table from rocking (instrumentally); if the coin were a rare issue, a collector might take pleasure in its possession (non-instrumental value) and a careless collector with a rocking table could regard it as being valuable in all these ways at the same time. Similarly, even if pleasure is uncontroversially non-instrumental, the pleasure of pain-relief might be instrumentally valuable in, for example, allowing one to focus on one's work and thereby meet a deadline.

There seems to be a difference between the pleasure of the coin collector and the value of the coin as nickel brass alloy, even though both could be regarded as belonging to the category of non-instrumental value. The value of the coin as alloy appears to have a more direct relation to the coin itself than the value of the pleasure experienced by the collector. The former is a value of the coin regardless of whether or not it has the purchasing power of a pound sterling or can be exchanged for currency which has equivalent purchasing power; the latter is dependent upon not only a response, but a response from an individual who can appreciate the particular features of the coin that produce the pleasure of the experience. The value of the coin to the collector may not be derivative, but it is related to something outside itself—that is, the collector, in a way which the value of the alloy is not.

Christine Korsgaard addresses this concern, questioning the naïve dichotomy between instrumental and non-instrumental value and proposing two distinctions rather than two categories of value:

> One is the distinction between things valued for their own sakes and things valued for the sake of something else—between ends and means, or final and instrumental goods. The other is the distinction between things which have their value in themselves and things which derive their value from some other source: intrinsically good things versus extrinsically good things. [12]

Dale Dorsey summarises Korsgaard's taxonomy as follows:

> *Final value:* φ is finally valuable if and only if it is valuable as an end.
> *Instrumental Value:* φ is instrumentally valuable if and only if it is valuable as a means.
> *Intrinsic Value:* φ is intrinsically valuable if and only if it is valuable in a way that supervenes only on the intrinsic properties of φ.
> *Extrinsic Value:* φ is extrinsically valuable if and only if it is valuable in a way that supervenes—at least to some extent—on the extrinsic properties of φ. [13]

Dorsey's summary introduces *properties* to the discussion of values. The values attributed to an entity are generally accepted to be supervenient on non-evaluative properties of that entity such that there cannot be a change in the evaluative properties of the object without a change in the non-evaluative properties.

Thomas Magnell identifies an ontological difference between intrinsic and extrinsic properties as follows:

1. Intrinsic properties: the properties that an entity possesses no matter what properties other entities possess.
2. Extrinsic properties: the properties that an entity possesses in relation to other entities.

He uses the example of a desk that is six feet in width. The property of being six feet wide is an intrinsic property, but the property of being a wide desk is extrinsic because it is dependent upon the lengths of other desks, which are standardly less than six feet in width. Magnell maintains that extrinsic properties are not identical with relational properties, but form a subclass thereof because of the relations that exist between the parts of a whole, which are both relational and intrinsic.[14]

My inquiry into literary value will consider the value of works of literature as a whole rather than parts thereof, however, and I shall follow Wlodek Rabinowicz and Toni Rønnow-Rasmussen in employing "the expression 'relational property' as short for 'externally relational property' (i.e., a property that an object has in virtue of its relation to something that is not one of its parts)".[15] I shall thus accept the identity of *non-relational* and *intrinsic* properties on the one hand and *relational* and *extrinsic* properties on the other, defining Korsgaard's second distinction as follows:

> *INTRINSIC VALUE*: ϕ is intrinsically valuable if and only if it is valuable in a way that supervenes only on the non-relational properties of ϕ.
>
> *EXTRINSIC VALUE*: ϕ is extrinsically valuable if and only if it is valuable in a way that supervenes—at least to some extent—on the relational properties of ϕ.

If one removes the terms "extrinsic" and "intrinsic" from my initial dichotomy above, one is left with:

1. instrumental or derivative value; value for the sake of (something else) or as a means (to an end); and
2. non-instrumental or non-derivative value; value for its own sake or (as an end) in itself.

Due to its characterisation as non-derivative, category (2) is also described as *final* or *telic* value. There is a debate between *monists*, who claim that there is only one non-derivative value, and *pluralists*, who claim that there is more than one non-derivative value. The existence of non-derivative value is uncontroversial, but its nature has proved notoriously difficult to specify. The standard solution—offered by Plato in *Protagoras*—is to elucidate this value in terms of pleasure, such that "we are no longer able to say 'by pleasure,'—for it has taken on its other name, 'the good' instead of 'pleasure'".[16] Plato associated non-derivative goodness with pleasure and non-derivative badness with pain, but did not hold a monistic view of value. Monists, such as Epicurus and John Stuart Mill, have tended to associate non-derivative value with either the absence of pain or with pleasure. Epicurus and Mill have therefore been described as hedonists, but the label belies the sophistication of their respective positions. Pluralists attribute non-derivative value to other forms of goodness—like truth and virtue—but both monists and pluralists recognise pleasure as non-derivatively valuable.

There is further debate about what types of entity—objects, properties, states of affairs, or facts—can be bearers of non-derivative value. I do not wish to contribute to this debate, but I shall accept that works of literature can be bearers of non-derivative value. Rabinowicz and Rønnow-Rasmussen identify ends as *facts* rather than *objects* and specify their concern, which is with objects, as value for its own sake rather than value as an end.[17] A literary work, and—in the institutional theory of literature I endorse in §3 below—the text upon which the work is based, is more accurately described as an object than a fact, so I shall follow Rabinowicz and Rønnow-Rasmussen in discounting value as an end in itself from category (2). Given my definition of intrinsic value above, value for its own sake is ambiguous because it could also be construed in terms of non-relational value. In order to be precise, I shall therefore characterise Korsgaard's first distinction in terms of derivation:

> *FINAL VALUE*: φ is finally valuable if and only if it is valuable in a way that is non-derivative.
> *INSTRUMENTAL VALUE*: φ is instrumentally valuable if and only if it is valuable in a way that is derivative.

Due to the frequency with which "intrinsic" is employed as a synonym for "final" when value is discussed, I shall use the terms "non-relational" and "relational" instead of "intrinsic" and "extrinsic" where possible—that is, employ the following pair of distinctions: "final" versus "instrumental" value on the one hand and "non-relational" versus "relational" value on the other.

The relation between these two distinctions is far from clear. G. E. Moore, for example, claims that final value supervenes on non-relational properties, whereas Korsgaard maintains that final value supervenes on both non-relational and relational properties, and Dorsey argues that instrumental value can be a form of both relational and non-relational value.[18] With regard to literature, I am a contextualist and hold that historical and cultural properties—both of which are relational—are relevant to work identity (which I discuss in §16 in chapter 4) and the value of a work *qua* literature (which I discuss in §4 below). Jerrold Levinson makes a convincing case for contextualism in his discussion of the ontology of a work of music, the consequence of which for literary art is that two identical texts could be different works if their production conditions differed.[19] Jorge Luis Borges parodies an extreme version of this view in his short story, "Pierre Menard, Author of the *Quixote*", where he contrasts the literary value of *Don Quixote* as written by Miguel de Cervantes with *Don Quixote* as written by Pierre Menard (a fictional contemporary author). I shall not attempt to explain the relation between the two distinctions, but I shall accept that final value neither supervenes upon non-relational properties alone nor upon relational properties alone.

3. LITERATURE, FICTION, AND ART

Peter Lamarque and Stein Haugom Olsen advance the following conception of fiction: *"the fictive dimension of stories (or narratives) is explicable only in terms of a rule-governed practice, central to which are a certain mode of utterance (fictive utterance) and a certain complex of attitudes (the fictive stance)"*.[20] To create a work of fiction in an oral or written tradition is to make a fictive utterance, and to experience that work as a work of fiction is to adopt the fictive stance. Just as a fictive work is conceived of as a fictive utterance, so a literary work is identified on the basis of the intention of the author—specifically *"the intention to invoke a literary response"*. Similarly, to read a text *as* literature is to adopt the literary stance: "Adopting the literary stance towards a text is to identify it as a literary work and apprehend it in accordance with the conventions of the literary practice. The mode of apprehension which the practice defines is one of *appreciation*".[21] To appreciate a work is to recognise its value; specifically, to grasp the literary value of a literary work. The concepts of fiction and literature are clearly not coextensive, however, as there are works of fiction that are not works of literature and works of literature that are not works of fiction.

In the former case, this may be because the work belongs to another art form, for example a cinematic work, such as Christopher Nolan's *Memento*; or because the work does not aspire to a distinctively literary kind of attention—for example, Agatha Christie's *And Then There Were None*. The category of literary works that are not fictional includes historical, documentary, and philosophical works—such as William H. Prescott's *History of the Conquest of Peru*, George Orwell's *Homage to Catalonia*, and Friedrich Nietzsche's *Thus Spoke Zarathustra, A Book for All and None*—which are judged to have literary value.[22] "Fiction" is a descriptive concept and "literature" an evaluative one: *Ulysses* and *And Then There Were None* are both fictional works; only *Ulysses* is a literary work—that is, both invites and rewards literary attention.

Despite the significance of the differences between fiction and literature, and the historical problems in the relationship to which Lamarque and Olsen allude, they hold that "literature for the most part consists of stories that are either invented by the author or are mythical or legendary in character".[23] Derek Attridge indicates his broad agreement with this classification when he claims that while *Middlemarch* can be read as fiction but not literature, it is "unlikely" that it could be read as literature but not fiction.[24] I shall regard the literary stance as characteristically incorporating the fictive stance, accepting Olsen's claim that "the assumption that literature is invention and imagination, 'story' and not 'history', is central to literary practice", employing "literature" to refer to this inventive, imaginative subcategory of works.[25]

Literature as described above is an art form and to adopt the literary stance to a text is to experience the text as a work of art. I do not wish to commit to a definition of art, but the characterisations of fiction and literature I have accepted—particularly the references to "practices" and "conventions"—are compatible with the institutional theory of art. George Dickie is the leading proponent of this theory and his version is based on a series of five interlocking definitions—artist, work, public, artworld, and artworld system—with a work of art defined as *"an artifact of a kind created to be presented to an artworld public"*.[26] Dickie is unconcerned by the circularity of the definition because its function is not identification, but the clarification and explanation of an already familiar term: "Virtually everyone can recognize some things as works of art".[27] I shall take this to be true of some works of literary art and focus on works whose status as literature is little contested (or at least uncontroversial), employing examples from the literary canon wherever possible.[28]

According to the institutional theory anything can be a work of art, but it does not follow that everything is a work of art. Dickie is clear that his theory is descriptive, but admits that the five interlocking definitions nonetheless have important evaluative implications.[29] An object must be presented to the public through the framework of the artworld system and the combination of public and system serves as a filter, granting some but not all objects the status "work of art". This filter can be understood in terms of artistic practices, which are constituted by artistic conventions. Lamarque and Olsen explain the relationships between institutions, practices, and conventions as follows:

> An institutional practice, as we understand it, is *constituted* by a set of conventions and concepts which both regulate and *define* the actions and products involved in the practice. . . . An institution, in the relevant sense, is a rule-governed practice which makes possible certain (institutional) actions which are defined by the rules of the practice and which could not exist without those rules.[30]

The literary stance and the author's intention to invoke this stance are reliant upon the practice of literature, the set of concepts and conventions that constitute the institutional framework within which literary works are presented and received. Olsen describes the consequences of the institutional theory of literature for the ontology of the literary work:

> The suggestion is that the literary work is an institutional object; that the specifically artistic features of a literary work are defined by the institutional conventions and have no existence independently of the institution; that therefore the literary work has no objectively given distinguishing features, but that

these features are the product of a set of descriptive and classificatory possibilities created by the institution.[31]

I shall return to the question of ontology in my discussion of work identity in chapter 4: §16. For the present, it is sufficient to state that literary art is a category of art such that to speak of a work *qua* literature is to speak of that work *qua* art.

There is a peculiar terminological issue to address when discussing works of the literary art form—that there is no generic word for a literary work of art. The oldest literary categories of art are poems and plays. Both have ancient origins, arising from an oral tradition where they were performed for audiences. While contemporary appreciators are much more likely to read a printed poem than hear a spoken one, performance has remained essential to plays. When I refer to a play as a work of literature, I shall be referring to the script of the play (whether heard or read) and excluding the performance elements essential to the art form of theatre. The third category of literature is the novel, which includes (shorter) novellas and (even shorter) short stories. Unlike its predecessors, the novel has a weaker link to performance such that to read a novel in silence and solitude is not to have an impoverished experience of the work. The prototype novels of the Enlightenment were also distinguished by being modelled on history and biography rather than poetry or plays. Short of providing a neologism, which seems pretentious, there is no way to overcome this problem. I shall strive to reach conclusions that are true for all literary works and, where necessary, be clear to differentiate between—in particular—poems and novels.

4. VALUES OF LITERATURE

Either there is a characteristically literary value or none of the many values associated with literature are characteristic of the practice. If there is no characteristic literary value, then it is difficult to see why the practice of literature matters or how it has been able to sustain the prolonged and consequential attention to which it has been subjected. My first claim, which I shall assume, is that there *is* a value characteristic of literature and that this value is literary value—that is, the value of literature *qua* literature. My employment of the term *literary value* will be restricted to this value alone. Literary value is distinct from the *values of literature*, which are all the values associated with literary works. Amongst these, there is a second distinction to be made: some, like cognitive and ethical values, will be of philosophical interest; others, like investment and adventitious values, will not.

My second claim, for which I shall argue, is that literary value is final rather than instrumental (as defined in §2 above) and that on the basis of this classification, literary value is autonomous (as defined in §5 below). My concern with the autonomy of literature is exclusively with whether literary value is final or instrumental and there is a related—but distinct—debate from which I must therefore distinguish my thesis.

Until the end of the twentieth century, the main employment of "autonomy" in a literary context was in the discussion of critical practice—specifically with the extent to which the interpretation of a literary work was independent of authorial intention. The debate was initiated in 1946, by Monroe Beardsley and W. K. Wimsatt with "The Intentional Fallacy".[32] Beardsley and Wimsatt argued for the complete rejection of *genetic reasons* and the partial rejection of *affective reasons* in the process of critical evaluation. They defined genetic reasons as those that refer to something that preceded the existence of the work, including intention, expression, originality, and sincerity. Affective reasons are those that refer to the psychological effect of the work on the person experiencing it, and include pleasure and emotional impact.[33] Beardsley maintained that the former category were entirely irrelevant to the judgement of aesthetic objects (including works of art) and the latter inadequate on their own. This debate is related to my concern with autonomy because Beardsley's rejection of genetic and affective criticism forms part of his aesthetic theory of art, which is closer to—although still distinct from—my concern. Regarding literary art, for example, Beardsley states, "What makes literature literature, in part, must be some withdrawal from the world about it, an unusual degree of self-containedness and self-sufficiency that makes it capable of being contemplated with satisfaction in itself".[34] I shall not employ "autonomy" in the sense in which it relates to either of the above fallacies.

The sense of autonomy with which I am concerned was popularised in the value interaction debate, initiated by Noël Carroll in 1996 with his paper "Moderate Moralism". The central dispute is whether a moral defect in a work of art is (also) an artistic or aesthetic defect—that is, whether there is a relation between these two spheres of value. Moralists answer in the affirmative, and autonomists, in the negative. Carroll identifies two types of *autonomism* as follows:

1. Radical Autonomism: the view that "it is inappropriate or even incoherent to assess artworks in terms of their consequences for cognition, morality, and politics".[35]
2. Moderate Autonomism: "A given artwork may legitimately traffic in aesthetic, moral, cognitive, and political value. But these levels are independent or autonomous".[36]

Carroll employs "aesthetic value" as inclusive of what I have called "literary value"—that is, the value of literature *qua* literature. This is standard usage in philosophical aesthetics and although I shall not discuss aesthetic value in isolation from literary value I shall take aesthetic value to be the value of literature (or art) *qua* literature (or art) unless otherwise specified. As I explain below, number (1) above is an implausible view. My interest in autonomy is with the notion expressed in (2) above as applied to literature—that literary value is independent of moral value, cognitive value, and political value. Within the value interaction debate, arguments for this view have been made by James Anderson and Jeffrey Dean, James Harold, and myself.[37] I shall not engage with the value interaction debate directly in this book as— for reasons which I have explained elsewhere—I believe the question of literary or artistic autonomy to be prior to the question of whether a moral defect is (also) an artistic defect.[38]

My claim that literature is autonomous is a claim about the characteristically literary value. Specifically, it is a claim that the characteristically literary value is *finally*, rather than *instrumentally*, valuable. In terms of my definition in §2 above, I am therefore stating that the characteristically literary value is non-derivative. I noted that there is a debate as to whether there is one or more final value and also that both monists and pluralists typically accept that pleasure is finally valuable. In a similar manner, those who agree with my view of literary value as final and those who disagree both agree that pleasure as a literary value is correctly characterised as final rather than instrumental (even if that pleasure has, as noted in §2 above, instrumental value). I shall follow Malcolm Budd in arguing that literary value is experiential—that is, that the value of a literary work is the value of the experience afforded by the literary work.[39] It should now be evident why I accepted Korsgaard's two distinctions in §2 above: regardless of whether literary value is final or instrumental, if it is experiential it cannot be non-relational— that is, experiential value is necessarily relational.

If the experience of reading, for example, Ernest Hemingway's *For Whom the Bell Tolls* is an experience that involves the formation of true, justified beliefs about the Spanish Civil War (or civil wars in general), then one might regard that experience as finally valuable if one holds that truth is finally valuable. Similarly, if the experience of reading J. M. Coetzee's "The Lives of Animals" is an experience that involves the recognition of animal suffering as morally relevant, then one might regard that experience as finally valuable if one holds that virtue is finally valuable. Alternatively, however, it could be argued that whether or not truth is finally valuable, it is a derivative value of the experience of *For Whom the Bell Tolls* that it educates. And whether or not virtue is finally valuable, it is a derivative value of the experience of "The Lives of Animals" that it educates morally.

Consider the analgesic pill mentioned in §2 above. I stated that there could be at least two types of pleasure involved: pleasure in tasting the pill and pleasure in the pain relief produced by the pill. The pleasure of pain relief is typically considered a derivative value of the pill and the pleasure of the taste, a non-derivative value. If the education in the experience of the two literary narratives is similar to the experience of pain relief, then they could also be considered as instrumental values of the work, and there is indeed a long tradition in philosophy and criticism of arguing for literature as being "good for" a wide variety of reasons.

Within this tradition, however, including defences of didactic literature—which I discuss in chapter 4: §17—there is assent that the value of literature lies not only in its capacity for instruction, but also in the manner in which it instructs, by "delighting" according to Sir Philip Sidney and by "pleasing" according to Samuel Johnson.[40] The claim that pleasure is a final value of literature is uncontroversial and is accepted by those who hold that literature is finally valuable for its pleasure, those who hold that it is finally valuable for other reasons, and those who claim that literary value is instrumental. Catherine Belsey makes an even stronger statement about the relationship between literature and pleasure:

> Deep down, most critics probably share his [Sidney's] assessment: the capacity of verbal artefacts in every form to solicit and secure the most rapt attention has never been seriously disputed. Indeed, works of fiction are available for us to read at all only on the grounds that they once gave pleasure to someone—a populace, an aristocratic audience, a monarch, or simply a single editor. That, amid a diversity of critical values and practices, is one widely shared conviction.[41]

Belsey refers to "fiction" rather than "literature", but I characterised literature as fictional in §2 above, so her view applies to literature on my account. The relation between literature and pleasure is taken for granted in both the theoretical and philosophical approaches to literature. From the analytic perspective, Olsen expresses a similar view:

> Literature is an activity which is highly valued. In our culture it has been found unfailingly interesting and rewarding for more than two thousand years. Yet the reward cannot be specified in terms of any further ends to which it contributes. It is therefore natural to conclude that the reward is in the practice of the activity itself, and that one reads literature because one enjoys it.[42]

I shall argue that the value of literature *qua* literature is a particular type of pleasure—*literary satisfaction*—which I explain in chapter 6: §22.

This conception may seem to trivialise the characteristically literary value, but the link between art and pleasure extends back to one of Plato's objections to poetry—that it corrupted by making immorality appealing.[43] I shall take Henry Sidgwick's definition of "pleasure" in terms of desire as my starting point: "I propose therefore to define Pleasure—when we are considering its 'strict value' for purposes of quantitative comparison—as a feeling which, when experienced by intelligent beings, is at least implicitly apprehended as desirable or—in cases of comparison—preferable".[44] An early attempt to describe the particular pleasure associated with the appreciation of art, nature, and beauty was made by Francis Hutcheson, who produced the first systematic study of aesthetics with *An Inquiry into the Original of Our Ideas of Beauty and Virtue*. He argued that "the ideas of Beauty and Harmony, like other sensible Ideas, are *necessarily* pleasant to us, as well as immediately so".[45] Immanuel Kant developed Hutcheson's prototypical theory in the *Third Critique* and claimed that aesthetic pleasure was a response to the type of perception involved in the judgement of beauty, which placed the cognitive faculties of imagination and understanding in harmonious "*free play*".[46] For Kant, the judgement of beauty necessarily produced a cognitive harmony that was experienced as a particular type of pleasure.

Although Kant's aesthetic theory came to be associated with the fine arts, as I discuss in §6 in chapter 2, his primary concern was with beauty in nature and his conception of pleasure comes with too much baggage to be useful here, embedded as it is in his complex views on the different categories of judgement, which are in turn embedded in his transcendental idealism. My conception of the particular pleasure associated with literature is nonetheless in broad agreement with Kant's conception of the particular pleasure associated with beauty in that I take literary satisfaction to be an essentially intellectual pleasure. As Olsen states, "literature demand[s] of the reader imagination, intelligence, intellectual rigour, self-discipline, and sensitivity both to detail and to language. These are qualities which are highly valued and, where found, they are the result of long and arduous training".[47] Pleasure is thus neither a controversial nor trivial candidate for literary value.

A consequence of my argument from literary thickness, completed in chapter 6: §24, is that the values of literature—as opposed to literary value—are all instrumental, which is a controversial claim. In order to avoid generalising I shall first divide the values of literature into three categories. First, there are the adventitious values of a literary work, from its value as a paperweight to resale and investment value to its value in impressing visitors when they see it in a private collection. It is not clear that any of these values are related to the literary experience afforded by the work as even the investment value is a function of facts about the author and facts about the particular token of the work rather than the value of the literary experience. I shall have nothing to say about the adventitious instrumental values of a literary work.

The second category is the family of values connected with the literary work as a source of entertainment. The entertainment value of a work of literature can be a consequence of the absorbing nature of literary satisfaction or from a less intense, less sophisticated "light read" of a literary work or favoured part thereof. This may be what Attridge has in mind when he mentions reading *Middlemarch* as fiction, but not literature. Entertainment value is also associated with non-literary works, primarily works of genre fiction, which are typically either formulaic or lack the complexity of literary works. Entertainment value may be *a* value of literature, but it is not *the* value of literature. I shall therefore have nothing to say about this type of instrumental value either, except to show why literary satisfaction cannot be reduced to the pleasure of entertainment in §22 in chapter 6. Finally, there are the values with which I am concerned, namely cognitive, religious, moral, and political values—all of which may be regarded as either instrumentally or finally valuable (or as both). I shall focus on the cognitive and moral value of works.

John Gibson introduces the former as follows: "Whatever 'cognitive' may mean in its various technical uses, as I will use the term here (and as it is generally used in the literature on aesthetics), it has the sense of asking whether literature can be seen as in some significant respect *informative* of extra-textual reality".[48] The question of the cognitive value of literature is thus directly related to the realist perspective on literature, which is in turn partly constitutive of literary humanism, the intuition that the institution of literature is concerned with reality, embodies socially significant meanings, is capable of transforming readers, and plays a distinct cultural role.[49] Gibson maintains that literature is informative in this way, but not in terms of acquiring propositional knowledge, the type of cognitive value often associated with literature. He is thus in agreement with Catherine Wilson, who claims that literature provides non-propositional knowledge and criticises propositional theorists such as Samuel Taylor Coleridge, Morris Weitz, John Hospers, and Peter Jones.[50] The propositional theory remains popular, however, and adherents include Carroll, Peter Kivy, and Catherine Elgin. It was defended in 2013 by Richard Gaskin: literary works "may have a cognitive value which is part and parcel of their aesthetic value, and . . . their cognitive value and aesthetic value, if they do have it, depends essentially on their referring to, and making true statements about, the world".[51] Gaskin's definition draws attention to the significance of the second question in the pair Katherine Thomson-Jones employs to distinguish *aesthetic cognitivism* from *aesthetic anti-cognitivism*: "(1) Can art provide knowledge? And, if it can, (2) how is this aesthetically relevant?"[52]

Aesthetic relevance requires a link between the capacity of an artwork to provide knowledge and its success or failure *qua* artwork, and this is what Gaskin aims to establish in his claim that cognitive value is *part and parcel* of the aesthetic value of literary works. Carroll holds a similar view, *clarificationism*, which I discuss in §7 in chapter 2. Although she rejects the propositional theories endorsed by Gaskin and Carroll, Wilson is also an aesthetic cognitivist, arguing that literature is a source of knowledge by means of "a modification of a person's concepts".[53] If one accepts that knowledge is "justified true belief" (or "justified true belief plus something"), then any position that links literary value to knowledge is concerned with the truth value of literature. Both Gaskin (explicitly) and Wilson (implicitly) therefore advance truth as a value of literature *qua* literature. *Pace* Gibson, who refers to himself as a cognitivist, but rejects truth and knowledge as literary values, I shall designate "literary cognitivism" as the thesis that *truth is, or can be, a value of literature* qua *literature*.

The second of the values of literature I shall discuss at length is *moral value*. Where the concept of literature having cognitive value is relatively straightforward—whether works can inform readers about the world or communicate truth—the case is more complex for moral value. There seem to be several answers to the question of how moral value can be attributed to works of literature. The emphasis in literary aesthetics and literary theory has tended to focus on immorality in literature and A. W. Eaton identifies five ways in which a work of art can be ethically defective:

1. the subject matter represented,
2. the character of the artist,
3. the methods of production,
4. the behavioural consequences, and
5. the vision or perspective embodied by the work.[54]

Setting aside the question of defects in particular, Eaton's list specifies five potential sources of moral valence. The first way (1) is based on the naïve view that some subjects—for example, human nudity or lifestyles that are immoral—should not be represented. I call this view naïve because it fails to acknowledge the significance of (5). Works of art can embody radically different perspectives on the same subject, and where that subject is immoral—such as rape—the work can embody a pro- or anti- attitude, as Eaton's discussion of the contrasting depictions of rape in Titian's *Rape of Europa* and Nicolas Poussin's *The Rape of the Sabine Women* demonstrates. I shall therefore have nothing further to say about (1). I noted the dispute about the relevance of genetic reasons—(2) and (3) above—to artistic criticism in my discussion of the intentionalist debate above. I also noted that I do not wish to contribute to the intentionalist debate and as both intentionalists and anti-intentionalists accept (5), but not (2) and (3), I shall ignore morally relevant genetic facts about the literary work. Finally, Wilson is one of several who warns against questions about "the mechanics of the influence of literary works" and Carroll points to the inconclusive or trivial results of studies of the behavioural consequences of the experience of works of art thus far.[55] I shall therefore follow Eaton in excluding (4) and restricting my interest to (5), such that the moral value of a literary work is the moral value of the perspective embodied by the literary work.

With this in mind, I can designate *literary moralism* as the claim that *the moral value of the embodied perspective of a literary work is, or can be, a value of literature* qua *literature*. In §3 above I stated that I would limit my employment of examples to the literary canon and it is an interesting feature of the canon, to which I shall return in §19 in chapter 5, that there is a paucity of works which embody morally reprehensible perspectives. This is why my rejection of (1) in favour of (5) above is so important: despite their respective subjects, Vladimir Nabokov's *Lolita* does not promote paedophilia any more than John Milton's *Paradise Lost* promotes Satanism.

Where immorality is found in canonical works it is often in the assumptions made by their authors, the moral background of the works rather than the perspective they endorse. A vast number of works in the literary canon were written in historical periods where the prevailing assumptions are now considered sexist and racist, and the immorality is often restricted to this moral framework. Arguments have been advanced for works such as William Shakespeare's *The Merchant of Venice* and Ezra Pound's *The Cantos* embodying immoral perspectives, but interpretations are disputed and the apparent lack of canonical examples of embodied immorality is often regarded as *prima facie* evidence that moral value is part and parcel of literary value. There are, however, several paradigmatic examples with which literary moralists must deal. These include surrealist and existentialist works that embody a vision of the world as devoid of all value and promote amoralism in response to this absence—for example, Louis-Ferdinand Céline's *Journey to the End of Night*, Henry Miller's *Tropic of Cancer*, Samuel Beckett's *Waiting for Godot*, and William S. Burroughs" *Naked Lunch*. If moral value is part and parcel of literary value, then the flawed perspectives of these works make them less valuable *qua* literature, even if only on a *pro tanto* basis.

5. AUTONOMY VERSUS HETERONOMY

In the argument to follow, I shall show that literary value is final, where final value is understood exclusively in terms of a type of pleasure, and that the value of a literary work *qua* literature is therefore distinct from the cognitive or moral value of that literary work. The literary value of *For Whom the Bell Tolls* is thus distinct from the value of the knowledge it imparts about civil wars, and the literary value of "The Lives of Animals" is distinct from the moral value of its embodied perspective on animal suffering. I want to emphasise from the outset that my conception of autonomy does not involve a commitment to the primacy of this characteristic value—that is, I am not stating that works of literature should always be judged as works of literature or that the literary value of a work of literature is more important than its cognitive or moral value. I shall, however, argue that literary value is independent of the other values associated with literature, that these values are an external influence from which literary value is free, and that literary value is to this extent self-sufficient. My position can thus be stated as:

> THE AUTONOMY OF LITERATURE: the value of a work of literature *qua* literature is the value of the experience afforded by the work and the experience afforded by the work is valuable to the degree that this experience is finally valuable—that is, produces literary satisfaction. As such, the literary value of a literary work is independent of the work's cognitive and moral values.

The idea of some kind of aesthetic, artistic, or literary autonomy has been debated since the Enlightenment, and was particularly popular in the early and mid-twentieth century. The list of autonomists, broadly construed as regarding aesthetic, artistic, or literary value as in some way independent of cognitive or moral value, includes Attridge, Roland Barthes, Beardsley, Clive Bell, A. C. Bradley, Benjamin Constant, R. G. Collingwood, Jacques Derrida, Dickie, Richard Eldridge, William Gass, Gibson, Harold, Hutcheson, Gary Iseminger, Roman Jakobson, Kant, Lamarque, Olsen, Walter Pater, Richard Posner, I. A. Richards, Michael Riffaterre, Roger Scruton, and Oscar Wilde. This list of twenty-five names alone comprises an extremely wide variety of perspectives, from the moderate (Gibson's neo-cognitivism and Harold's autonomism) to the radical (Wilde's aestheticism, Bell's formalism, and Derrida's anti-realism). Artistic autonomy is, in particular (sometimes deliberately), conflated with two more extreme positions, which many of those in the above list hold: aesthetic theories of art and artistic formalism. Aesthetic theory, formalism, and aestheticism are all versions of artistic autonomy, but they do not exhaust the autonomist position and my thesis is distinct from all three.

Bradley describes aestheticism as the "doctrine that Art is the whole or supreme end of human life".[56] This doctrine has been associated with the Aesthetic Movement, which is usually dated from around 1870 to 1900. The origin of the movement is contested, but it seems to have been inspired by Constant's coining of the phrase "l'art pour l'art" (art for art's sake) in 1804 and motivated by reaction to the didacticism of John Ruskin and Matthew Arnold. Aestheticism was dominated by British artists, advocated unity amongst the arts, and valued beauty above all else. Members included James Abbott McNeill Whistler, Albert Moore, Wilde, and Algernon Charles Swinburne. In art criticism, Pater became the voice of the movement, beginning with his collection titled *Studies in the History of the Renaissance* in 1873. The most well-known statement of aestheticism is probably from Wilde in his preface to *The Picture of Dorian Gray*, where he makes claims such as:

1. *"There is no such thing as a moral or an immoral book. Books are well written, or badly written. That is all."*[57]
2. *"An ethical sympathy in an artist is an unpardonable mannerism of style"*.[58]

The preface ends with the famous statement that: *"All art is quite useless"*.[59] Wilde's point seems to be that it is inappropriate to judge art in terms of its moral value—which is reminiscent of the view Carroll calls "radical autonomism". Radical autonomism about art is nonetheless a far cry from making art *the supreme end of human life* and *The Picture of Dorian Gray* is itself a warning against taking aestheticism to such extremes. My autonomy thesis is clearly distinct from both aestheticism and radical autonomism.

Bell's *Art*, published in 1913, was highly influential (particularly in the visual arts) and he is probably the best-known formalist. Bell maintained that the representational and cognitive elements of art were irrelevant to art *qua* art and that the essence of visual art was *significant form*, which was characterised in terms of provoking "aesthetic emotion".[60] Bell thus located the value of a painting in the combination of lines and colours in the work to the exclusion of what those lines and colours represented, and his theory inspired formalists such as Roger Fry, Albert Barnes, and (subsequently) Clement Greenberg. Simultaneously, a parallel movement called "Russian Formalism" was underfoot in literary criticism, led by Viktor Shklovsky, Jakobson, and others. Formalism in literary theory was similarly influential, although it is also something of an umbrella term that includes theories as diverse as New Criticism, Structuralism, and Post-Structuralism, and comprises the work of John Crowe Ransom, Cleanth Brooks, Wimsatt, Beardsley, Tzvetan Todorov, Barthes, Michel Foucault, and Derrida, amongst others. Literary formalism is often associated with the anti-realist perspective on literature, the view that literature is—to use Gibson's terminology from §4 above—*not* "in some significant respect *informative* of extra-textual reality".[61] Bradley characterises formalism as the view that all artistic value lies in the form rather than the content of the work and Bell appears to have adopted precisely such a view when he proposed the irrelevance of representational and cognitive elements to artistic evaluation. Bradley terms poetic formalism "form for form's sake", although *poetry for form's sake* would be more accurate.[62] My autonomy thesis is distinct from all theories that locate the value of literature in literary form exclusively because my argument for the final value of literature is based on the salience of both literary form and literary content, as I shall emphasise throughout the rest of this book.

Aesthetic theories of art advance aesthetic properties or qualities as necessary and sufficient conditions for works of art. The most well-known aesthetic theorist is probably Beardsley, while Iseminger's New Aestheticism is highly regarded by both allies and opponents.[63] Eldridge argues for an aesthetic theory that is based on a particular relationship between artistic form and artistic content: "The aesthetic quality possession of which is necessary and sufficient for a thing's being art is the satisfying appropriateness to one another of a thing's form and content".[64] Eldridge's *appropriateness* is very similar to—if not identical with—the relation between literary form and literary content I shall describe as *literary thickness*. In order to formulate a theory of art, a condition that is both necessary *and* sufficient must be identified, however, and I shall argue only that literary thickness is a necessary condition of literature. In §2 above, I stated that although I do not wish to commit to a definition of art, the characterisation of literature I accept is compatible with the institutional theory. If a work is a work of literature it must therefore not only satisfy the demand for literary thickness, it must also either be created with the intention to invoke a literary response or—in cases such as Outsider Art—be appropriated with the intention of invoking a literary response by someone other than the author. I shall propose neither thickness nor intention—nor a combination of thickness and intention—as sufficient conditions of literature and cannot thus be accused of formulating an aesthetic theory of literature.

In my argument for literary autonomy I shall draw most heavily on the work of Bradley, Attridge, and Lamarque. My position is less extreme than Bradley's as my version of autonomy is weaker. Bradley appears to favour an anti-realist autonomy that severs poetry from the world, claiming that the nature of poetry is "to be not a part, nor yet a copy, of the real world (as we commonly understand that phrase), but to be a world by itself, independent, complete, autonomous; and to possess it fully you must enter that world, conform to its laws, and ignore for the time the beliefs, aims, and particularly conditions which belong to you in the other world of reality".[65] I shall argue for literary value as independent of cognitive and moral value, but I propose no such separation between work and world—*contra* Bradley, I hold that a particular connection between work and world, which I describe in §19 in chapter 5, is essential to literary value.

In contrast, my autonomy thesis is clearly stronger than Attridge's. He explicitly rejects conceptions of literature that involve "carrying away from the text some conceptual substance for my further use or entertainment" and can thus be considered an autonomist in the terms I have set out.[66] His literary theory is based on three cornerstones: singularity (which I discuss in chapter 4: §15), inventiveness (creativity), and otherness. The first two are closely related to the third: "The singular inventiveness of the work is what constitutes its *otherness*—not as an absolute quality, but one that is meaningful only in relation to a given context; otherness is always otherness *to* a particular self or situation".[67] Responsiveness to this otherness simply *is* ethical responsibility. Attridge argues that responsiveness to the absolutely new is a form of responsibility, and that inventiveness is therefore responsibility for the other conceived as the (meta-)ethical responsibility of the self for the other. While he rejects reading a work for the moral lesson it provides, the experience of a work *qua* literature is nonetheless essentially ethical: "Reading a work of literature entails opening oneself to the unpredictable, the future, the other, and thereby accepting the responsibility laid upon one by the work's singularity and difference. There is also abundant evidence that *writing* a literary work is often a similar experience. In a sense, the 'literary' is the ethical".[68] My argument proposes no necessary relation between literary value and moral value—at either the normative or meta-ethical levels. Nor do I accept a fundamental link between creativity and responsibility: Literary creativity can just as easily be turned to inhuman purposes as humanitarian. I do not deny that works of literature usually are morally valuable, only that there is a necessary relation between the moral and literary values of a work.

I have defined my autonomy thesis in terms of the literary value of a work being independent of the work's cognitive and moral values. This independence has been denied on the basis of artistic heteronomy—the view that the structure of artistic value is such that it is essentially bound up with other values rather than being *sui generic*. Heteronomy is indeed the dominant view and the list of heteronomists, broadly construed as regarding cognitive or moral value as part and parcel of literary value, includes Arnold, Jonathan Bate, Carroll, Cora Diamond, Horace, Terry Eagleton, Gaskin, Alan Goldman, Gordon Graham, Johnson, D. H. Lawrence, F. R. Leavis, György Lukács, Colin McGinn, Iris Murdoch, Martha Nussbaum, Plato, Hilary Putnam, Ruskin, the Third Earl of Shaftesbury, Friedrich Schiller, Percy Bysshe Shelley, Sidney, Thomson-Jones, and Wilson. It should be noted that this list and its predecessor above are not mutually exclusive; Scruton and Schiller, for example, might appear on either depending upon one's definition of "autonomy". All of those in this list, however, promote views of literary value that are incompatible with my autonomy thesis.

Opposition to my thesis comes from two main directions, exemplified by Carroll and Nussbaum respectively. Carroll's objection to literary autonomy is twofold. First, "the cognitive dimension of aesthetic experience is its primary locus of value"—that is, the experience of a work of art *qua* art should be valued for the knowledge communicated before the pleasure produced.[69] Carroll maintains that some works of art have the capacity to yield "propositional knowledge about the conditions of application of our concepts" and this propositional knowledge is part and parcel of the works' aesthetic/artistic value.[70] With respect to narrative works of art and moral understanding in particular, Carroll advances "Clarificationism", the theory that the narratives in question offer insight into virtue concepts and thereby clarify moral understanding.[71] For Carroll both cognitive and moral value are part and parcel of aesthetic/artistic value, but I shall focus on his cognitive challenge to autonomy. Second, he holds that the autonomy thesis, understood as the conception of art as promoting *sui generic* value, severs not only art and the artworld from life and society, but also aesthetics from other branches of philosophy. In this respect, realist narratives play a particularly important role for Carroll because it is an essential element of the realist narrative that it communicates knowledge about the world and the realist novel thus constitutes a powerful counterexample to autonomism.[72]

Nussbaum also has a twofold objection to literary autonomy. First, "certain truths about human life can only be fittingly and accurately stated in the language and forms characteristic of the narrative artist".[73] A subcategory of realist novels, exemplified by Henry James and Charles Dickens, are indispensable to moral philosophy because they communicate non-propositional ethical knowledge which cannot be communicated in another form. In these works, the moral value is "absolutely central" to the literary value—that is, moral value is part and parcel of literary value.[74] These novels convey this distinctive knowledge by means of the sustained exploration of morally relevant particulars and the imaginative engagement characteristic of the experience of reading literature. Second, such novels can assist "public deliberations in democracy . . . by both cultivating and reinforcing valuable moral abilities".[75] This is an empirical claim about the moral effects of reading James's and Dickens's works as literature and although Nussbaum focuses on the moral value of the experience of reading, she also maintains that this experience will, *ceteris paribus*, exert a positive influence on the morality of the reader. In the next chapter, I set out Carroll's art in three dimensions and Nussbaum's literature as moral philosophy approaches in detail, selected as providing the two most compelling objections to my argument from literary thickness.

NOTES

1. Peter Carey cited in Nicholas Wroe, "Fiction's Great Outlaw," *The Guardian*, 6 January 2001, http://www.guardian.co.uk/books/2001/jan/06/fiction.petercarey (accessed 22 December 2015).

2. Paul Eggert, "The Bushranger's Voice: Peter Carey's 'True History of the Kelly Gang' (2000) and Ned Kelly's 'Jerilderie Letter' (1879)," *College Literature 34* (2007), 120–39: 123.

3. Peter Carey, *True History of the Kelly Gang* (London: Faber & Faber, 2001 [2000]), 22.

4. Carey, *True History*, 264.

5. Kelly cited in Eggert, "Bushranger's Voice," 127. There is no *[sic]* after "postrate", but the error is Kelly's rather than Eggert's. Eggert quotes from the first printed transcription of the *Jerilderie Letter*, which appears in Alex McDermott's *The Jerilderie Letter* (Melbourne: The Text Publishing Company, 2001).

6. Carey, *True History*, 159.

7. See, for example: Carey, *True History*, 187, 193, 287 & 308. Carey's Kelly does not have a physical relationship with his mother, but he certainly has an unnaturally strong attachment to a woman who demonstrates very little concern for him and betrays him several times.

Ultimately Kelly chooses his mother over Mary, refusing to escape to America with her and their child.

8. Carey, *True History*, 329. This sentence is actually appropriated from the *Jerilderie Letter*. See: Eggert, "Bushranger's Voice," 128–9. Emphases here and in all quotes in the manuscript appear in the original.

9. Eggert, "Bushranger's Voice," 123.

10. Carey, *True History*, 183.

11. Carey, *True History*, 299.

12. Christine Korsgaard, "Two Distinctions in Goodness," *The Philosophical Review 92*, no. 2 (1983), 169–95: 170.

13. Dale Dorsey, "Can Instrumental Value Be Intrinsic?" *Pacific Philosophical Quarterly 93*, no. 2 (2012), 137–57: 137.

14. Thomas Magnell, "Evaluations as Assessments, Part I: Properties and Their Signifiers," *The Journal of Value Inquiry 27*, no. 1 (1983), 1–11.

15. Wlodek Rabinowicz & Toni Rønnow-Rasmussen, "A Distinction in Value: Intrinsic and for Its Own Sake," *Proceedings of the Aristotelian Society 100* (1999), 33–51: 35.

16. Plato, *Protagorus*, trans. S. Lombardo & K. Bell, in J. M. Cooper, ed., *Plato: Complete Works* (Indianapolis, IN: Hackett, 1997), 746–90, 355c: 4–6.

17. Rabinowicz & Rønnow-Rasmussen, "A Distinction in Value," 47–48.

18. G. E. Moore, "The Conception of Intrinsic Value," in *Philosophical Studies* (New York: Harcourt, Brace & Co., 1922), 255–75; Korsgaard, "Two Distinctions in Goodness"; and Dorsey, "Can Instrumental Value Be Intrinsic?"

19. Jerrold Levinson, "What a Musical Work Is," *The Journal of Philosophy 77* (1980), 5–28.

20. Peter Lamarque & Stein Haugom Olsen, *Truth, Fiction, and Literature: A Philosophical Perspective* (Oxford: Clarendon, 2002 [1994]), 32.

21. Lamarque & Olsen, *Truth, Fiction, and Literature*, 256.

22. Lyric poetry could also be categorised as literary non-fiction.

23. Lamarque & Olsen, *Truth, Fiction, and Literature*, 268.

24. Derek Attridge, *The Singularity of Literature* (New York: Routledge, 2004), 96.

25. Stein Haugom Olsen, *The End of Literary Theory* (New York: Cambridge University Press, 1987), 160.

26. George Dickie, *The Art Circle* (New York: Haven, 1984), 80.

27. Dickie, *Art Circle*, 79.

28. Membership of the canon is of course itself disputed, but the canon remains the most reliable guide to literary value available.

29. George Dickie, "Art and Value," *British Journal of Aesthetics 40* (2000), 228–41: 240–41.

30. Lamarque & Olsen, *Truth, Fiction, and Literature*, 256.

31. Olsen, *End of Literary Theory*, 22.

32. Monroe Beardsley & W. K. Wimsatt, "The Intentional Fallacy," *Sewanee Review 54* (1946), 468–88. The paper was revised and republished in W. K. Wimsatt, *The Verbal Icon: Studies in the Meaning of Poetry* (Lexington: University Press of Kentucky, 1954), 3–18.

33. This "fallacy" was initially discussed in Monroe Beardsley & W. K. Wimsatt, "The Affective Fallacy," *The Sewanee Review 57* (1949), 31–55.

34. Monroe Beardsley, *Aesthetics: Problems in the Philosophy of Criticism* (New York: Harcourt, Brace & World, 1958), 436–37.

35. Noël Carroll, "Moderate Moralism," *British Journal of Aesthetics 36* (1996), 223–38: 224.

36. Carroll, "Moderate Moralism," 231.

37. See: James C. Anderson & Jeffrey T. Dean, "Moderate Autonomism," *British Journal of Aesthetics 38* (1998), 150–66; James Harold, "Autonomism Reconsidered," *British Journal of Aesthetics 51* (2011), 137–47; Rafe McGregor, "Moderate Autonomism Revisited," *Ethical Perspectives 20* (2013), 403–26.

38. See: Rafe McGregor, "A Critique of the Value Interaction Debate," *British Journal of Aesthetics 54* (2014), 449–66.

39. Malcolm Budd, *Values of Art* (London: Penguin, 1995). I discuss Budd's theory of value, including his particular use of "intrinsic", in §22 in chapter 6.

40. Sir Philip Sidney, *A Defence of Poesy* [e-book] (Oregon: Renascence Editions), available at: University of Oregon, http://darkwing.uoregon.edu/%7Erbear/defence.html (accessed 11 July 2015); Samuel Johnson, "Preface to the Edition of Shakespeare's Plays," in S. Johnson, *Samuel Johnson on Shakespeare* (London: Penguin, 1989 [1765]), 120–65: 126. The e-text I have used for the former is a copy of the facsimile of the first authorised edition, by William Ponsonby in 1595, and therefore contains neither paragraphing nor pagination. An unauthorised edition, titled *An Apologie for Poetrie*, was published by Henry Olney in the same year.

41. Catherine Belsey, *A Future for Criticism* (Malden, MA: Wiley-Blackwell, 2011), 17.

42. Stein Haugom Olsen, *The Structure of Literary Understanding* (Cambridge: Cambridge University Press, 1978), 220.

43. Plato, *Republic*, trans. G. M. A. Grube & C. D. C. Reeve, in J. M. Cooper, ed., *Plato: Complete Works* (Indianapolis, IN: Hackett, 1997), 971–1223, X595b: 3–6.

44. Henry Sidgwick, *The Methods of Ethics* (Cambridge: Hackett, 1981 [1874]), II.2.§2: 127.

45. Francis Hutcheson, *An Inquiry into the Original of Our Ideas of Beauty and Virtue* (Indianapolis, IN: Liberty Fund, 2008 [1726]), §1: 11.

46. Immanuel Kant, *Critique of the Power of Judgment*, trans. P. Guyer & E. Matthews (Cambridge: Cambridge University Press, 2001 [1790]), §9: 217.

47. Olsen, *Structure of Literary Understanding*, 215.

48. John Gibson, *Fiction and the Weave of Life* (Oxford: Oxford University Press, 2007), 82.

49. Gibson, *Fiction and the Weave of Life*, 2.

50. Catherine Wilson, "Literature and Knowledge," *Philosophy 58* (1983), 489–96.

51. Richard Gaskin, *Language, Truth, and Literature: A Defence of Literary Humanism* (Oxford: Oxford University Press, 2013), vii.

52. Katherine Thomson-Jones, "Inseparable Insight: Reconciling Cognitivism and Formalism in Aesthetics," *The Journal of Aesthetics and Art Criticism 63* (2005), 375–84: 376.

53. Wilson, "Literature and Knowledge," 495.

54. A. W. Eaton, "Where Ethics and Aesthetics Meet: Titian's *Rape of Europa*," *Hypatia 18* (2003), 159–88.

55. Wilson, "Literature and Knowledge," 495; Noël Carroll, *Art in Three Dimensions* (Oxford: Oxford University Press, 2012 [2010]), 240–41. There are similar problems in a related area which has been the subject of much more intensive study: the causal relation between media violence and violent crime. The prevailing opinion appears to be that the proposed causal relation is inconclusive or—at best—disputed. The actual effect that reading literature has on cognitive ability and ethical behaviour is even less clear, with much less empirical evidence.

56. A. C. Bradley, "Poetry for Poetry's Sake," in A. C. Bradley, *Oxford Lectures on Poetry* (London: Macmillan, 1959 [1901]), 3–34: 5.

57. Oscar Wilde, *The Picture of Dorian Gray* (Ware, Herts: Wordsworth Classics, 1992 [1890]), 5.

58. Wilde, *Picture of Dorian Grey*, 6.

59. Wilde, *Picture of Dorian Grey*, 6.

60. Clive Bell, *Art* (New York: Frederick A. Stokes, 1913), 12.

61. Gibson, *Fiction and the Weave of Life*, 82

62. Bradley, "Poetry for Poetry's Sake," 7.

63. See: Gary Iseminger, *The Aesthetic Function of Art* (Ithaca, NY: Cornell University Press, 2004).

64. Richard Eldridge, "Form and Content: An Aesthetic Theory of Art," *British Journal of Aesthetics 25* (1985), 303–16: 308.

65. Bradley, "Poetry for Poetry's Sake," 5.

66. Attridge, *Singularity of Literature*, 111.

67. Derek Attridge, *J. M. Coetzee and the Ethics of Reading: Literature in the Event* (London: University of Chicago Press, 2004), 11.

68. Attridge, *J. M. Coetzee and the Ethics of Reading*, 111. Attridge has recently modified his position such that it is more, rather than less, compatible with my own. See: Derek Attridge, *The Work of Literature* (Oxford: Oxford University Press, 2015).

69. Carroll, *Art in Three Dimensions*, 102fn.

70. Carroll, *Art in Three Dimensions*, 189.

71. Noël Carroll, "Art, Narrative, and Moral Understanding," in J. Levinson, ed., *Aesthetics and Ethics: Essays at the Intersection* (Cambridge: Cambridge University Press, 1998), 126–60: 142.

72. Carroll, *Art in Three Dimensions*, 471.

73. Martha Nussbaum, *Love's Knowledge: Essays on Philosophy and Literature* (New York: Oxford University Press, 1990), 5.

74. Martha Nussbaum, "Exactly and Responsibly: A Defense of Ethical Criticism," *Philosophy and Literature 22* (1998), 343–65: 360.

75. Nussbaum, "Exactly and Responsibly," 346.

Chapter Two

Literary Education

The purpose of this chapter is to set out the two most compelling objections to the theory of literary value I shall propose—Noël Carroll's art in three dimensions and Martha Nussbaum's literature as moral philosophy. I provide a summary of Carroll's approach in §6, explaining why he regards the cognitive dimension of artistic experience as its primary locus of value. Section §7 isolates two specific objections to literary autonomy: Carroll's theory of clarificationism, where moral understanding is part and parcel of the literary value of narratives; and the claim that the autonomy thesis cannot account for realist novels. In §8 I provide a summary of Nussbaum's approach, explaining why she regards certain realist novels as being able to communicate a unique kind of moral knowledge. I isolate two specific objections to literary autonomy in §9—that the moral value is part and parcel of the literary value of the realist novels of Charles Dickens, Henry James, Marcel Proust, and Richard Wright; and that the experience of reading these works *qua* literature is a means to moral improvement.

6. ART IN THREE DIMENSIONS

Art in Three Dimensions is an impressive achievement. In twenty-five, self-contained papers prefaced by a detailed introduction, Carroll offers an always coherent and often convincing account of many of the central concerns of the philosophy of art and analytic aesthetics. At the end of the introduction, he states his goal with typical clarity: "If Clive Bell, that arch-aesthetic theorist, advocated art as a means to escape the stream of life, it is the ambition of this book to plunge it once again back into the flow of our vital personal and cultural concerns".[1] There can be no doubt that Carroll succeeds, demonstrating several times over why Bell's formalism fails. Carroll's target extends beyond formalism, however, and includes art for art's sake, artistic autonomy, and aesthetic theories of art—all of which he classifies as "art in one dimension". He accounts for the popularity of these flawed approaches to art in terms of analytic philosophy, being suited to a search for essences, with the autonomy thesis and artistic essentialism having a particularly close affinity.

Carroll identifies the aesthetic theory of art as having begun with Hutcheson and Kant, both of whom argued that aesthetic judgements—judgements of beauty—were characterised by disinterested pleasure. *Disinterest* was associated with attending to an object as an end rather than a means and *pleasure* with the value of attending to the object in such a manner. For Hutcheson and Kant, beauty was thus finally valuable. Carroll notes that it was a small step, which may have been taken by Constant, from the theory of final value to a theory of art, a theory which posits this final value as the essence of art: "For Constant, this appears to signify that art is not useful and that it has no purpose other than to be beautiful. Art is, so to speak, for its own sake and not for the sake of something else, like moral education or edification".[2]

Carroll explains the endurance of aesthetic theory by its concurrence with "The Modern System of the Arts" or "'Art' with a capital 'A'", the origin of which he attributes to Charles Batteux's *The Fine Arts Reduced to a Single Principle*, first published in 1747.[3] Carroll notes that the idea of poetry, painting, sculpture, music, and dance belonging to the same ontological kind was not widely accepted before Batteux's proposal, and wishes to replace *Art* the ontological kind with *art*—a widespread practice aimed at both the transmission of a culture's ethos and the promotion of aesthetic experience. Regardless of one's view of Batteux's system, it is clear that the separation of art from other spheres of human interest is a relatively recent historical development. Carroll is not only critical of what he regards as a disproportionate emphasis on these Enlightenment theories in art criticism and aesthetics, but also maintains that the "Modern System of the Arts" failed very quickly—that is, Batteux's conception of the fine arts was based on their shared commitment to revealing reality through representation and the popularisation of absolute music soon presented a counterexample. Any initial coherence was therefore short-lived.

Carroll agrees with aesthetic theorists that aesthetic experience is central to understanding art, but differs on two points: first, as noted above, aesthetic experience is one of two artistic functions; and second, aesthetic experience is not only characterised in terms of pleasure, but also expression. Similarly, Carroll agrees with the view of literary or artistic satisfaction I shall propose in chapter 6: §22—the interactive and simultaneous experience of sensory, imaginative, affective, and intellective pleasure—but maintains that such experiences "redundantly encode useful cultural knowledge about conspecifics and the environment across several faculties, thereby rendering it both more entrenched in memory and easier to access than it might otherwise be".[4] The primary purpose of art is thus to transmit the ethos of a culture and this transmission is achieved by means of aesthetic experiences, which are primarily valued for their cognitive dimension. In the terms I set out in §4 in chapter 1, Carroll is a paradigmatic aesthetic cognitivist—that is, works of art provide knowledge (of the cultural ethos) in a manner that is aesthetically relevant (by means of aesthetic experiences). Aesthetic experience is therefore a means to the cognitive end of art and Carroll embraces the instrumentalist label: "The instrumental value of aesthetic experience alone, it would appear, gives us what we need—our simplest explanation".[5] Carroll also maintains that the moral and political values of art are instrumental and is thus in agreement with the classification I present in chapter 6: §23. He provides the following account of aesthetic experience:

> A specimen of experience is aesthetic if it involves the apprehension/comprehension by an informed subject in the ways mandated (by the tradition, the object, and/or the artist) of the formal structures, aesthetic and/or expressive properties of the object, and/or the emergence of those features from the base properties of the work, and/or of the manner in which those features interact with each other and/or address the cognitive, perceptual, emotive, and/or imaginative powers of the subject.[6]

In contrast, the explanations of aesthetic experience offered by aesthetic theorists and artistic autonomists are lacking in content and they are therefore better served by associating the aesthetic with the formal. Indeed, Carroll claims that autonomists have historically kept on returning to form for form's sake, which is the most extreme of the one-dimensional views, necessarily anti-realist and therefore also necessarily anti-humanist.

Carroll's heteronomy draws on historic and prehistoric precedent. He maintains that art appeared independently at different times and places and his conception of the origin of art is compatible with Dickie's account of the evolution of art from features of religious worship and the practice of magic:

> With the passage of time the techniques would have become more polished and specialists have come to exist and their products would have come to have characteristics of some interest (to their creators and others) over and above the interest they had as elements in the religious or whatever other kind of activity in which they were embedded. At about this point it becomes meaningful to say that primitive art had begun to exist, although the people who had the art might not yet have had a word for it as art.[7]

Carroll notes that premodern arts—*ars* in Latin and *techne* in Greek—were skills which required training to master and included practices such as medicine and archery. The development of those arts identified by Batteux was thus intimately associated with instrumental values due to their origin. Carroll continues,

> Premodern art, in short, functioned as one of the—if not the most—powerful disseminators of the ethos of a people and it was widely recognized to possess this capacity. Art was a *comprehensive* source of enculturation in the sense that it very frequently engaged the whole person—simultaneously setting in motion one's mind and one's body (one's senses, emotions, desires, and pleasures).[8]

With evident exasperation, Carroll wonders why the instrumental role of art—which has persisted to the present day and was not questioned for two millennia—is now regarded as controversial. He makes several interesting claims about the modernist-inspired alienation of the artworld from society and the concomitant alienation of aesthetics from the other branches of philosophical inquiry before offering the following remedy:

> The antidote, broadly stated, is that artists once again have to become involved in the life of the culture, taking up many of the responsibilities that modern art has shed under the sign of the autonomy of art. This includes re-entering the ethical realm, not only, I stress, in the role of social critic, but also as transmitter and shaper of that which is positive in the ethos of their audience.[9]

The notion of artistic autonomy is a recent one, which goes against the grain of the practice of art through history and across cultures, and the burden of proof is thus on the autonomist.

Carroll's instrumental values include moral value and he regards the exploration of morality as one of art's primary functions. He makes an accurate summary of the autonomist's position—that works with moral content are subject to moral evaluation but that evaluation *qua* art is independent thereof: "That is, an artwork may be evil, but that evil need not figure at all in the question of whether it is aesthetically good or bad".[10] The only way that the moral content can be relevant to the autonomist's artistic evaluation is if the content impacts upon the unity or coherence of the work and the autonomist must once again therefore rely on form to maintain the independence from moral value which he seeks. The result is that the autonomist can claim that a moral defect/merit in an artwork is never a formal defect/merit. But this recourse to formalism is readily refuted by Carroll:

> It would be an error in the design, *ceteris paribus*, in an artwork predicated on raising a sense of injustice in normal audiences, were it to represent as utterly saintly the commandant of a heinous slave camp. That is, it would be a formal error insofar as the way in which the commandant has been designed impedes the work's functioning as intended.[11]

Carroll holds that the restriction of the value of art *qua* art to *sui generic* value, which forms the basis of the one-dimensional views of art, separates art from life, and that this anti-realist perspective is not only fallacious but also undesirable.

7. CLARIFICATIONISM AND LITERARY REALISM

Several of Carroll's objections to my position as defined in §5 in chapter 1 will be evident from my summary in §6 in this chapter, but I am going to focus on the two strongest, which I shall present as explicit challenges to my argument to follow. Crucial to my argument will be the proposal that the value of literature *qua* literature—literary value—is the value of the experience afforded by the work, the literary experience. Where I refer to *literary experience* Carroll refers to *aesthetic experience* and he claims that the primary value of this experience is its cognitive dimension: the experience is a literary means to achieve a cognitive end. Literary works are thus valued primarily—although not exclusively—for their cognitive value, for the conceptual clarification that they provide. Carroll has labelled this approach *clarificationism* and he offers a paradigmatic example in the moral clarification literary narratives provide by means of virtue wheels. [12] Clarificationism challenges my thesis because it offers evidence that literary value is—in my terminology as well as Carroll's—instrumental.

Carroll maintains that some works of literature can function as philosophical thought experiments or counterexamples. Analytic philosophers make frequent use of thought experiments as tools of clarification in conceptual analysis, and thought experiments are both fictional narratives and enthymematic arguments. Literary narratives are also, by my definition in §3 in chapter 1, fictional so the question is whether literary narratives are sufficiently analogous to thought experiments to be considered enthymematic. If so, then it seems that the cognitive value of literary narratives can no more be rejected than the cognitive value of thought experiments, regarding which there is no doubt. Carroll does not discuss this similarity at length, but there appears to be little need because extracts or paraphrases from literary narratives are often employed as thought experiments (or counterexamples) in philosophy. He states: "It is my contention that conceptual discrimination occurs in art, especially in literature, quite frequently, or, at least, much more than heretofore suspected, and that this justifies our speaking of certain literary thought experiments as analogous . . . to philosophical thought experiments". [13] Literary narratives can thus function as a type of thought experiment and "engender the sort of reflection that yields propositional knowledge about the conditions of application of our concepts". [14] In such works, the truth value of the propositional knowledge is not only part and parcel of the literary value, but also its primary value.

Clarificationism is particularly evident in the relation between literary narratives and moral understanding. Carroll is careful to ward off the objection that the knowledge yielded by literary narratives is banal or platitudinous, maintaining that the refinement of virtue concepts is cognitively valuable: "For, though literary thought experiments of this variety tread conceptual terrain that in some sense we already inhabit, they cultivate our grasp of what is known with finer distinctions".[15] Carroll demonstrates the value of this refinement in his description of the means by which clarificationism operates—the deployment of a structure called a *virtue wheel*:

> A virtue wheel or virtue tableau comprises a studied array of characters who both correspond and contrast with each other along the dimension of a certain virtue or package of virtues—where some of the characters possess the virtue in question, or nearly so, or part of it, while others possess the virtue, but only defectively, or not at all, even to such an extent that their lack of the virtue in question amounts to the vice that corresponds to the virtue.[16]

One of the examples he employs is *Great Expectations*, where the following characters are compared in terms of their virtues as parents (or guardians): Joe Gargery, Abel Magwitch, Miss Havisham, and Mrs Gargery. To this list, one could add a similar array of minor characters as smaller spokes in the wheel, which would include: John Wemmick, Matthew Pocket, and Molly. The novel is structured so as to juxtapose these characters, situating each at a different position on the virtue wheel. The correspondence and contrast between the virtues and vices displayed by these characters in their respective roles as parents or guardians in the novel provides a sustained exploration of the concept of parenting by the studious variation of similarity and difference. Readers are prompted to respond to the characters in terms of their respective virtues and vices and the practice serves to sharpen reader recognition ability and make explicit the criteria for the application of the relevant concept. The virtue wheel provides a conceptual clarification that is of particular use in moral cases, where concepts are typically vague or abstract, and is consequently an effective instrument of moral education.

Virtue wheels in works such as *Antigone*, the mystery play *Mankind*, *Great Expectations*, and *Howards End* share the function of conceptual clarification with thought experiments and thus demonstrate that literary works are sufficiently like thought experiments to be considered enthymematic. As such, both literary narratives and thought experiments are valuable as means to a cognitive end. Carroll offers evidence for virtue wheels in his interpretations of *Great Expectations* and *Howards End* and is quick to address the charge that they serve as nothing more than organisational devices aimed at preserving the coherence and unity of the work. Virtue wheels do serve this purpose, but they also prompt self-reflection on the part of readers:

> Once the reader has begun to contemplate the pertinent virtues and their puta-
> tive status in a given literary work, it is natural for her or him to reflect on how
> the characterizations implied by the text apply outside the text. How are we to
> determine which virtues are true and which are false without considering the
> application of the relevant concepts outside the text? [17]

The evidence Carroll offers for virtue wheels thus combines the theoreti-cal (a rewarding interpretation of the respective works) with the empirical (the actual audience appreciation). He maintains that audiences typically discuss the virtues and vices of the fictional characters after attending a play (or film) and that these discussions are indicative of the nature of solitary reflections on the work. Drawing on his analysis of art history, Carroll offers further evidence that art has served a didactic purpose across not only time, but also across space: "unquestionably, in many of the artistic traditions of Asia, Africa, and Europe, art from time immemorial has served as a means for teaching about and meditating upon virtue and vice, often by example". [18] This long didactic tradition justifies the practice of responding to virtue wheels in this way such that the autonomist cannot claim that attending to literary narratives as means to the end of moral education is unwarranted. Clarificationism thus establishes literary value as essentially instrumental rather than final.

Carroll's second challenge to my thesis is derived from his view that one-dimensional approaches to art, which include artistic autonomy, sustain the separation of art from life that was caused by the combination of Enlighten-ment aesthetics and art theory and has resulted in the isolation of the artworld from society and aesthetics from philosophy. One-dimensional theories of art focus entirely on one or more of form, final value, or aesthetic value and are therefore anti-realist. This flawed overemphasis not only has undesirable consequences for the institution of art, but it is also fallacious in producing specious appreciations of individual works of art. One-dimensional ap-proaches frequently ignore what is most important about the value of a work *qua* art; this failure is most clearly demonstrated in the case of realist art, with literary realism serving as the paradigm. One-dimensional critics or philosophers cannot appreciate a realist novel or play because they do not accept the cognitive and moral values essential to realist works as relevant to their literary value. [19] The communication of knowledge is a necessary condi-tion for realist literature such that realist literary works recall art to life and culture and away from the aesthetic realm. Clarificationism and realism thus both present arguments for cognitive value as partly constitutive of literary value. While the appreciation of an individual literary work by means of a virtue wheel might be contested, the significance of psychological and social insights to realist literary works appears indisputable.

Prior to his discussion of literature, Carroll defines realist artworks as "artworks that represent the social and psychological dimensions of human affairs in such a way that the works are intended to impart knowledge or understanding, among other things, to viewers and readers".[20] The truth value of the representational content of realist literary works is crucial to their literary value because if the representation is inaccurate then the author's intention to impart knowledge will fail, and if the work does not impart knowledge then it is precluded from classification as realist. Carroll employs Honoré de Balzac's *Comédie humaine* and Arthur Miller's *Death of a Salesman* as examples. In Balzac's series of novels and Miller's play the authentic representation of society is crucial to the value of the respective works *qua* literature—that is, the cognitive value is part and parcel of the literary value. This is to some extent true for all literature in Carroll's account, but the relation is particularly strong in realist works such that the cognitive merits (the degree to which the psychological and social representations are accurate) are literary merits and the cognitive defects (the degree to which the psychological and social representations are inaccurate) are literary defects. The strength of the relation between work and world in literary realism is further demonstrated by the fact that realist authors are expected to be expert observers of humanity and to represent their observations faithfully: "The talent for comprehending social conditions is not a dispensable responsibility for the realist novelist".[21]

Carroll notes that it is not open to the advocate of one-dimensional approaches to literature to claim that the revelation of social facts is mere journalism while the unity of character and event under an overarching theme constitutes the literariness of the work.[22] He is thus claiming that I cannot answer the literary realism challenge by stating that a literary work such as *True History of the Kelly Gang* can be read in more than one way—for example, *qua* autobiography and *qua* literature. Reading *Death of a Salesman qua* literature would, according to Carroll, involve consideration of the accuracy of the psychological and social representations—that is, the cognitive value of the work. I think that a subtle—and potentially fatal—challenge to my argument arises at this point. Realist works of literature appear to be a counterexample to the claim I shall make in §20 in chapter 5—that the aboutness relation that holds between work and world and is consequent upon the demand for literary thickness is necessarily anti-cognitivist. Why, in other words, does form-content inseparability entail that truth is not a literary value? If one demands form-content inseparability of *Death of a Salesman*— that is, attends to the combination of literary form and literary content—then there seems no reason that the accuracy of the psychological and social representations should not play a role in appreciation. It seems plausible that the accuracy of the representational content in the literary work should be (at least) a *pro tanto* literary merit. In other words, the category of realist literature appears to present numerous examples of works that reward the demand for literary thickness, but where literary value is instrumental rather than final.

8. LITERATURE AS MORAL PHILOSOPHY

Nussbaum is one of the few professional philosophers whose work has reached a popular audience and she has produced a vast oeuvre in addition to spending a significant proportion of her career actively involved in the promotion of human and animal rights across the globe. Her writing is passionate, compelling, and assured, and I am deeply sympathetic to her desire to promote the importance of literature and the humanities. Her particular combination of celebrity and adversarial style has, however, resulted in caustic criticism from both the philosophical and theoretical traditions, epitomised by judge and economist Richard Posner and literary critic Geoffrey Galt Harpham respectively.[23] Nussbaum has published two books dedicated to her theory of *aesthetic education*, the thesis—which originated with the Third Earl of Shaftesbury and was popularised by Friedrich Schiller– that the experience of art provides a moral (and political) education.[24] The first, *Love's Knowledge*, is a themed collection of essays that includes her initial papers on the subject, published from 1983 to 1988: "Flawed Crystals: James' *The Golden Bowl* and Literature as Moral Philosophy", "'Finely Aware and Richly Responsible': Literature and the Moral Imagination", and "Love's Knowledge". The second, *Poetic Justice*, is a monograph that assesses the impact of the novel on the public sphere.[25] Three other books published from 1986 to 2002—*The Fragility of Goodness: Luck and Ethics in Greek Tragedy and Philosophy*, *The Therapy of Desire: Theory and Practice in Hellenistic Ethics*, and *Upheavals of Thought: The Intelligence of Emotions*—also discuss the relationship between literature and philosophy.

Nussbaum's view of literary education is thus expounded in at least five books across two decades and the claims she makes are not entirely consistent. Posner, for example, is justified in reading literary education as holding for all novels despite Nussbaum's claims to the contrary in her defence of ethical criticism.[26] There are also times when her rhetorical skills appear to disguise flaws in her arguments and Harpham compares Nussbaum to Derrida in terms of both the quantity and quality of her philosophy, notwithstanding her criticism of literary theory in general and Derrida in particular.[27] I shall attempt to present the most rewarding reading of her work, drawing on the most concise and rigorous presentations of her position. In this respect the paper titled "Exactly and Responsibly: A Defense of Ethical Criticism", from her exchange with Posner in the journal *Philosophy and Literature*, is exemplary. Of the two books dedicated to literary education *Poetic Justice* is the clearest and most focused, while the introduction to *Love's Knowledge* provides a detailed overview of her argument for the moral value of literature.

Nussbaum's ultimate aim is to replace deontological and teleological approaches to ethics with an Aristotelian perspective and she envisages literature as playing a crucial role in this project. As quoted in §5 in chapter 1, she holds that certain truths can only be conveyed in the form of narrative art such that there is a unique kind of non-propositional ethical knowledge communicated in the "realist Anglo-American" and "realist social" novels of Dickens, James, Proust, and Wright.[28] Nussbaum begins *Love's Knowledge* by taking form-content inseparability for granted: "Literary form is not separable from philosophical content, but is, itself, a part of content—an integral part, then, of the search for and of the statement of truth".[29] Form-content inseparability plays an essential role because of the resultant resistance to paraphrase. If the moral content of a realist novel could be paraphrased without loss of identity then there would be no need to experience the work and literature would not communicate a unique kind of knowledge.

Nussbaum maintains that the substantive view of life expressed in the narrative structure of realist novels has several points in common with the Aristotelian ethical perspective: noncommensurability of values, priority of the particular, ethical value of the emotions, and ethical relevance of uncontrolled happenings. Novels are especially suited to the Aristotelian conception because of their structural complexity, open-endedness, and concern with the ordinary and the everyday. They extend life horizontally by broadening the reader's experience of people, places, and events, and vertically by the precision and richness of their representations. This extension is facilitated by the relationship between literature and life: (1) literature is like life in that the reader has an emotional involvement and an awareness of her own limitations; (2) literature is unlike life in that the reader maintains a distance from the work and is able to maintain an "(ethically concerned) aesthetic attitude" towards the narrative; and (3) literature creates a community of mutual respect between author and readers.[30] Nussbaum elaborates on the aesthetic attitude by introducing Adam Smith's notion of the *judicious spectator*. Smith's idea is that when one is a witness to—rather than a victim of—a wrongdoing, one's emotion is less excessive, partisan, and debilitating such that one is better placed to make rational judgements. Nussbaum notes that Smith employed readers of literature and spectators of dramas to illustrate the concept, and claims that literary appreciation is paradigmatic because "we are not prejudicially located" when we read a novel.[31] Thus, "When we read a novel such as *Hard Times*, reading not as literary theorists asking about theories of interpretation, but as human beings who are moved and delighted, we are, I have argued, judicious spectators, free from personal bias and favour".[32]

Nussbaum uses *The Golden Bowl* and Proust's *Remembrance of Things Past* as examples of novels that do not just provide lessons in Aristotelian ethics, but lessons that impart exclusive ethical knowledge that could not be conveyed in works of philosophy. There are two ways in which novels are unique in this respect. First, works make claims about value and imperfection that can only be made in the context of a sustained exploration of character and event, and which would be difficult to make in a philosophical argument. The novel thus constitutes an elaboration of the good life, a life that Aristotle claimed only to have outlined in his philosophy, and which required clarification by means of both lived and literary experience. Second, the appreciation of novels requires imaginative and emotional engagement on the part of the reader, abilities which are exercised and developed in the reading of the novel in a way that philosophy has difficulty achieving.[33] Referring to James and *The Golden Bowl*, Nussbaum proposes that moral knowledge is not merely an intellectual understanding of propositions, but also a perception— that is, the ability to discern the salient moral features of one's specific situation.[34] The literary experience thus not only involves the communication of a unique type of moral knowledge, but also cultivates moral capacities that are required in order to understand moral philosophy. Philosophical works play an important role in locating a particular literary work in the context of moral writing as a whole, but philosophy has a subordinate role to the novel in moral education.[35]

Nussbaum initially proposes a necessary relation between realist novels and a unique type of moral knowledge; subsequently she makes the even stronger claim that novels promote liberal democracy and she thus elevates literary education from the moral realm to the political, following in the footsteps of Shaftesbury and Schiller. The moral aspects of this political value are the virtues of egalitarianism and compassion. Regarding the former, she states of *Hard Times. For These Times*, "Reading a novel like this one makes us acknowledge the equal humanity of members of social classes other than our own, makes us acknowledge workers as deliberating subjects with complex loves and aspirations and a rich inner world".[36] The mechanism in operation is that in order to appreciate the novel one must engage not only with the people, places, and events described, but also with the point of view from which they are described. In Nussbaum's terms, one cannot appreciate the novel without accepting that the factory workers are fully human. *Hard Times* embodies a liberal democratic vision in its form, enacting this vision in its structure. Realist novels promote compassion as well as egalitarianism because "concern for the disadvantaged is built into the structure of the literary experience".[37]

Literary understanding contributes to the dismantling of negative stereotypes. Using the example of Wright's *Native Son*, Nussbaum claims that novels equalise in two ways: (1) by making the misery plain, and (2) by focusing on an individual character. She quotes Walt Whitman on the democratising mission of poetry, which she describes as "a mission of imagination, inclusion, sympathy, and voice. The poet is the instrument through which the 'long dumb voices' of the excluded come forth from their veils into the light".[38] The literary imagination promotes—and teaches—empathy and attention to the historical and social contexts of moral judgement. In making a moral judgement of an action or individual, the literary judge will attempt to imagine herself in the situation and consider context carefully.

The imaginative engagement with literature is crucial to the ethical value of literature and is characterised by Nussbaum in terms of Aristotle's observation on the difference between history and literature (to which I shall return in chapter 5: §20): "Unlike most historical works, literary works typically invite their readers to put themselves in the place of people of many different kinds and to take on their experiences".[39] There is thus an immediacy that is lacking in the respective engagements with history, biography, and philosophy. The most important feature of the literary imagination is the balance between the universal and particular, which is built into the form of realistic novels such that they present an invitation to imagine concrete situations in terms of a general conception of human flourishing. The imaginative engagement with realist novels is concerned with the agency of the characters portrayed therein and is thus essentially, rather than contingently, moral. "If we think of reading in this way, as combining one's own absorbed imagining with periods of more detached (and interactive) critical scrutiny, we can already begin to see why we might find in it an activity well suited to public reasoning in a democratic society".[40]

Nussbaum's concern with the literary imagination involves moral perception, which is—as noted above—the ability to discern the salient features of a particular situation. This emphasis on particulars prompts Mavis Biss to construe Nussbaum's approach to the role of imagination in moral reasoning as a *way of seeing*—"the apprehension of morally salient particulars, which may encompass empathy and mental framing of particulars as well as other elements such as emotional balance and self-awareness".[41] Biss maintains that practical reason consists of three elements: (1) moral perception, which is a responsiveness to particulars; (2) moral judgement, which relates the perceived particulars to universals; and (3) moral imagination, which presents possibilities for achieving moral ends.[42] Biss's characterisation of Nussbaum's moral imagination as restricted to perception leaves Nussbaum with an incomplete approach on Biss's model, involving (1) and (2), but not (3). Biss fails to do justice to the sophistication of Nussbaum's position, however, and my reading of Nussbaum is that she associates literary content with moral perception, literary form with moral judgement, and the literary imagination with moral imagination. If form and content are inseparable, then the responsiveness to particulars cannot be isolated from the play back and forth between the particular and the universal, and the literary imagination therefore opens up possibilities for moral deliberation and action. The literary imagination involves more than the perception of moral particulars and the judgement of those particulars in terms of universals because the experience of reading combines absorbed imagining with critical scrutiny and thus facilitates the reflection on achieving moral ends that makes literature useful to public reason. This reading of Nussbaum also explains why literature has such an important role to play in moral education: literature provides a unique type of moral knowledge, literature "develops moral capacities without which citizens will not succeed in making reality out of the normative conclusions of any moral or political theory", and literature opens up new possibilities for realising moral ends. [43]

9. ETHICAL CRITICISM AND MORAL IMPROVEMENT

The general incompatibility of Nussbaum's position on the relationship between literature and moral philosophy with my position should already be evident from my summary in §8 above, but I shall focus on what I consider the two strongest challenges to literary autonomy, both of which she makes explicit in her defence of ethical criticism against Posner, whose position is similar (though not identical) to my own. As noted in §5 in chapter 1, Nussbaum maintains that the moral value of realist novels is *absolutely central* to their literary value: literary form and moral content cannot be separated and the unique moral knowledge communicated by novels is part and parcel of their literary value. As such, the "ethical properties" of these novels is salient to their value *qua* literature and literary criticism can "legitimately invoke ethical categories". [44] With regard to *Hard Times*, therefore, moral content and narrative form unite to produce a liberal democratic vision which is a literary merit in virtue of the moral merit of the vision, as well as the aesthetic merit of the way in which the content is integrated with the form. A crude but accurate way of putting this point is that *a moral merit in a realist novel is a literary merit*. [45]

Nussbaum admits that readers bring a diverse array of interests to novels and therefore concurs with my view that works of literature can be read *qua* philosophy, *qua* history, or—as she puts it—for their "rhetorical and grammatical interest" (i.e., attention to their form alone). [46] When they are read *qua* literature, with attention to both form and content, they are, however, read ethically. Responsible, ethical readings of novels do not presuppose a homogenous moral background for readers and the different responses by readers are part of the ethical value of literature. This diversity also applies to the literary value of the works themselves, because works that are defective in one way can be meritorious in another. Nussbaum thus shows that novels with immoral perspectives do not constitute counterexamples to her position. "Literature has great seductive power: it can get us to sympathize with class privilege, the oppression of women, war and pillage, and . . . hideous racism".[47] All that this diversity entails for Nussbaum is that the category of works upon which her theory is based must be selected with great care. Once the appropriate novels and the context of their impact are specified, these works "nourish the ascription of humanity, and the prospect of friendship".[48]

Nussbaum addresses literary autonomy, which she calls the "aesthetic-autonomy argument", as an objection to her theory. She begins her response by reiterating that not all art—and not even all literary works of art—address the Aristotelian question of how to live. Nonetheless, those novels she has identified both address this question and provide an answer in their invitations to readers to respond to the suffering they depict with compassion: "It seems to me impossible to conceive of an attentive and responsive reader of Dickens who did not pose the question, 'How should we live?' and who did not connect this reflection with thought about the social condition of the poor".[49] The combination of moral content and narrative form in Dickens is designed to promote the value of egalitarianism, and the failure to read Dickens ethically is a failure to read his novels *qua* literature. Egalitarianism is not only relevant to the literary value of his works, but also essential, such that the novels cannot be appreciated without an evaluation of egalitarianism. Literary criticism of Dickens that omits ethical criticism therefore omits judgement of one of the aspects—perhaps the most important aspect—of the literary value of his works. The novels of Dickens, James, Proust, and Wright are paradigmatic cases of moral value being part and parcel of literary value and thus counterexamples to my thesis.

In §5 in chapter 1, I stated that Nussbaum's theory posed a twofold problem for my thesis, in terms of both a theoretical and empirical claim about literary appreciation. Nussbaum is explicit about the practical consequences of reading realist novels *qua* literature:

> I make two claims, then, for the reader's experience: first, that it provides insights that should play a role (though not as uncriticised foundations) in the construction of an adequate moral and political theory; second, that it develops moral capacities without which citizens will not succeed in making reality out of the normative conclusions of any moral or political theory, however excellent.[50]

Nussbaum's claim is empirical rather than behavioural and she admits that the moral capacities developed during the literary experience need not play a dominant role in the reader's moral judgement; nor will an increase in the time spent reading produce a greater likelihood of this dominance. In a similar manner to that in which the moral merits of Dickens are also literary merits, so the literary experience offered by his work is also a moral experience. The experience of reading Dickens, of imagining the particulars represented in terms of the general conception of human flourishing presented, is an experience which is morally valuable and—as noted in §8 above—an experience that opens up possibilities for achieving moral ends. Nussbaum identifies her concern as "the interaction between novel and mind during the time of reading" and maintains that "if the novels are ethically good it will have a good influence, other things equal".[51] These practical effects of the literary experience are precisely why realist novels are so useful a tool in legal instruction, because the imaginative engagement cultivates and reinforces moral abilities—such as the awareness of the significance of the context in which an action occurs—in moral deliberations. The literary experience afforded by these novels is therefore an experience in which the reader's satisfaction is accompanied by moral development.

Once more, Nussbaum is careful to make the scope of this empirical claim clear:

> I begin from the assumption that we are thinking about good citizenship in connection with the situation of the poor and excluded, and I intend simply to convince people already interested in these same issues that they can get some assistance from literature, even though many views of rationality around in the academy will have suggested to them that they cannot.[52]

Reading Dickens will not thus make liberal democrats of Ku Klux Klan or al-Qaeda members, even if they are able to overcome their respective prejudices and read his works responsibly. If, however, one is receptive to the values of compassion and egalitarianism, then reading Dickens will develop one's moral capacities in addition to communicating unique moral knowledge that one would not be able to learn by reading philosophy. Despite these limitations, Nussbaum leaves no room for doubt that the imaginative engagement with realist novels has an effect on the receptive and responsible reader. Referring to the compatibility of her position with Wayne Booth's, she states,

> Our thesis about the effects of literature is only in part a causal thesis, a thesis about what reading literature does to the personality. It is also, clearly, a conceptual thesis. We claim that the activities of imagination and emotion that the involved reader performs during the time of reading are not just instrumental to moral conduct, they are also examples of moral conduct, in the sense that they are examples of the type of emotional and imaginative activity that good ethical conduct involves. It is by being examples of moral conduct that they strengthen the propensity so to conduct oneself in other instances.[53]

The literary experience of realist novels (i.e., reading them *qua* literature) develops one's imaginative abilities and these abilities are useful in both literary appreciation and moral judgement.

The emphasis on *conduct* in the above passage suggests that Nussbaum's empirical claim may actually be a behavioural claim—that is, the literary experience develops the moral faculties and in doing so makes readers more likely to act in a moral manner. I shall take her to be arguing for the former alone. To state her position crudely but accurately again, *reading realist novels responsibly and receptively will* ceteris paribus *improve one's moral judgement.* The literary value of a realist novel is therefore partly derived from its value as a means to the end of moral improvement. I shall discuss Nussbaum's own classification of her theory of literary education in terms of final and instrumental value in §28 in chapter 7, but regardless of whether one considers the communication of moral knowledge a final or instrumental value of literature, it is difficult to construe moral improvement as anything other than an instrumental value. Her position is of particular concern to me as our approaches concur on at least three important points: (1) works of literature can be read in different ways, including *qua* literature; (2) when works of literature are read *qua* literature, the experience is the locus of value; and (3) form-content inseparability is crucial to understanding literary value. Nussbaum's emphasis on form-content inseparability presents the greatest problem: Both elements of her literary education—moral knowledge and moral improvement—are based on this relation. Moral merits are literary merits because the moral content cannot be extracted from the literary work without loss of identity and the irreducible combination of the realist novel's form and content affords an experience that causes moral improvement. My argument for literary autonomy is the argument from literary thickness, and literary thickness is a particular conception of form-content inseparability. In the next chapter I lay the foundations of this argument by examining the relationship between poetic form and poetic content in the experience of poetry *qua* poetry.

NOTES

1. Noël Carroll, *Art in Three Dimensions* (Oxford: Oxford University Press, 2012 [2010]), 16.
2. Carroll, *Art in Three Dimensions*, 11.
3. Carroll, *Art in Three Dimensions*, 2.
4. Carroll, *Art in Three Dimensions*, 94. Carroll also uses the term *intellective*, which is central to my conception of literary satisfaction.
5. Carroll, *Art in Three Dimensions*, 95.
6. Carroll, *Art in Three Dimensions*, 101–2.
7. George Dickie, *Art Circle* (New York: Haven, 1984), 56.
8. Carroll, *Art in Three Dimensions*, 143.
9. Carroll, *Art in Three Dimensions*, 162.

10. Carroll, *Art in Three Dimensions*, 178.

11. Carroll, *Art in Three Dimensions*, 195.

12. Carroll actually specifies *artistic* narratives, which presumably include all narrative art forms, but his most detailed examples are all literary.

13. Carroll, *Art in Three Dimensions*, 215.

14. Carroll, *Art in Three Dimensions*, 189.

15. Carroll, *Art in Three Dimensions*, 216.

16. Carroll, *Art in Three Dimensions*, 217.

17. Carroll, *Art in Three Dimensions*, 233.

18. Carroll, *Art in Three Dimensions*, 225.

19. Carroll, *Art in Three Dimensions*, 466.

20. Carroll, *Art in Three Dimensions*, 458.

21. Carroll, *Art in Three Dimensions*, 468.

22. Carroll, *Art in Three Dimensions*, 469.

23. See: Richard Posner, "Against Ethical Criticism," *Philosophy and Literature 21* (1997), 1–27; Richard Posner, "Against Ethical Criticism: Part II," *Philosophy and Literature 22* (1998), 394–412; and Geoffrey Galt Harpham, "The Hunger of Martha Nussbaum," *Representations 77* (2002), 52–81.

24. See: Third Earl of Shaftesbury (Anthony Ashley-Cooper), *Characteristicks of Men, Manners, Opinions, Times, Volumes I–III* (Indianapolis, IN: Liberty Fund, 2001 [1714]); Friedrich Schiller, *On the Aesthetic Education of Man: In a Series of Letters*, trans. Elizabeth M. Wilkinson & L. A. Willoughby (Oxford: Clarendon Press, 1967 [1794]). Shaftesbury's theory is spread across all three volumes of the *Characteristicks*.

25. Martha Nussbaum, *Love's Knowledge: Essays on Philosophy and Literature* (New York: Oxford University Press, 1990); and Martha Nussbaum, *Poetic Justice: The Literary Imagination and Public Life* (Boston: Beacon Press, 1995).

26. Posner, "Against Ethical Criticism," 5 & 16–17; Martha Nussbaum, "Exactly and Responsibly: A Defense of Ethical Criticism," *Philosophy and Literature 22* (1998), 343–65: 346.

27. Harpham, "Hunger of Martha Nussbaum," 55–56; Nussbaum, *Love's Knowledge*, 170–71. Patrick Fessenbecker has a stronger view, maintaining that Nussbaum and Derrida share the same critical project and identifying "neo-Aristotelian moral philosophers and Levinasian poststructuralists" as being at the core of the recent revival in ethical criticism ("In Defense of Paraphrase," *New Literary History 44* [2013], 117–39: 118).

28. Nussbaum, *Poetic Justice*, 10 & 87. I shall hereafter employ the term *realist novels* to denote this subcategory alone.

29. Nussbaum, *Love's Knowledge*, 3. Note that her subsequent discussion does not limit "content" to philosophical content.

30. Nussbaum, *Love's Knowledge*, 48.

31. Nussbaum, *Poetic Justice*, 75.

32. Nussbaum, *Poetic Justice*, 83. See also: Adam Smith, *The Theory of Moral Sentiments* (Indianapolis, IN: Liberty Fund, 1982 [1759]), especially Part I, §1.

33. Nussbaum, *Love's Knowledge*, 139–43.

34. Nussbaum, *Love's Knowledge*, 152.

35. Nussbaum, *Love's Knowledge*, 161.

36. Nussbaum, *Poetic Justice*, 34.

37. Nussbaum, *Poetic Justice*, 87.

38. Nussbaum, *Poetic Justice*, 119.

39. Nussbaum, *Poetic Justice*, 5.

40. Nussbaum, *Poetic Justice*, 9.

41. Mavis Biss, "Moral Imagination, Perception, and Judgment," *The Southern Journal of Philosophy 52* (2014), 1–21: 4.

42. Biss, "Moral Imagination," 12–14.

43. Nussbaum, *Poetic Justice*, 12.

44. Nussbaum, "Exactly and Responsibly," 358 & 344.

45. Stating Nussbaum's position in this way situates her within the value interaction debate, mentioned in §4 in chapter 1 of this book, and her exchange with Posner is indeed often regarded as a significant contribution to that debate.

46. Nussbaum, "Exactly and Responsibly," 356.

47. Nussbaum, "Exactly and Responsibly," 355.

48. Nussbaum, *Poetic Justice*, 39.

49. Nussbaum, "Exactly and Responsibly," 359.

50. Nussbaum, *Poetic Justice*, 12.

51. Nussbaum, "Exactly and Responsibly," 353.

52. Nussbaum, "Exactly and Responsibly," 351.

53. Nussbaum, "Exactly and Responsibly," 355.

Chapter Three

Poetic Thickness

The purpose of this chapter is to demonstrate that the experience of a poem *qua* poem is an experience of *poetic thickness*—that is, an experience in which poetic form and poetic content are inseparable. In §10 I introduce the philosophical interest in the relationship between form and content and discuss Morris Weitz's scepticism about the value of the distinction.[1] I present a critical analysis of A. C. Bradley's "Poetry for Poetry's Sake" lecture in §11, indicating both the strengths and weaknesses of his conception of resonant meaning. Section §12 draws on subsequent work by I. A. Richards and Peter Lamarque to advance my account of the relationship in question—poetic thickness—understood as a demand made of a poem rather than a property discovered therein. I discuss four objections to form-content unity from Peter Kivy in §13: perfect circularity, ubiquitous unity, the sugar-coated pill tradition, and the defence from tradition. I show that all these objections fail against poetic thickness and that poetic thickness is therefore a necessary condition of poetry.

10. FORM AND CONTENT

In everything that can be called art there is a distinction between a work's form and a work's content.[2] The possible exception is pure or absolute music (music without non-musical components), which is thought to have no content and therefore be an instance of pure form. It is the apparent absence of this distinction in music that prompts Walter Pater to state:

> All art constantly aspires towards the condition of music. For while in all other kinds of art it is possible to distinguish the matter from the form, and the understanding can always make this distinction, yet it is the constant effort of

47

art to obliterate it. That the mere matter of a poem, for instance, its subject, namely, its given incidents or situation—that the mere matter of a picture, the actual circumstances of an event, the actual topography of a landscape—should be nothing without the form, the spirit, of the handling, that this form, this mode of handling, should become an end in itself, should penetrate every part of the matter: this is what all art constantly strives after, and achieves in different degrees.[3]

Pater refers to form as *mode of handling* and content as *subject* and *matter*. There are numerous ways to characterise the distinction, the most common of which are: form/content, style/substance, manner/matter, and medium/message.

Plato distinguished the "style" of stories from their "content" and while there has been philosophical interest in the relationship between form and content ever since, Bradley's "Poetry for Poetry's Sake" lecture marks the beginning of the contemporary concern.[4] Bradley employs the terms "form", "style", "versification", "treatment", and "handling" to describe one side of the distinction in poetry;[5] and "matter", "subject", "content", "substance", "the 'moral'", "the 'idea'", and "meaning" for the other.[6] Subsequently, Richards employed "sequences of sounds" and "inherent rhythm" for form; and "meanings of the words" and "sense and feeling" for content.[7] Moving from poetry to literature, Attridge distinguishes between form as "sounds and shapes" and content as "meaning and feeling"; and Gaskin between "sense and reference".[8]

Literary form includes structure, morphology (the patterns of word formation), syntax (the rules of sentence formation), metre (the arrangement of words in regularly measured, patterned, or rhythmic lines or verses), and tropes (all literary or rhetorical devices that use words in other than their literal sense). Content includes subject, theme, characters, settings, and events. Recent discussions of narrative have introduced new versions of the distinction, such as Berys Gaut's narration/narrative and Gibson's narrative/story.[9] The proliferation of terms is a source of potential confusion: "sense" is content for Richards and form for Gaskin; "narrative" is content for Gaut and form for Gibson. In order to avoid ambiguity, I shall employ *form* and *content* wherever possible. Following Plato, Bradley offers a simple and effective description of the distinction, which I shall take as my starting point: *form* is *how* a poet says something; *content* is *what* the poet says.[10]

An obvious objection to my thesis is that in basing my argument for the autonomy of literature on the relationship between literary form and literary content I am overvaluing a dichotomy which is not in fact enlightening or useful. According to Morris Weitz, the distinction is not only uninformative, but actively misleading, "responsible for more of the difficulties in contemporary aesthetic thought than any other".[11] He refers to the *what-how* characterisation of Bradley's as a "commonsense" distinction between the elements of a work and their organisation and identifies three variants:

1. content as the subject, theme, or idea of a work; form as the medium in which this content is presented;
2. content as the subject, theme, or idea of a work; form as the manner in which this content is expressed; and
3. content as a work's terms or elements; form as all the relations among these elements. [12]

Weitz rejects all three usages and reconceptualises the dichotomy in terms of his Organic Theory of Art, which identifies a work as "an organic complex or integration of expressive elements embodied in a sensuous medium". [13] Content and form are defined as identical: "*the organic unification of the several expressive constituents of the work of art*" and "the same coördination of elements, characteristics, and relations". Weitz's revision of the distinction is in fact a rejection, as he is explicit that there is "*no* distinction" between artistic form and artistic content. [14] He also maintains that this analysis—the identity of form and content—has been appropriated by Bradley.

Bradley is unclear about the precise relationship he has in mind, and there is indeed evidence for identity:

1. "And this identity of content and form, you will say, is no accident";
2. "This unity has, if you like, various 'aspects' or 'sides,' but they are not factors or parts; if you try to examine one, you find it is also the other". [15]

Bradley does not, however, appear to mean "identical" in the strict philosophical sense of indiscernible identicals. Prior to the mention of identity in (1) he notes that form and content "are one" in the experience of a poem, but not in the analysis or critique thereof. [16] If the relation was one of strict identity for Bradley, then form and content would be identical in both the experience and analysis of a poem. Kivy characterises Bradley's relation as follows: "inseparability", "indistinguishable", "the thesis of form-content identity", "the form-content identity assumption", "the assumption of form-content unity", "indissolubility", and "total fusion of form with content". [17] Kivy favours *identity*, but this is hardly surprising as he is arguing against Bradley. Richards is critical of the term, maintaining that talk of identity has resulted in "mystery and obscurity" regarding the relationship and I am inclined to agree. [18] I explain Bradley's conception of form-content unity in terms of inseparability in §11 below.

Returning to Weitz, my preliminary characterisation of *what-how* matches his third usage: content as a work's terms or elements and form as all the relations amongst these elements.[19] The first usage conflates "artistic form" with "art form" (which is often, but not necessarily, related to the artistic medium), and Weitz is right to disambiguate between the two employments of "form". I cannot accept the second usage because it is unnecessarily restrictive: even if one takes "expression" to include structure, morphology, syntax, metre, and tropes, basic elements such as character, setting, and action are excluded from content. This usage could also be considered a subcategory or instantiation of the third if the subject is an element of the work and expression is determined by the way in which the elements are related. I therefore agree with Weitz that the first two distinctions are erroneous, but I shall argue that the *what-how* distinction understood in terms of elements and relations not only does justice to the literary art form, but also grounds a literary humanism that does not entail a commitment to either literary cognitivism or literary moralism.

Weitz's alternative, the identity claim, is unconvincing because both of the definitions quoted above are reducible to my preferred *what-how* distinction: "organic unification" and "coordination" appear to be referring to form, and "expressive constituents" and "elements", to content. Despite Weitz's rejection of the form-content distinction, therefore, he fails to offer an alternative that cannot itself be understood in terms of the very distinction he is rejecting. Although I stand by my reading of Weitz, I make mention of Thomson-Jones's interpretation here. In my understanding, she maintains that Weitz's claim is one of indistinguishablility: form and content are not identical, but they cannot be distinguished.[20] If Weitz is arguing for this weaker relation, then he is even more susceptible to the objection I have just expressed as the different parts of his definition clearly *are* distinguishable in *what-how* terminology.

11. RESONANT MEANING

Bradley's inaugural address at Oxford was intended to convince his audience of *poetic autonomy*, the view that the experience of a poem is valuable in itself regardless of any instrumental value it may possess. He does not argue for the final value of poetry, but simply assumes that the poetic "experience is an end in itself, is worth having on its own account, has an intrinsic value",[21] before attempting to answer three objections: (1) autonomy is a commitment to aestheticism; (2) autonomy severs poetry from life; and (3) autonomy is a commitment to formalism.[22]

The argument for form-content unity is part of Bradley's attempt to distinguish autonomy from *formalism*, which he conceives as the view that all poetic value lies in the form of a poem and that its content is irrelevant—that poetry is in fact *form for form's sake*. Bradley attempts to show that an autonomist is not committed to formalism, and he does this by arguing against two "heresies", one that assigns poetic value exclusively to form, and the other that assigns poetic value exclusively to content.[23] If he can prove that the value of the poem lies in the form *and* the content, then he will have distinguished his position from the formal heresy—hence the argument for form-content unity.

Lamarque characterises the relation for which Bradley argues as being "that neither can be specified or identified independently of the other. In this sense form and content are united, indivisible and mutually dependent".[24] I take the evidence Bradley offers to support a relation of *inseparability*, such that once form (or content) is separated from the work (the form-content unity), it is no longer identical with the form (or content) in that work. This relation—as distinct from both identity and indistinguishability—is consistent with Thomson-Jones's work on form and content, and Bradley's approach can be further classified in terms of her taxonomy. Thomson-Jones divides accounts of form-content unity in art into three categories: container, functional, and semantic. The first describes the relation between *organising* and *organised* elements in a work; the second describes form in terms of the function of a work; and the third "describes content as the meaning of a work, or what it is about, and form as the mode of presentation or expression—the way meaning is made manifest".[25] Bradley's form-content inseparability is a semantic account of the relation and poetic thickness will follow suit.

One of Bradley's most important premises is only made explicit towards the middle of his lecture, but should be kept in mind at the outset: the poem *is* the poetic experience—that is, the reader's experience of the poem.[26] His argument begins with a clarification, distinguishing the *subject* from the other elements of content. The subject of a poem is what it is about in a sense that is both general and informed. The example Bradley provides is *Paradise Lost*, which has the Fall of Man as its subject. The Fall is a non-specific description of what the poem is about and is informed because one has to know something of religious doctrine in order to comprehend the subject. The opposite of the subject is not the form of the poem, but the poem itself because the subject is not exclusive to the poem: many poems and even different works of art can share the same subject. The Fall, for example, is also the subject of the painting on the ceiling of the Sistine Chapel, the sculpture on the west façade of Notre Dame Cathedral in Paris, and the book of *Genesis*; the subject could furthermore be communicated by any method, including non-artistic ones such as a newspaper report or textbook. Given that the subject is external to the poem, Bradley states: "it is surely obvious that the poetic value cannot lie in the subject, but lies entirely in its opposite, the poem".[27]

The second antithesis is form versus content and both sides of this antithesis exist within the poem.[28] Lamarque explains the relation as follows: content is *"the-subject-as-realised-in-the-poem"*, and form, *"the-mode-of-realisation-of-the-subject-in-the-poem"*.[29] The content of *Paradise Lost* is the characters and events as portrayed *in the poem*, and although they are similar to the characters and events in the story of The Fall, they are not identical. Satan, for example, in *Paradise Lost* is not identical with his counterparts in C. S. Lewis's *Perelandra*, the *Qu'ran*, or the *Book of Mormon*. Bradley then claims that the heresies he has identified will either both be false or nonsensical.[30] If subject is confused with content and the fallacious antithesis form-subject established, then both heresies will be false because they rely on something that is external to the poem. If form is *the-mode-of-realisation-of-the-subject-in-the-poem* and content *the-subject-as-realised-in-the-poem*, then the heresies both

> imply that there are in a poem two parts, factors, or components, a substance and a form; and that you can conceive of them distinctly and separately, so that when you are speaking of the one you are not speaking of the other. . . . But really in a poem, apart from defects, there are no such factors or components; and therefore it is strictly nonsense to ask in which of them the value lies.[31]

Bradley appeals to the imaginative experience of the poem and holds that when one is reading a work, one does not appreciate the sound of the words and the meaning of the words separately. His most convincing analogy is the experience of a smile: one does not understand the lines on a person's face and the feeling they express separately. One can conceive of the two as distinct later on, when recalling someone's smile, but to do so is to analyse two aspects of a single experience in isolation, an isolation that alters the aspects under consideration. One can similarly dissect the unity of form and content after experiencing the poem, analysing form or content in isolation, but this isolation takes place in the mind of the critic—it is not in the poem.[32] And if one makes a value judgement based on something external to the poem, then—whether one finds the value in isolated form or isolated content—one's claim will be false (as with the form-subject antithesis above). The poem is the poetic experience and this cannot be achieved by recombining what one has dissected, only by re-experiencing the poem. In poetry "the meaning and the sounds are one: there is, if I may put it so, a resonant meaning, or a meaning resonance".[33] The poem is the experience of the poem and the experience of the poem is the experience of *resonant meaning*.

12. POETIC THICKNESS

Resonant meaning lies at the core of Bradley's argument for form-content inseparability, but aside from the brief analogy with a smile he offers little explanation of the concept. This is perhaps understandable given the context of the lecture, but nonetheless requires extrapolation if it is to convince. Richards explains the phenomenon Bradley describes as follows: "the effect of a word as a sound cannot be separated from its contemporaneous other effects. They become inextricably mingled at once".[34] He holds that it is impossible to dissociate the formal features of a poem, such as rhythm and metre, from the sense and expression of its content.[35] The evaluation of a poem's rhythm cannot be made without considering the meaning of the words because the rhythm one ascribes to a poem is in part a function of one's *apprehension of the meaning* of the words in the poem. The sounds—the *inherent rhythm*—operate in conjunction with sense and feeling, producing the poetic experience, which is an experience of *ascribed rhythm*.[36]

Richards demonstrates this by comparing phrases with identical sound but different meanings. He contrasts "Deep into a gloomy grot" with "Peep into a roomy cot", stating that the "ascribed rhythm, the movement of the words, trivial though it be in both cases, is different".[37] Although the sound is (almost) identical, the rhythm differs due to the meaning of the words. He employs the following lines to show that poetic value cannot lie in form alone, but they serve as an example of the difference between inherent rhythm and ascribed rhythm:

> J. Drootan-Sussting Benn
> Mill-down Leduren N.
>   Telamba-taras oderwainto weiring
> Awersey zet bidreen
> Ownd istellester sween
>   Lithabian tweet ablissood owdswown stiering
> Apleven aswetsen sestinal
> Yintomen I adaits afurf I galas Ball.[38]

This, Richards believes, is as much a masterpiece of inherent rhythm as stanza XV of Milton's "On the Morning of Christ's Nativity":

> Yea Truth, and Justice then
> Will down return to men,
>   Th' enameld *Arras* of the Rainbow wearing,
> And Mercy set between,
> Thron'd in Celestiall sheen,
>   With radiant feet the tissued clouds down stearing,
> And Heav'n as at som festivall,
> Will open wide the Gates of her high Palace Hall.[39]

Inherent rhythm (form) combines with meaning (content) to produce ascribed rhythm (form-content inseparability). If inherent rhythm could be isolated, then the above two verses would have a similar poetic value. If meaning could be isolated, then a poem and a paraphrase of the poem would have a similar poetic value. Both of these claims are false, and Richards proposes a reciprocal relationship between sound, rhythm, and metre on one hand and sense, meaning, and feeling on the other that is completely compatible with Bradley.

Further evidence for Richards's ascribed rhythm can be found in an observation by Martin Heidegger on the everyday experience of sound: "What we 'first' hear is never noises or complexes of sounds, but the creaking wagon, the motor-cycle. We hear the column on the march, the north wind, the woodpecker tapping, the fire crackling. It requires a very artificial and complicated frame of mind to 'hear' a 'pure noise'".[40] I do not wish to contribute to the contemporary debate on nonconceptual mental content, but Heidegger is correct in that one usually hears sounds experienced as the *sound-of* something rather than *noise*.[41] On the rare occasions when one hears first a noise and then discovers its source, the transition from noise to sound-of draws attention to the difference Richards proposes between inherent rhythm and ascribed rhythm. Take, for example, the experience of a supersonic jet passing overhead: one hears, first, a loud noise whose origin is often difficult to ascertain due to the difference in the speeds of light and sound; when the aircraft is spotted and the source confirmed, the experience of the sound—no longer noise, but the sound-of a jet—changes, albeit subtly. The actual sound hasn't changed, but the identification of the noise as a sound-of alters the aural experience. Similarly, the pure noise of inherent rhythm is affected by the apprehension of the meaning of the words such that the poetic experience is the experience of the sound-of words-with-meaning.[42]

The influence of rhythm on meaning is more difficult to determine, but Angela Leighton provides an example of the former affecting the latter in her discussion of James Cousins's description of Yeats's method of composition. Cousins recalls Yeats murmuring sound sequences for periods of up to three hours at a time, and Leighton maintains that Yeats "would start with the rhythm, and through its repetition, 'trial and alteration', would find words to match".[43] Iambic feet were thus of paramount—even obsessive—importance to him. Leighton draws attention to the frequency of representations of human and animal feet in his poems and suggests that Yeats's poetry is "projecting the sound of its own rhythm as a kind of content".[44] Leighton's claim is both intriguing and compelling, but the manner in which rhythm affects meaning is nonetheless elusive and Solomon Fishman criticises Richards in particular and structuralist poetics in general for failing to provide an explanation.[45] Patrick Suppes sketches a neuroscientific account of how rhythm enhances associative meaning in poetry that draws attention to the significance of rhythm in the activities of humans and animals. Interestingly, in the light of Leighton's commentary on Yeats, these activities include walking and running as well as breathing and the beating of the heart.[46] Suppes's account is based on the following claim: "The rhythms of the words lock in phase with the rhythms of the brain. Or, rather to put it the other way around, the brain's processes phase-lock to a poem's rhythm".[47] Suppes's thesis can be read as a direct defence of Richards against Fishman's accusation, but I prefer Anna Christina Ribeiro's simpler account, where formal devices augment understanding by inviting the comparison and contrast of words with a similar sound which are presented in particular patterns.[48]

I do not intend to offer a complete answer to the question of how rhythm and meaning exert reciprocal influences upon each other. It is sufficient for my purpose to note that there is strong evidence for the existence of this reciprocity in poetry, even if there is an absence of a consensus as to the mechanism—or *mechanisms*—by which it operates. I shall, however, discuss one of the consequences of this reciprocity for the appearance of real people, places, and events in poems. Consider, as an example, the opening of T. S. Eliot's "Gerontion":

> Here I am, an old man in a dry month,
> Being read to by a boy, waiting for rain.
> I was neither at the hot gates
> Nor fought in the warm rain
> Nor knee deep in the salt marsh, heaving a cutlass,
> Bitten by flies, fought.
> My house is a decayed house,
> And the Jew squats on the window sill, the owner,
> Spawned in some estaminet of Antwerp,
> Blistered in Brussels, patched and peeled in London.[49]

In chapter 5: §19 I shall argue for a pro-reference view of literature, which I pre-empt here by stating that "London" in "Gerontion" refers to London. My interest is in what images one is licensed to invoke and what connotations one must bring to mind in one's imaginative engagement with the poem when one reads "London". Does "Gerontion" licence one to bring an image of, for example, "the city that hosted the 2012 Summer Olympics" to mind?

According to Richards, the language of a poem—the literal meaning of "London" in this instance—must be understood as the means by which the poet communicates *feeling*, *tone*, and *intention*.[50] As "London" only appears once in the poem, its connotations and relevant associations can be ascertained from the first stanza, the rest of which reads:

> The goat coughs at night in the field overhead;
> Rocks, moss, stonecrop, iron, merds.
> The woman keeps the kitchen, makes tea,

> Sneezes at the evening, picking the peevish gutter.
>   I an old man,
> A dull head among windy spaces.[51]

The line "Blistered in Brussels, patched and peeled in London" is an expression of Eliot's feeling of disgust for the landlord, who, like the speaker, may not be a discrete character but a symbol. As part of the trio completed by Brussels and Antwerp, London is one of Europe's main commercial centres, and suggests the anti-Semitic stereotype of the Jewish businessman motivated primarily by the pursuit of profit. The three cities also bring to mind the figure of the "wandering Jew", another negative image, which is augmented by the use of *blistered*, *patched*, and *peeled*, words that describe the landlord as deformed, unclean, and cursed. Resignation dominates the tone at this point, with the speaker showing no desire to act on the disgust he feels by removing himself from the decaying house, squatting landlord, and goat droppings. Eliot's intention seems to be the communication of a vision of a morally and spiritually bankrupt civilisation that has destroyed itself in war and sold itself to ignoble foreign influences. Crucially in this respect, the Jew owns the house and the speaker lives in rented accommodation, a relationship that holds for both character and symbol.[52] According to Richards, therefore, "London" does not licence one to bring to mind just any images of its referent, because many of those images would detract from the feeling, tone, and intention of the poem. An image of "the city that hosted the 2012 Summer Olympics" would not contribute to the feeling of disgust which is being expressed and the positive associations of the Olympic Games would mar the tone and intention of the poem as well. "London" is an instance of resonant meaning in "Gerontion" and invites an imaginative engagement that is determined by the combination of its reference with feeling, tone, and intention. "London" in the poem is thus not "London" in its full extension, but *London-in-"Gerontion"*—that is, London imagined as an instrument of the feeling, tone, and intention of "Gerontion".[53] I shall return to the question of extension in my discussion of narrative opacity in chapter 4: §15.

Bradley maintains that the form-content distinction is useful and even necessary to the analysis and criticism of poetry—as long as the critic realises that he or she is extracting the form or the content from the poem and therefore discussing something that is external to the poem.[54] Both Bradley and Richards admit that there are times when form and content can, however, be separated in the experience of the poem, as opposed to in criticism. Bradley holds that separation occurs in poetry which is not free from defects, "true", "quintessential", or "pure".[55]

Form-content inseparability is actually a benchmark or criterion for great poetry as opposed to the merely good, mediocre, or bad because form and content can be separated in even "good poetry" and Shakespeare's work shows evidence of this flaw.[56] If *P* is a poem, and form-content inseparability holds for *P*, then *P* is a great poem. Where inseparability holds for a poem one will not be able to paraphrase it, and this inability to admit of paraphrase also identifies great poetry: "When poetry answers to its idea and is purely or almost purely poetic, we find the degree of purity attained may be tested by the degree in which we feel it hopeless to convey the effect of a poem or passage in any form but its own. Where the notion of doing so is simply ludicrous, you have quintessential poetry".[57]

Richards restricts form-content inseparability to *good* poetry, implying that the relation will differ for mediocre or bad poetry. Regarding metrical form, he writes,

> But it cannot be judged apart from the sense and feeling of the words out of which it is composed nor apart from the precise order in which that whole of sense and feeling builds itself up. The movement or plot of the word-by-word development of the poem, as a structure of the intellect and emotions, is always, in good poetry, in the closest possible relation to the movement of the metre, not only giving it its tempo, but even distorting it, sometimes violently. Readers who take up a poem as though it were a bicycle, spot its metre, and pedal off on it regardless of where it is going, will naturally, if it is a good poem, get into trouble. For only a due awareness of its sense and feeling will bring its departures from the pattern metre into a coherent, satisfying whole.[58]

A consequence of ascribed rhythm is thus that form is not something which can be experienced in isolation from content in a good poem.

Lamarque offers insight into form-content inseparability as a poetic criterion, noting first that Bradley's central concern is poetic *value* and then that "reading a poem *as poetry* demands the assumption of form-content unity. The indivisibility of form and content is not something that is *discovered* in works—more in this, less in that, not in this one at all—it is something that the practice of reading poetry *imposes* on a work".[59] Form-content inseparability is not therefore an objective feature of a text, but an imputed feature arising from a particular kind of attention paid to a work. Lamarque's emphasis recalls Northrop Frye on Blake: "'Every poem must necessarily be a perfect unity,' says Blake: this, as the wording implies is not a statement of fact about all existing poems, but a statement of the hypothesis which every reader adopts in first trying to comprehend even the most chaotic poem ever written".[60]

The reconceptualisation of form-content inseparability as a demand imposed by the reader does not mean that every text or work will meet the demand. Some works will reward this particular type of interest, others will not. Whether one refers to the former category as *true*, *quintessential*, *pure*, or *good* poetry—or just *poetry*—will depend upon whether "poetry" is used as a descriptive or evaluative term. My preference is for the latter, in which case form-content inseparability is a necessary condition for poetry *simplicit-*

er; if "poetry" is employed as a descriptive term, then form-content inseparability will be a necessary condition for a subcategory of paradigmatic poetry.
The terminology used is not particularly important; what is significant for my
argument is (1) Bradley's identification of resonant meaning as a criterion
of—or necessary condition for—poetry, and (2) Lamarque's emphasis on
that criterion as a demand (which may or may not be met) rather than a
discovery. Henceforth, I shall combine the conceptions of Bradley, Richards,
and Lamarque to argue for my own version of form-content inseparability in
poetry:

> *POETIC THICKNESS*: the inseparability of poetic form and poetic content in
> the experience of a work of poetry such that neither form nor content can be
> isolated. Poetic thickness is a demand which is satisfied by a work rather than
> a property of a text, and is characteristic of poetry such that if a work is a work
> of poetry, it will reward the demand for poetic thickness.

13. OBJECTIONS

Kivy has mounted the most sustained attack on form-content inseparability,
arguing first against Bradley, and then against two defences of him, one by
Lamarque and the other by Kelly Dean Jolley.[61] Kivy begins his critique of
Bradley by noting that form-content inseparability is meant to apply to all of
the arts and states his intention to demonstrate that the inseparability thesis is
false for literature and the visual arts, because form can be separated from
content; and for music, because absolute music has no content.[62] I shall
consider only his argument against inseparability for poetry and restrict my
focus to his most telling criticisms, the first of which is that Bradley submits
no evidence for form-content inseparability, merely defining poetry in terms
of it—that is, his argument for inseparability is circular.

Kivy observes, with accuracy, that Bradley is making a normative claim
about the correct manner in which to read poetry, and asks:

> How do we know when we are properly experiencing a poem, experiencing it
> "as poetically as we can"? Why, when we are experiencing form and content
> as fused. And why should we think that is the only proper way of experiencing
> the poem, the way that is "as poetically as we can"? Because, in a word, the
> form-content identity thesis is true—which is to say, we have moved in a
> perfect circle.[63]

According to Kivy, Bradley's argument for form-content inseparability is:

P_1 The poem is the experience of the poem.
P_2 The experience of the poem is (properly) the experience form-content
inseparability.

C_1 Therefore form and content are inseparable in a poem.

The argument can be rearranged as follows to define a poem:

P_{1*} The poem is the experience of the poem.
P_{2*} Form and content are inseparable in a (proper) poetic experience.
C_{1*} Therefore the poem is the experience of form-content inseparability.

Kivy's accusation of perfect circularity appears accurate. Circularity aside, he is unimpressed with Bradley's definition that "until someone comes along to convince me that any *single* way of reading poetry is *the* only *echt* way of reading it, qua poetry, I will continue to take *echt* poetry reading practice to be just those many ways in which competent readers do indeed read poetry".[64]

There is evidence to suggest that Bradley regards form-content inseparability as a necessary *and* sufficient condition for poetry, but I deliberately restricted poetic thickness to the former in §12 above. If one ignores Bradley's apparent definition of poetry in terms of form-content inseparability, the following argument for form-content inseparability can be extracted from his lecture:

P_1 The experience of a poem is an experience of form-content inseparability—that is, resonant meaning.
P_2 The isolation of the poem's form or the poem's content alters the resonant meaning (and therefore the experience of the poem).
C_1 Therefore form and content cannot be separated in a poem.

The problem with *this* argument is not that it is circular, but that it is largely unsubstantiated in the lecture. Bradley provides evidence for P_1—I noted the smile analogy in §11 above—but not P_2. If Bradley's claim is to convince, it must be embellished, and this is precisely what I have done in §12 above, by recourse to Richards's notion of ascribed rhythm, the example of *On the Morning of Christ's Nativity*, and Heidegger's distinction between sound and noise. Kivy is correct to criticise Bradley's argument, which is either circular or ambiguous, but his objection does not succeed against the above argument or against my account of poetic thickness.

Following from the perfect circularity criticism, Kivy maintains that Bradley's strong thesis of form-content unity fails to describe the actual experience of a poem, which is more accurately described by his own moderate thesis:

> Sometimes we experience the medium and the message as one rather than two objects of attention; sometimes we are not aware of the medium and the message but only the medium-and-message, undifferentiated. But sometimes, too, our attention flits rapidly back and forth from one to the other or concentrates for a while on one rather than the other.[65]

Kivy holds that Bradley cannot accept this moderate thesis because it extends to all linguistic expression and thus fails to distinguish poetry. He notes that when one reads a newspaper and textbook one must experience the message (content) through the medium (form). There is, he claims, a better argument for form-content unity in these nonpoetic and non-literary cases because one is concerned with the message to the extent that the form becomes transparent: this constitutes a perfect fusion of form and content, unlike poetry and literature where the medium and message both demand attention. He concludes, "So it appears that, far from the experience of form-content fusion being exclusive to poetry, it is linguistically ubiquitous and more prevalent in nonpoetic forms to boot. The form-content identity thesis for poetry again comes to nought". [66]

Kivy has replaced Bradley's thesis with his own because he believes that the former is inaccurate, but he leaves himself open to the following defence: Bradley would simply reject the moderate thesis and therefore the objection that form-content unity is ubiquitous. A more telling objection to Bradley is to examine the linguistic ubiquity of the *strong* thesis in terms of Kivy's *perfect fusion of form and content*. Bradley offers (2) as a paraphrase of (1):

1. "To be or not to be, that is the question".
2. "'What is just now occupying my attention is the comparative disadvantages of continuing to live or putting an end to myself'". [67]

When I read (1) I attend to both the content of the statement and its form; I take pleasure in the combination of *what* Hamlet says with *how* he says it. When I read (2) as a paraphrase, I attend to content alone: Hamlet is contemplating suicide. Kivy's claim that the medium is transparent holds for (2) but not (1) and his proposal that perfect fusion is more prevalent in nonpoetic language appears to have some force.

I have two objections to Kivy's ubiquity claim: the first is a minor point; the second, more serious. I noted above that Kivy rejects form-content unity across the arts due to absolute music, which he regards as having no content. Subsequently, he cites newspapers and textbooks as paradigmatic examples of form-content fusion because the form is transparent such that one penetrates straight to the message without attending to the medium. [68] I think there is an inconsistency in the way in which these examples are used. If one accepts that content-free absolute music is a counterexample to form-content unity, why should textbooks not be regarded in a similar manner—that is, as texts that have content, but no form? The textbooks with which Kivy is concerned certainly lack artistic or literary form—that is why they are transparent. In order to maintain consistency, Kivy should either accept that the absence of form (transparency) in textbooks and lack of content ("reflectivity", perhaps) in absolute music are both counterexamples to form-content unity, or take both textbooks and absolute music as examples of form-content fusion. I concede that Kivy may be able to avoid this criticism by differentiating between absolute music artworks and non-artistic textbooks, but there remains an apparent contradiction in his approaches.

The claim that a newspaper or textbook is a (perfect) fusion of form and content is deeply problematic. The paraphrase of Shakespeare above is not an example of form-content fusion, but an employment of language that fails to reward attention to its form.[69] The value of the paraphrase lies in its content. The line from Shakespeare is an example of form-content unity because Hamlet's soliloquy rewards attention to both the form and the content of the language employed. In many linguistic expressions that are not literary, there is likely to be little reward in attending to the form of the utterance. Kivy admits this when discussing newspapers and textbooks:

> The medium is "transparent" to me. Of course, I must *experience* the medium to get the message. But just because I do not pay particular attention to it, it is perfectly fused with its meaning. It is quite different with poetry, and literary language in general, just because the medium is thick, interesting, and so, far more frequently, the object of my attention: attention-getting, in fact.[70]

Kivy is associating unity with *transparency* instead of *opacity*. In his own terms, *thin* media are non-literary and transparent, and *thick* media, literary and opaque. If thin media are transparent, there is nothing to unify—and this lends weight to my previous objection, because absolute music is not a perfect unity of form and content, it is an absence of content.[71] Similarly, a thin medium is one where form is not attention-getting, such that there is no form to unify with content. In contrast, *Hamlet* is instantiated in a thick medium, which is opaque, and this opacity is constituted by the combination of attention-getting form and attention-getting content. Kivy's claim that form-content inseparability is ubiquitous is therefore erroneous.

One of Kivy's objections to the ineffability of poetic meaning that Bradley describes is to offer a pair of counterexamples in Lucretius's *De rerum natura* and Parmenides's *Way of Truth*. He states of these two didactic works that: "for the Greeks and Romans it was as natural to convey philosophical and 'scientific' results at the cutting edge in poetry as it is natural for us to convey the former in learned journals and the latter in mathematics".[72] Lucretius, Kivy claims, wrote his poem to communicate his philosophical and scientific doctrine—that is, precisely for the purpose of having its didactic content separated from its poetic form. Part of this content had already been expressed in nonpoetic form by Lucretius and readers who learned from his work could paraphrase its content without alteration of meaning. Kivy quotes Lucretius's theory of poetry as explicated in the *De rerum natura*, where the poet compares the presentation of his "harsh doctrine" in poetic form to a doctor administering wormwood to a child by sweetening it with honey.[73] Kivy states: "Lucretius had a clear concept of what he was doing, shared by his contemporaries, that was generalizable to at least a large part of the poetic enterprise and might justly be termed the 'sugar-coated pill' theory".[74] Kivy thus establishes *De rerum natura* as a counterexample to Bradley because the work is both: (1) a poem and (2) a case where the content can be separated from the form without loss of identity. The didactic nature of the poem is important for Kivy; as it was designed to convey philosophical and scientific knowledge, the propositional content which is extracted from the poem is the *same* content that appears in the poem.[75]

Lamarque's response to Kivy's counterexamples is worth quoting in full:

> The reason that *De rerum natura* is not a counterexample to form-content unity is simply that our interest in that poem characteristically is not *as a poem*; the versification, as Lucretius himself admits, is extraneous to what is of interest in the work. Were we to read the work as a poem we would indeed assume form-content indivisibility and seek out what Bradley calls the "poetic experience". Then it would not just be the subject—Epicureanism—that concerns us, even the subject-as-conceived-by-Lucretius, which could no doubt be paraphrased or rewritten, but *the-subject-as-realised-in-the-poem*, which rests on a unique "mode of realisation".[76]

Lamarque notes that one should not regard the verse form as an invitation to read the work as poetry. Supporting evidence is found in other sources, for example from Nigel Fabb, who explains that verse is simply the division of text into lines and has no necessary connection to poetry.[77] One may read Lucretius's work *qua* philosophy *or qua* poetry; if the latter, then one demands form-content inseparability and attends to the experience of poetic thickness. Given Lucretius's stated intent, it seems likely—for the very reasons Kivy describes—that reading *De rerum natura* as a poem will be less rewarding than attending to it as a philosophical treatise.

Kivy has a second point which is both essential in his reply to Lamarque and related to the sugar-coated pill tradition objection. He maintains that Lamarque is mounting a defence of Bradley from tradition in this passage:

> Am I not defining the practice of reading poetry in terms of form-content unity and then saying that anything not conforming to the practice is not poetry, or not reading as poetry? But the charge of arbitrariness or mere stipulation won't stick. I haven't invented the practice of reading poetry—it is of ancient lineage (the inter-relation of "thought" and "diction" in Aristotle's account of tragedy is but one example).[78]

Kivy then identifies three types of tradition defences explained in terms of the following practices:

1. The tradition of serving bitter herbs at a Seder.
2. The tradition of driving on the left-hand side of the road in the United Kingdom.
3. A Polynesian tradition of scattering lotus blossoms in the ocean at a particular time of year to appease a particular deity. [79]

Kivy claims that Lamarque cannot be referring to (1) because the tradition has an explanation (the bitter herbs are a reminder of the bitter suffering of the Israelites in Egypt) where Lamarque is using the tradition *as* an explanation. Nor can he be referring to (2) because the choice to drive on the left is arbitrary and, given that the rest of the world drives on the right, should perhaps be abandoned. Lamarque's tradition defence is therefore of the third type, and (3) "absolutely depends upon there being an *unbroken* tradition". [80]

Kivy believes that the historical evidence is contrary to any such unbroken tradition of experiencing poetry as a unity of form and content. The evidence he offers includes Plato, Lucretius, Horace, and Pope, and he attributes Lamarque's error to his Romantic sentiments. [81] I do not have space to discuss all the poets he mentions, but his comments on Plato are instructive. Kivy conceives of Plato's antagonism towards tragic poetry in terms of a separation of form and content. [82] A convincing account can be constructed for both Plato's moral and epistemic objections: poetry corrupts because its appealing form disguises its immoral content, and it misleads because its persuasive form leads audiences to believe that they are being addressed by experts in content. [83] Both objections offer evidence against an unbroken tradition of reading poetry as unity of form and content because they focus on the interaction of two *separate* elements of the work. Plato's criticisms are consistent with Lucretius's sugar-coated pill theory, although for Plato the pill is poisonous rather than curative.

Kivy claims that the type of tradition to which Lamarque appeals to justify the practice of reading poetry as a unity of form and content requires complete continuity. In his example, he asks an anthropologist why the Polynesians can't use apple blossoms instead of lotus blossoms in their ritual. The reply is that the use of apple blossoms would constitute a different tradition. To be clear about the parallel Kivy is proposing:

1. Q_1: Why do Polynesians scatter lotus blossoms in the ocean?

    A_1: The practice is a tradition.
    Q_2: Why can't they use apple blossoms instead?
    A_2: Because that is a different practice and would initiate a new tradition.

2. Q_{1*}: Why do we demand form-content unity of poetry?

A$_{1*}$: The practice is a tradition.

Q$_{2*}$: Why can't we read poetry as a sugar-coated pill?

A$_{2*}$: Because that is a different practice and would initiate a new
tradition.

I simply fail to see why either practice requires the *unbroken* tradition upon
which Kivy is so insistent. If Polynesians in Pago Pago continued to use lotus
blossoms, but those in Auckland switched to more readily-available apple
blossoms, one might say either that the tradition had evolved in Auckland or
that it had been replaced by a new tradition. The choice of which of the two
descriptions of the same event to employ does not appear to be especially
important. If, after a hundred years of using apple blossoms, the New Zea-
landers switched back to lotus blossoms one might say that the tradition had
either evolved again or that they had reverted back to an earlier tradition. The
dialogue I have set out in (1) above would be the same in Pago Pago or
Auckland because the tradition explains the practice in both cases, even if it
has been interrupted and renewed.

The tradition defence is invoked by Lamarque in order to escape the
charge of arbitrariness, however, so the following pair of questions would be
more pertinent:

1. Why should Polynesians scatter lotus blossoms in the ocean?
2. Why should we demand form-content unity of poetry?

Lamarque's answer to (2) consists of two parts, one explicit and one implicit.
The explicit part is that the practice is, as he notes, of ancient lineage, stretch-
ing at least as far back as Aristotle. The implicit part is that this practice has
value—*had* value and *continues to have* value. The value of the practice also
shows why the Polynesian example is a poor one. If I received A$_1$ in response
to Q$_1$ my next question would probably be, "But they are all atheists or
Christians now, so why do they continue the pagan tradition?" The answer is
likely to be something along the following lines, "The original purpose of the
ritual was to appease the Polynesian god, but it has persisted because it is
now considered valuable in other ways".[84] The appeal to tradition in the
Polynesian example implies that the practice has value. Practices that do not
have value fall into Kivy's second category of tradition, which are completely arbitrary, like the decision to drive on either the left or right side of the
road. Lamarque appeals to the history of the tradition as evidence in support
of its value, as a supplement to Bradley's thesis, but the practice is not
dependent upon either the length or continuity of the tradition; they are only
relevant as an indication of its value. If Kivy's objection to Lamarque is to
convince, he must show what is *wrong* with that tradition. Kivy makes no
such demonstration, nor is he likely to given his pluralistic approach to the

practice of reading poetry, quoted in above, as "just those many ways in which competent readers do indeed read poetry".

My conclusion is that while Bradley's conception of form-content insepa-rability in poetry is correct, he fails to present a compelling argument in favour thereof. I strengthened Bradley's resonant meaning with Richards's notion of ascribed rhythm and Lamarque's reconception of form-content inseparability as a demand rather than a discovery in order to advance poetic thickness as characteristic of poetic experience. I then considered all four of the objections Kivy levels against Bradley and Lamarque as objections to my thesis of poetic thickness. In each case I demonstrated that the objection failed. Until a more convincing critique of form-content inseparability is forthcoming, I therefore take poetic thickness to be both the experience of a poem *qua* poem and a necessary condition of poetry. In the next chapter, I consider whether a similar thesis of form-content inseparability will hold for nonpoetic literature.

NOTES

1. Morris Weitz, *Philosophy of the Arts* (New York: Russell & Russell, 1964 [1950]).

2. Even those who are sceptical of the value of this distinction—like Weitz—acknowledge its existence.

3. Walter Pater, *The Renaissance: Studies in Art and Poetry* (London: Macmillan, 1922 [1888]), 135.

4. Plato, *Republic*, trans. G. M. A. Grube & C. D. C. Reeve, in J. M. Cooper, ed., *Plato: Complete Works* (Indianapolis, IN: Hackett, 1997), III: 392c5–7. Peter Kivy explains both Plato's antagonism towards poetry and Kant's play of cognitive faculties in terms of form and content. I discuss the former briefly later in this chapter in §13. See: Peter Kivy *Philosophies of Arts: An Essay in Differences* (New York: Cambridge University Press, 1997), 89–91 & 94–96.

5. A. C. Bradley, "Poetry for Poetry's Sake," in A. C. Bradley, *Oxford Lectures on Poetry* (London: Macmillan, 1959 [1901]), 7–8.

6. Bradley, "Poetry for Poetry's Sake," 7 & 18–19.

7. I. A. Richards, *Practical Criticism: A Study of Literary Judgment* (London: Routledge, 1978 [1929]), 227 & 233.

8. Derek Attridge, *The Singularity of Literature* (New York: Routledge, 2004), 108–9; Richard Gaskin, *Language, Truth, and Literature: A Defence of Literary Humanism* (Oxford: Oxford University Press, 2013), 304. Gaskin is making use of Frege's terminology: "It is natural, now, to think of there being connected with a sign (name, combination of words, letter), besides that to which it refers, which may be called the reference of a sign, also what I should like to call the *sense* of the sign, wherein the mode of presentation is contained" ("On Sense and Reference," in P. T. Geach & M. Black, eds., *Translations from the Philosophical Writings of Gottlob Frege*, trans. Peter Geach [Oxford: Blackwell, 1970 (1892)], 56–78: 57).

9. See: Berys Gaut, "Telling Stories: Narration, Emotion, and Insight in *Memento*," in N. Carroll & J. Gibson, eds., *Narrative, Emotion, and Insight* (University Park: Pennsylvania State University Press, 2011), 23–44: 26; and John Gibson, "Thick Narratives," in N. Carroll & J. Gibson, eds., *Narrative, Emotion, and Insight* (University Park: Pennsylvania State University Press, 2011), 69–91: 71–72.

10. Plato, *Republic*, III: 394c8–10; Bradley, "Poetry for Poetry's Sake," 7–8.

11. Weitz, *Philosophy of the Arts*, 35.

12. Weitz, *Philosophy of the Arts*, 39–40.

13. Weitz, *Philosophy of the Arts*, 51.

14. Weitz, *Philosophy of the Arts*, 48.

15. Bradley, "Poetry for Poetry's Sake," 15.

16. Bradley, "Poetry for Poetry's Sake," 14.

17. Kivy, *Philosophies of Arts*, 84–86. See also: Peter Kivy, *Once-Told Tales: An Essay in Literary Aesthetics* (Chichester, UK: Wiley-Blackwell, 2011), 165; and Peter Kivy, "Paraphrasing Poetry (For Profit and Pleasure)," *The Journal of Aesthetics and Art Criticism 69* (2011), 367–77: 368–70.

18. Richards, *Practical Criticism*, 233.

19. Weitz's delineation of both *elements* and *relations* is broad: "The what, or content, of a work of art is its terms or elements, which may include dramatic entities like people as well as colors, lines, or shapes, tones, etc., in the case of the arts other than painting; and the how, or form, is all the relations—spatial, temporal, or causal—among the elements" (*Philosophy of the Arts*, 39).

20. Katherine Thomson-Jones, "Inseparable Insight: Reconciling Cognitivism and Formalism in Aesthetics," *The Journal of Aesthetics and Art Criticism 63* (2005), 375–84: 377.

21. Bradley, "Poetry for Poetry's Sake," 4. According to the taxonomy I set out in §2 in chapter 1, Bradley is one of several philosophers and critics who conflates the two distinctions in value: between *final* and *instrumental* value on the one hand (non-derivatively valuable versus derivatively valuable) and *intrinsic* and *extrinsic* value on the other (non-relationally valuable versus relationally valuable). Understood in these terms, poetic autonomy is a statement of the final value of poetry.

22. Bradley, "Poetry for Poetry's Sake," 5–6, 6–7 & 7–25. Interestingly, Malcolm Budd performs a similar operation in *Values of Art* (London: Penguin, 1995, 9–11). I think it is incumbent upon autonomists to distinguish their theories from these positions. I distinguished my thesis from aestheticism, formalism, and aesthetic theories of art in §5 in chapter 1; I discuss the relationship between literature and life in detail in §26 in chapter 7.

23. Bradley, "Poetry for Poetry's Sake," 24.

24. Peter Lamarque, "The Elusiveness of Poetic Meaning," *Ratio 22* (2009), 398–420: 409.

25. Thomson-Jones, "Inseparable Insight," 377.

26. Bradley, "Poetry for Poetry's Sake," 15.

27. Bradley, "Poetry for Poetry's Sake," 9–10. The subject is external to the poem in that it is shared by other poems, art forms, and methods of communication; but it is also internal in that it is part of the content of the poem.

28. Bradley, "Poetry for Poetry's Sake," 12.

29. Lamarque, "Elusiveness of Poetic Meaning," 407.

30. Bradley, "Poetry for Poetry's Sake," 13–14.

31. Bradley, "Poetry for Poetry's Sake," 14.

32. Bradley, "Poetry for Poetry's Sake," 15.

33. Bradley, "Poetry for Poetry's Sake," 14. I shall employ the term *resonant meaning* exclusively in the future.

34. I. A. Richards, *Principles of Literary Criticism* (London: Kegan Paul, Trench, Trübner & Co., 1930 [1924]), 136.

35. Richards, *Principles of Literary Criticism*, 142.

36. Richards, *Principles of Literary Criticism*, 233.

37. Richards, *Practical Criticism*, 231.

38. Richards, *Practical Criticism*, 232.

39. John Milton, *Poems of Mr. John Milton* [e-book] (London: Humphrey Moseley, 1645), 7–8.

40. Martin Heidegger, *Being and Time*, trans. John Macquarrie & Edward Robinson (New York: Harper & Row, 1962 [1927]), §34: 163–64.

41. The debate concerns whether mental states require conceptual content in order to represent the world. Those who argue that concepts are required—and Heidegger does not, despite the implication of the above quote—include: John McDowell, *Mind and World* (Cambridge, MA: Harvard University Press, 1994); Bill Brewer, *Perception and Reason* (Oxford: Oxford University Press, 1999); and Alva Noë, "Thought and Experience," *American Philosophical Quarterly 36* (1999): 257–65. Arguments for nonconceptual content have been made by Gareth

Evans, *The Varieties of Reference* (Oxford: Oxford University Press, 1982); Christopher Peacocke, *A Study of Concepts* (Cambridge, MA: MIT Press, 1992); and Michael Tye, *Ten Problems of Consciousness* (Cambridge, MA: MIT Press, 1995).

42. This observation is restricted to the apprehension of the denotation of the words—"understanding the language of a poem" for John Gibson. Gibson contrasts understanding the language with understanding the poem and makes a convincing case for poetic meaning as both latent and twofold. A discussion of how poetic meaning affects inherent rhythm is beyond the scope of my inquiry, but the greater complexity of meaning is likely to offer more rather than less evidence for poetic thickness. *Poetic meaning* is of course notoriously elusive and Gibson begins his exposition by identifying the philosophical problem posed by the term itself. See: John Gibson, "The Question of Poetic Meaning," *Nonsite* 4 (2011), http://nonsite.org/article/the-question-of-poetic-meaning (accessed 24 December 2015).

43. Angela Leighton, *On Form: Poetry, Aestheticism, and the Legacy of a Word* (Oxford: Oxford University Press, 2008 [2007]), 158–59.

44. Leighton, *On Form*, 156.

45. Solomon Fishman, "Meaning and Structure in Poetry," *The Journal of Aesthetics and Art Criticism 14* (1956), 453–61: 456.

46. Patrick Suppes, "Rhythm and Meaning in Poetry," *Midwest Studies in Philosophy 33* (2009), 159–66: 161.

47. Suppes, "Rhythm and Meaning," 165.

48. Anna Christina Ribeiro, "Toward a Philosophy of Poetry," *Midwest Studies in Philosophy 33* (2009), 61–77: 72–73.

49. T. S. Eliot, *The Complete Poems and Plays of T. S. Eliot* (London: Book Club Associates, 1979 [1969]), 37.

50. Richards, *Practical Criticism*, 187–88.

51. Eliot, *Complete Poems and Plays*, 37.

52. Regrettably, anti-Semitism appears as a motif in several of Eliot's works. For a detailed discussion, see: Anthony Julius, *T. S. Eliot, Anti-Semitism, and Literary Form* (London: Thames & Hudson, 2003).

53. My brief example of poetic meaning has drawn on Richards's *total meaning*, but other accounts could be employed to make the same point. I indicated my preference for Ribeiro above. Gibson's account involves an application of his neo-cognitivist theory of literature to lyric poetry ("The Question of Poetic Meaning"). Fishman advances John Crowe Ransom as providing a satisfactory account of the relationship between the phonetic and semantic components of poetic language by means of an organic model ("Meaning and Structure," 460–61), which recalls Weitz's organic unification, discussed in §10, earlier in this chapter.

54. Bradley, "Poetry for Poetry's Sake," 16.

55. Bradley, "Poetry for Poetry's Sake," 14, 19 & 23.

56. Bradley, "Poetry for Poetry's Sake," 23.

57. Bradley, "Poetry for Poetry's Sake," 22–23.

58. Richards, *Practical Criticism*, 230.

59. Lamarque, "Elusiveness of Poetic Meaning," 411.

60. Northrop Frye, *Anatomy of Criticism: Four Essays* (Princeton, NJ: Princeton University Press, 1957), 77.

61. See: Kelly Dean Jolley, "(Kivy on) The Form-Content Identity Thesis," *British Journal of Aesthetics 48* (2008), 193–204.

62. Kivy, *Philosophies of Arts*, 85–86.

63. Kivy, *Philosophies of Arts*, 109.

64. Kivy, "Paraphrasing Poetry," 374.

65. Kivy, *Philosophies of Arts*, 110–11.

66. Kivy, *Philosophies of Arts*, 111.

67. Bradley, "Poetry for Poetry's Sake," 20.

68. I do not actually approve of identifying the form-content distinction with the medium-message distinction as the latter oversimplifies the former, but I employ Kivy's terminology in order to make my objection more pertinent.

69. Given the conception of poetic thickness I have advanced, the paraphrase is not an example of nonpoetic language, but an example where the typical reader does not demand form-content inseparability. I shall, however, continue to respond to Kivy on his own terms.

70. Kivy, *Philosophies of Arts*, 111. I have derived my description of form-content inseparability as "thickness" from this passage.

71. Assuming, of course, that one accepts that absolute music has no content.

72. Kivy, *Philosophies of Arts*, 87.

73. Kivy, *Philosophies of Arts*, 89. Kivy quotes from Book I, lines 936–50 and notes that Lucretius repeats himself almost to the word in Book IV, lines 1–25.

74. Kivy, *Philosophies of Arts*, 88.

75. It would be pointless to use poetic form to make philosophy and science more palatable if the paraphrased content differed from the poetic content.

76. Lamarque, "Elusiveness of Poetic Meaning," 411.

77. Nigel Fabb, "Why Is Verse Poetry?," *PN Review 36* (2009), 52–57: 52.

78. Lamarque, "Elusiveness of Poetic Meaning," 412.

79. Kivy, "Paraphrasing Poetry," 368–69.

80. Kivy, "Paraphrasing Poetry," 369.

81. Kivy, "Paraphrasing Poetry," 370–71.

82. Kivy, *Philosophies of Arts*, 89–91.

83. For an example of the former objection, see: Plato, *Republic*, X: 595b3–6; for an example of the latter objection, see: Plato, *Apology*, in J. M. Cooper, ed., *Plato: Complete Works*, trans. G. M. A. Grube and C. D. C. Reeve (Indianapolis, IN: Hackett, 1997), 22b4–c6.

84. Such as maintaining family and community relations or being recognised as finally valuable.

Chapter Four

Narrative Thickness

The purpose of this chapter is to demonstrate that the experience of a literary narrative *qua* literary narrative is an experience of *narrative thickness*—that is, the inseparability of literary form and literary content. I discuss the application of poetic thickness beyond poetry in §14 and explain why I have chosen to argue for a different—albeit related—instantiation of form-content inseparability in literary narratives. Section §15 synthesises elements of Derek Attridge's literary theory with elements of Peter Lamarque's theory of narrative opacity to propose narrative thickness as characteristic of literary narratives, understood as a demand made of a narrative rather than a property discovered therein. In §16 I explain the implications of narrative thickness for work identity. Section §17 considers the subcategory of didactic literature, which appears to include examples of works that are both literary and fail to reward the demand for narrative thickness. Using J. M. Coetzee's "The Lives of Animals" as a potentially paradigmatic counterexample to my thesis, I conclude that narrative thickness is indeed a necessary condition of literary narratives.

14. LITERARY NARRATIVES

In chapter 1: §2, I distinguished three categories of literary artworks: poems, plays, and novels. Thus far, I have only demonstrated that form-content inseparability holds for the first of these. A. C. Bradley twice extends his proposal to all art in his lecture:

1. "And this identity of content and form, you will say, is no accident; it is of the essence of poetry in so far as it is poetry, and of all art in so far as it is art".[1]

2. "Poetry in this matter is not, as good critics of painting and music often affirm, different from the other arts; in all of them the content is one thing with the form".[2]

My concern is restricted to literature, and Bradley does not comment on the extension of the particular version of form-content inseparability he articulates beyond poetry. Clearly, *poetic thickness* as established in chapter 3 cannot be employed to explain the relationship between form and content in painting, sculpture, music, dance, and architecture; the question is whether it can perform this function for plays and novels.

There are certainly reasons to resist the move. One is the greater emphasis on sound and non-literal meaning in poetry. Nigel Fabb states,

1. "Poetry is formally rich: it is associated with the regulation of many forms at the same time—for example, not only metre, but also rhyme, and perhaps optional alliteration, and a bit of parallelism".[3]
2. "Poetry is more difficult to interpret than prose, because it is more ambiguous, less direct and more open to figurative language such as metaphor, or just less easy to understand in general".[4]

Anna Christina Ribeiro reiterates these two characteristics as typically—but neither necessarily nor exclusively—distinctive of poetry.[5] Another reason is that the formal features of plays and novels standardly differ from those of poems such that the form of the former pair cannot be explained in the same terms as the form of the latter. These formal aspects are, I propose, those in virtue of which plays and novels are narratives. I shall therefore present a second argument for form-content inseparability in literature, which applies to the inseparability of narrative form and narrative content in literary narratives.

I am not suggesting that poetry and narrative are exclusive categories. Narratives are found in the literary, visual, and musical arts, and within literature there are narrative plays, narrative novels, and narrative poems. Ribeiro, for example, divides poems into three subcategories: lyric, dramatic, and epic.[6] Epic poems are distinguished by having a narrator, but dramatic poems—distinguished by characters having their own voices—are also likely to be narratives. My aim in presenting an argument for form-content inseparability in poetry and an argument for form-content inseparability in narrative literature is to show that inseparability holds across the literary art form. The majority of works of literature are *either* poems *or* narratives and form-content inseparability is explained by poetic thickness in the former case and narrative thickness in the latter.

Narrative poems, such as *Paradise Lost*, may exhibit both types of inseparability, as may novels such as *Ulysses*, where the sound of the words is an integral element of narrative form. One would expect examples of this nature to be rare—because of the exceptional skill required to sustain the formal intensity associated with poetry over the length required to depict the characters, settings, and action typical of narratives—and this appears to be the case. It is, furthermore, a strength of my account of form-content inseparability that it draws attention to the greater intimacy of the relationship between literary form and literary content in the cases where these poetic and narrative elements are combined.

Drawing on the work of the Russian Formalists, Todorov differentiates *fabula*, real or imagined events, from *sjužet*, the way in which these events are presented.[7] Peter Brooks notes that the translation of *fabula* as "story" and *sjužet* as "plot" has been subject to much criticism and it does indeed misrepresent both his and Todorov's discussions.[8] The distinction with which they are concerned is between a *sequence of events* and a *story*. The distinction with which I am concerned, and which is crucial to understanding narrative, is between a *representation of a sequence of events* (real or imagined) and a *story*. I shall employ "narrative" as synonymous with "story" and address the question of whether every representation of a sequence of events is a narrative.

Hayden White identifies three types of historical representation—annals, chronicles, and histories—and claims that the first two are not narrative. He maintains that non-narrative historians such as Alexis du Tocqueville, Jacob Burckhardt, Johan Huizinga, and Fernand Braudel "did not impose upon it [the perceived reality] the form of a story" and explains the distinctions between the three historiographies.[9] His discussion of histories and chronicles is not relevant to my inquiry, but the annal is a paradigmatic example of a non-narrative representation of a sequence of events.

This is an extract from White's translation of the *Annals of Saint Gaul*:

709. Hard winter. Duke Gottfried died.
710. Hard year and deficient in crops.
711.
712. Flood everywhere.
713.
714. Pippin, Mayor of the Palace, died.[10]

Two features of the annal are striking: the absence of entries for the years 711 and 713, and the absence of a connection between the represented events. The gaps draw attention to a characteristic of both non-narrative and narrative representations of sequences of events—that they are *selective*. According to White, "every narrative, however seemingly 'full,' is constructed on the basis of a set of events which *might have been included but were left out*; and this is as true of imaginary as it is of realistic narratives".[11] The lack of connection between the events is indicative of one of the essential differences between non-narrative and narrative representations. Not only is there no link between the events described in different years, but nothing connects the events described within each year. Did the hard winter of 709 put paid to the duke or was his death unrelated? Was 710 a hard year because the crop yield was poor or were there additional hardships? Were some of these hardships a result of the duke's death? The text contains neither explicit nor implicit answers to these questions, and there is a complete absence of what Peter Goldie refers to as *coherence*—that is, causal and other connections in the represented sequence of events.[12]

A third feature of the annal is revealed in White's translation of the final entries:

> 1056. The Emperor Henry died; and his son Henry succeeded to the rule.
> 1057. 1058. 1059. 1060. 1061. 1062. 1063. 1064.
> 1065. 1066. 1067. 1068. 1069. 1070. 1071. 1072.[13]

The representation lacks *closure*, which White describes as "that summing up of the 'meaning' of the chain of events with which it deals that we normally expect from the well-made story".[14] White's description matches Goldie's observations on the characteristic features of narratives that take human beings as their subject: they are not only coherent but meaningful, and have evaluative and emotional import—that is, offer the narrator's judgement of—and emotional response to—the represented sequence of events.[15] Both coherence and closure can be subsumed under the concept of *plot*, which is "a structure of relationships by which the events contained in the account are endowed with a meaning by being identified as parts of an integrated whole" for White and "the active process of *sjužet* working on *fabula*, the dynamic of its interpretive ordering" for Brooks.[16] I shall designate *plot* as the feature that distinguishes narratives from non-narrative representations of sequences of events.[17] My interest is in narratives which are works of literature. In chapter 1: §2, I stated that the literary stance characteristically incorporates the fictive stance, and I take this to be true of the relationship between literary narratives and fictional narratives such that literary narratives are works of fiction, literature, and narrative. In the remainder of this chapter, I shall—unless otherwise specified—employ "narrative" to mean "literary narrative".

15. NARRATIVE THICKNESS

Derek Attridge is explicitly sceptical of the "tradition of 'organic form'" due to its reliance upon the combination of two separate elements.[18] His alternative is a particularly intimate relationship between literary form and literary content, where content is *constitutive* of form: "Meaning is not therefore something that appears in defining opposition or complementary apposition to form, but as something already taken up within form; forms are made out of meanings quite as much as they are made out of sounds and shapes".[19] One of Bradley's claims is, as noted in §11 in chapter 3, "This unity has, if you like, various 'aspects' or 'sides,' but they are not factors or parts; if you try to examine one, you find it is also the other".[20] This could be interpreted as a claim of constitution rather than inseparability, but neither Bradley nor Attridge appear to mean "constitution" in the strict philosophical sense. In David Wiggins's classic example of the coincident objects explanation of material constitution, the tree T is constituted by W, the aggregate of its cellulose molecules at a particular time.[21] T can change while W remains the same (if the tree is cut up in such a way so as not to damage any cells) and W can change while T remains the same (when the tree is pruned). T and W thus coexist spatially and temporally. The relationship between T and W is clearly different from that between form and meaning because meaning cannot be altered without a corresponding change in form—a symmetry I discuss below. One of Attridge's main concerns is the relationship between the institution of literature (as opposed to individual literary works) and ethical responsibility. This concern manifests itself in a defence of literary form against accusations of insignificance in comparison with ethics and his rejection of the form-content opposition is in service of this end. If one sets this issue aside, however, it is perfectly plausible to consider Attridge's *staging* as a thesis of form-content *inseparability* in literary works, as I shall demonstrate.

Attridge begins his re-elaboration of literary form by advancing the work as "an act-event" or "performance".[22] A performance should be understood as a particular reading of a particular work by a particular individual rather than a performance in terms of acting or reading aloud and is thus not dissimilar to Bradley's focus on the experience of the poem.[23] The work (act-event) of literature is constituted by responsiveness to its singularity. Singularity "is a uniqueness derived from a capacity to be endlessly transformed while remaining identifiable—within the institutional norms—as what it is".[24] Singularity is based on the paradox Derrida identifies in the signature: the signature is both unique (the legal system recognises an individual's signature to represent that individual alone), but also repeated and—on each repetition— slightly different (no two signings will be exactly the same).[25] The signature thus represents not only an individual entity, but an act of signing by that individual which has a context (time and place). Similarly, the literary work (as experience) is both the same (in its created uniqueness) and different (because no two readings—even by the same person—will be exactly the same). Singularity also describes the way in which literary works are characterised by the potential for interpretation and reinterpretation.[26]

Singularity is a necessary characteristic of literature and is linked to both literary form and literary value: "Responding to the work as literary means responding to the singularity of its meaningful, affective moment, occurring in the renewable act of my performance; what it does not mean is carrying away from the text some conceptual substance for my further use or entertainment".[27] Like Bradley, Attridge is distinguishing the value of literature *qua* literature from the instrumental values that a literary work may have. This passage is an explicit statement of form-content inseparability as the substance cannot be removed from the work (the combination of substance and style). Attridge also shares Bradley's concern with resonant meaning and claims that words are composed of sounds and shapes: "These sounds and shapes are nexuses of meaning and feeling, and hence deeply rooted in culture, history, and the varieties of human experience. The formal sequence therefore functions as a *staging* of meaning and feeling".[28] Staging is realised in "performative reading", an experience of the work that activates its linguistic power and involves the simultaneous experience of its conceptual, emotional, and physical qualities.[29] Staging is essential to appreciating literature and is in fact the source of the pleasure taken in literature *qua* literature. Like form-content inseparability for Bradley, staging is the criterion for the literary, and a work is defined as literary if it is "open to such a staging of the primary functions of language and discourse".[30]

Just as a director stages a play, so literary form stages literary content and staging is the means by which form is re-elaborated such that it is (partly) constituted by content. While Attridge rejects the *tradition of organic form* in favour of *constitution*, the constitution relation is—unlike identity—asymmetrical, so if content constitutes form, form does not constitute content. It is not only substance that cannot be removed from a work without loss of identity for Attridge, however, as formal features are apprehended as "*already meaningful*".[31] He states, "The sounds and shapes of the text are always already meaningful sounds and shapes, and there is no moment, not even a theoretical one, at which it is possible to isolate a purely formal property—at least not without turning the literary work into something else".[32] When one does isolate a formal property of the work, one therefore moves outside the literary act-event and is no longer discussing the work, in the same way that poetic form and poetic content in isolation are no longer the poetic work for Bradley. The relationship proposed by both Attridge and Bradley is symmetrical—neither content nor form can be isolated without loss of identity—and thus more accurately characterised as inseparability than constitution.

There is further evidence of staging as an inseparability relation in the claim that staging includes the mobilization of meanings, or rather of the events of meaning—

their sequentiality, interplay, and changing intensity, their patterns of expectation and satisfaction or tension and release, their precision or diffuseness. It does not include any extractable sense, information, image, or referent that the work lays before the reader. Through this mobilization of meanings, the work's linguistic operations such as referentiality, metaphoricity, intentionality, and ethicity are staged.[33]

Staging as the *mobilisation of meanings*—or *forming of content*—matches Bradley's resonant meaning very closely. Attridge and Bradley are both concerned with the experience of the literary work, the close relation of sound and meaning in this experience, and its final value. I shall henceforth take "staging" to describe the relation of form-content inseparability in literary works, once again understood as a demand imposed upon a work rather than discovered therein.[34] If staging functions as a necessary condition for literature in general, then Attridge's theory indicates how Bradley's thesis of form-content inseparability can be manipulated to extend beyond poetry. I shall now explain the operation of staging in literary narratives in particular by means of Lamarque's work on narrative opacity.

Lamarque identifies the type of narratives which are opaque as follows:

> Only where the mode of narration is salient—in other words where the form in which a story is told matters in the appraisal of the narrative—will co-referential substitutions be blocked. Those narratives primarily concerned with imparting information—from homely conversational narratives to those of history or biography—will normally invite a transparent construal of their proper names and other referential devices.[35]

The mention of the salience of the mode of narration recalls Attridge's argument: "What we respond to in performing a literary work is evidently a complex involving both the formal and the semantic".[36] Narrative opacity is distinct from, but related to, W. V. O. Quine's referential opacity. Quine identifies several referentially opaque contexts, where the truth of a sentence depends upon something other than the referent such that truth is not preserved in coreferential substitutions. For example, although "Tegucigalpa" and "the capital of Honduras" have the same referent, coreferential substitution transforms true statement (1) into false statement (2):

1. "Philip believes that Tegucigalpa is in Nicaragua".
2. "Philip believes that the capital of Honduras is in Nicaragua".[37]

Narrative opacity is not concerned with the preservation of truth, but with the preservation of the identity of the fictional work, specifically with the constraints it places on one's imaginative engagement with that work. Lamarque's discussion of narrative opacity in terms of the relation between form and content focuses on the issue of paraphrase, about which I shall have more to say in §16 below, but he is explicit that "narrative opacity also shows how form helps determine content in prose narrative".[38] Content is always shaped by form in a literary narrative such that the narrative is not transparent—that is, one does not penetrate through the form straight to the content as one would in a philosophical or historical work.

Narrative content is therefore "not merely loosely or contingently connected to its mode of presentation, but is partially constituted by it".[39] People, places, and events thus appear under a description, which constitutes a perspective on them. Two examples from Dickens are instructive; the first describes Coketown in *Hard Times*:

> It was a town of red brick, or of brick that would have been red if the smoke and ashes had allowed it; but as matters stood it was a town of unnatural red and black like the painted face of a savage. It was a town of machinery and tall chimneys, out of which interminable serpents of smoke trailed themselves for ever and ever, and never got uncoiled. It had a black canal in it, and a river that ran purple with ill-smelling dye, and vast piles of building full of windows where there was a rattling and a trembling all day long, and where the piston of the steam-engine worked monotonously up and down, like the head of an elephant in a state of melancholy madness. It contained several large streets all very like one another, and many small streets still more like one another, inhabited by people equally like one another, who all went in and out at the same hours, with the same sound upon the same pavements, to do the same work, and to whom every day was the same as yesterday and tomorrow, and every year the counterpart of the last and the next.[40]

This is not simply a representation of a fictional town, but a representation which is so laden with negative terminology and imagery that one responds with ever-increasing distaste as the description unfolds. The point of view from which Dickens introduces Coketown is such that one cannot both engage with the novel and imagine the town as appealing or attractive in any way. The perspectival description of the fictional setting is paradigmatic form-content unity because the content, Coketown, is shaped by the form, the point of view from which it is presented, such that the content is not separable from the form-content unity which constitutes the work.

This is true of all narratives where the mode of narration is salient, including those that employ real rather than fictional people, places, or events. Jacob's Island (a rookery in Bermondsey), for example, is presented under an aspect in *Oliver Twist; or, The Parish Boy's Progress*:

> In such a neighbourhood, beyond Dockhead in the Borough of Southwark, stands Jacob's Island, surrounded by a muddy ditch, six or eight feet deep and fifteen or twenty wide when the tide is in, once called Mill Pond, but known in the days of this story as Folly Ditch. It is a creek or inlet from the Thames, and can always be filled at high water by opening the sluices at the Lead Mills from which it took its name. At such times, a stranger, looking from one of the

wooden bridges thrown across it at Mill Lane, will see the inhabitants of the houses on either side lowering from their back doors and windows, buckets, pails, domestic utensils of all kinds, in which to haul the water up; and when his eye is turned from these operations to the houses themselves, his utmost astonishment will be excited by the scene before him. Crazy wooden galleries common to the backs of half-a-dozen houses, with holes from which to look down on the slime beneath; windows, broken and patched, with poles thrust out, on which to dry the linen that is never there; rooms so small, so filthy, so confined, that the air would seem too tainted even for the dirt and squalor which they shelter; wooden chambers thrusting themselves out above the mud, and threatening to fall into it—as some have done; dirt-besmirched walls and decaying foundations; every repulsive lineament of poverty, every loathsome indication of filth, rot, and garbage; all these ornament the banks of Folly Ditch. [41]

The perspectival aspect under which Jacob's Island is presented differs from that of Coketown in diction and tone, but shares its negative point of view as Dickens creates an atmospheric setting for the villainous Sikes's final bolt-hole—where he meets his ignominious and much-deserved end by accidentally hanging himself while attempting to escape from an angry crowd. Numerous parts of London are described in great detail in *Oliver Twist*, but because *the form in which the story is told matters in the appraisal of the narrative* the geographical content is not presented transparently. The lack of transparency means one cannot invoke just any information about London in one's imaginative engagement with the novel if the identity of the work is to be preserved. Like "Gerontion", *Oliver Twist* does not authorise one to imagine "the city that hosted the 2012 Summer Olympics" when one reads "London". "London" refers to London, but "London" is presented under an aspect rather than in its full extension. "London" in *Oliver Twist* is not therefore London *per se* (i.e., "London" in its fully extensional use), but *London-in-*Oliver-Twist (i.e., London under the aspect *Oliver Twist* licences one to imagine). Lamarque states,

> The content of literary fictional narrative is infused with a kind of opacity. The content is given and thus constituted, as we might say, "under a description". This is not true just for the fictional characters and fictional incidents described in the narrative, which acquire their nature and very existence from the modes of their presentation, but also for any real world setting, both material and moral, which itself is presented under a perspective. [42]

The relation in opaque narratives is one of inseparability, which Lamarque calls "form-content indivisibility" because the point of view (form) and the person, place, or event (content) cannot be separated: one cannot separate either Coketown or London from the point of view Dickens offers on each in the respective novels.[43] Narrative thickness and poetic thickness thus have an identical effect on the extension of proper names.

I argued above, *contra* Attridge, that staging was an instantiation of form-content inseparability. Less controversially, I have interpreted narrative opacity as a function of form-content inseparability. I regard staging as a development of Bradley's resonant meaning that can be extended to all literary works and opacity as the mechanism by which form-content inseparability operates in those literary works that are also narratives. The respective conceptions of staging and opacity complement each other and Attridge's literary singularity matches Lamarque's formal salience: Where formal salience is absent or limited, a narrative will be transparent as one penetrates through the form to the content. Transparent narratives, such as newspaper reports, will not be singular because each performance of the narrative will be much the same as the last and unlikely to be open to different interpretations. I proposed staging as a necessary condition of literature and the notion that opacity is a necessary condition of literary narratives is implicit in Lamarque, a "standing assumption".[44] The combination of the two concepts produces a version of poetic thickness that is applicable to literary narratives rather than poetry:

> *NARRATIVE THICKNESS:* the inseparability of literary form and literary content in the experience of a literary narrative such that neither form nor content can be isolated. Narrative thickness is a demand which is satisfied by a work rather than a property of a text, and is characteristic of literary narratives such that if a work is a literary narrative, it will reward the demand for narrative thickness.[45]

16. WORK IDENTITY

In Lamarque's discussion of paraphrase, he demonstrates the strength of the inseparability relation by questioning the restriction of the prohibition against the substitution of words with synonyms to poetry. He maintains that the value of even novel-length, literary narratives is likely to be affected by such changes:

> A Jane Austen or Charles Dickens novel, let's say, gets its identity, and through that its literary value, in the precise words—give or take minor issues of textual corruption and so forth—written by the author. Wilful changes, even preserving sense, would be unacceptable and undermine work identity. Even more significantly it could never be said with confidence than any given synonym substitution is "harmless" to a literary narrative.[46]

The idea that the substitution of a single word alters *work identity* is relatively uncontroversial for poems, but not for novels, due to the typical differences mentioned in §14 above. Lamarque wants to extend the resistance to paraphrase accepted for poetry to literary narratives and his strategy is reliant upon the similarity in the kind of attention paid to each by readers. He quotes Ian Ousby on the use of the word "peep" in *Bleak House* and a similar example can be constructed from the use of the words "human" and "humane" in *Oliver Twist*, particularly in the first ten (of fifty-three) chapters of the novel.

The first instance occurs when the authorities are "humanely resolved" to send the orphan Oliver to a workhouse.[47] Subsequently, Mr Bumble states, "You are a humane woman, Mrs Mann", a sentence that drips with dramatic irony in a sincere exchange between two of the most bestial inmates in the narrative's well-populated menagerie.[48] There is also the worrying juxtaposition between "humane" and "Mann", which suggests that Mrs Mann might be an everyman, representative of the species—and indeed there is precious little humanity, fellow feeling, or responsibility demonstrated by any of the characters until Oliver meets the Artful Dodger, who manipulates him as a means to his own ends. Shortly after the conversation between Mr Bumble and Mrs Mann, Gambfield explains how the practice of setting fire to the feet of trapped chimney sweeps is "humane", causing them to renew their struggles to escape as it does.[49] Dickens then writes of "what a beautiful thing human nature can be" when describing Noah, yet another villain whose path Oliver has the misfortune to cross.[50] In London, human nature is characterised in terms of the passion for "*hunting something*" as Oliver is pursued by a crowd on his first outing with the Artful Dodger (a sentiment that will be confirmed when another crowd hounds Sikes to his death).[51] The vision of humanity and human nature that emerges in the initial chapters of *Oliver Twist* is extremely—absolutely, even—bleak, and this perspective is at least in part created by the repetition of the words in an ironic tone, and the restriction of the words to ironic employment until the appearance of Mr Brownlow, who really does "have a heart large enough for any six ordinary old gentlemen of human disposition".[52] Even here, however, the hyperbole implies how rare an individual of Mr Brownlow's admittedly considerable— but one would hope not exceptional—kindness is in the human species.

With respect to "peep" in *Bleak House*, Lamarque concludes, "A single word in so long a novel might seem of marginal significance—and thus easily substitutable—but the lesson from narrative opacity is that there is a standing assumption that form of narration *counts* in the characterisation of content".[53] The content of a literary narrative is essentially—*not merely loosely or contingently*—constituted by the perspectival description and the narrative is therefore necessarily narrated in the particular mode of the author. This necessary relation means that to realise the content of the novel in a different mode is to lose work identity. If one is reading a poem or novel *qua* literature, then form *counts*. Substitution with synonyms may preserve content in its entirety, but the form will differ, even if only to a small extent, and the alteration therefore results in a loss of work identity—when one is reading a work *qua* literature.

I have proposed narrative thickness as a necessary condition of literary narratives and I am therefore committed to the view that work identity is lost if either content or form are altered. To adapt Dickie's terminology from §3 in chapter 1, a literary work is a text that has been presented to and accepted by the literary public for appreciation, and survives as a work in virtue of being embedded in the institution of literature. Olsen maintains that the "literary work is therefore logically tied to the author/reader relationship and can only be understood as a transaction between these two institutional roles".[54] A work is thus an abstract object, a type, that is constituted by—but not identical to—a text, which is itself a sequence of words. A consequence of narrative thickness is that the alteration of, for example, one of the 355,000-odd words of *Bleak House* alters work identity, producing another distinct type rather than a token of the type *Bleak House*. A further consequence, which is more plausible but nonetheless counter-intuitive, is that all translations of literary works are also new types rather than tokens of the originals. These apparently unpalatable consequences might be taken as a *reductio ad absurdum* against narrative thickness.

In chapter 1: §2, I stated that I was a contextualist with regard to literature and that I therefore regard historical and cultural facts about literary works as relevant to both work identity and literary appreciation. I mentioned Borges's "Pierre Menard" and acknowledged that two different works could be constituted by two identical texts. Text identity is only a necessary condition for work identity. A second necessary condition can be established by adapting Jerrold Levinson's proposal for works of music to literature: Literary works must be such that authors writing in different literary-historical contexts (including a single author on separate occasions) who produce identical texts invariably create distinct literary works. I shall refer to this necessary condition, the identity of the literary-historical context in which a work is created, as "provenance identity".[55] Text identity and provenance identity are jointly sufficient conditions for work identity.

Nelson Goodman and Catherine Elgin disagree, holding that text identity is a sufficient condition of work identity and that Menard is simply replicating Cervantes's work such that both Cervantes's manuscript and Menard's manuscript are tokens of the type Cervantes's *Don Quixote*.[56] Despite this difference, Goodman and I are in agreement regarding the consequences of an alteration in the text for work identity: "Even replacement of a character in a text by another synonymous character (if any can be found in a discursive language) yields a different work".[57] The reason for this ostensibly extreme view can be found in Goodman's discussion of music which he characterises like literature, as an *allographic* art form—that is, an art form where exact duplications of artworks are regarded as genuine rather than forgeries.[58] He argues that complete compliance with the score is a necessary and sufficient condition for an instance of a work of music, with the result that "the most miserable performance without actual mistakes does count as such an instance, while the most brilliant performance with a single note wrong does not".[59] Goodman notes that this consequence is both counter-intuitive and contrary to the ordinary employment of language, but warns against collapsing the distinction between ordinary and theoretical vocabulary.

> The innocent-seeming principle that performances differing by just one note are instances of the same work risks the consequence—in view of the transitivity of identity—that all performances whatsoever are of the same work. If we allow the least deviation, all assurance of work-preservation and score-preservation is lost; for by a series of one-note errors of omission, addition, and modification, we can go all the way from *Beethoven's Fifth Symphony* to *Three Blind Mice*.[60]

The same point about the transitivity of identity can be made for any work of literature: one could begin with the claim that *Ulysses* is identical to *Ulysses*-minus-one-word and end with the claim that *Ulysses* is identical to *And Then There Were None*. *Ulysses* is a particularly good example because of the numerous mistakes—up to five thousand– in its first publication, by Shakespeare and Company in 1922.[61] If the errors do indeed reach several thousand, then the claim that the 1922 and 1984 editions of the novel are different works is less controversial than it first appears, but the dispute over the number of errors draws attention to an important issue. Goodman's argument against work identity in the case of a single erroneous note can be regarded as a Sorites Paradox which is applicable to literary works: if one allows a single substitution, then one will either have to accept that two completely different works are identical or make what will inevitably be an arbitrary decision about the number of words that can be substituted before identity is lost. It is no less implausible to claim that the substitution of a single word alters work identity than it is to claim that, for example, twenty-five words or one percent of the words can be substituted without loss of identity. A boundary between identity and difference will have to be established at some point and, despite intuitions to the contrary, setting that boundary at a single difference is the least arbitrary point in the case of a literary work, as it can be justified by recourse to authorial intention (about which I shall have more to say in chapter 6: §21).

My account of literary value is experiential—that is, the literary value of a literary work is the value of the experience afforded by the literary work. While I am committed to the view that a single substitution or error produces a different work, my concern is with the experience afforded by that work.

The experience afforded by *Ulysses* and *Ulysses*-minus-one-word would be almost identical such that is difficult to imagine a context in which the difference is salient. Furthermore, the value of the two experiences would be either identical or indistinguishable. The experience afforded by the 1922 original and 1986 Bodley Head standard editions respectively is also similar—perhaps very similar—but it differs to the extent that critics and philosophers are careful to read the latter when writing about the work (unless they have a specific interest in the 1922 edition). A translation is a particular type of paraphrase, one that aims at reproducing identical content in a completely different form, a form which is partly dictated by the syntax and tropes of the second language. If one considers literary value in terms of the value of the experience afforded by the literary work, then it is evident that the experience of, for example, Joyce's *Ulysses* will be significantly different from the experience of M. Auguste Morel's *Ulysse* (the first French translation, published in 1929) when reading each *qua* literature. A faithful and skilful translation may produce an experience which is similar and has equivalent value, but both the experience and the value will differ from that afforded by the original. This distinction is, once again, reflected in critical and philosophical practice. Counter-intuitive though it may be, *Ulysse* is therefore a different work of literary art and a type in itself rather than a token of *Ulysses*.

17. DIDACTIC THINNESS?

A decisive objection to narrative thickness as a necessary condition of a literary narrative would be an example of a work that was literary, but "thin"—that is, did not satisfy the demand for form-content inseparability. The category of didactic literature appears to offer many such counterexamples, works that contain a "message" or "moral" that is independent of the work and is intended specifically for—in Attridge's terms—*carrying away from the text for further use*. Vladimir Nabokov is keen to distance himself from such works: "I am neither a reader nor a writer of didactic fiction, and, despite John Ray's assertion, *Lolita* has no moral in tow".[62] Bradley holds that in didactic poems "the poet had a truth or fact—philosophical, agricultural, social—before him, and then, as we say, clothed it in metrical and coloured language".[63] Didactic poems are not problematic for him as they are not "pure poems" and there is thus no requirement that the demand for form-content inseparability be rewarded. Hemingway offers a similar view in the claim that: "No good book has ever been written that has in it symbols arrived at beforehand and stuck in", which recalls Cleanth Brooks's warning against conceiving of form as a "beautified envelope" containing content.[64] Hemingway and Brooks's observations are direct challenges to the notion that the demand for narrative thickness will be rewarded by didactic literary works.

The adjective "didactic" denotes the property of being characterised by instruction or having instruction as an aim. Until recently, the instructive value of literature was simply assumed, but the historical weight of literary didacticism has occasionally been ignored in the twentieth century. Beardsley, for example, mentions Plato, Arnold, Shelley, and others, but dismisses three thousand years of instruction as a literary value in two sentences: "Unfortunately, as far as I can see, nobody has ever given any plausible reasons for the Didactic Theory. There is therefore nothing to refute".[65] Didactic theory deserves more attention than he is prepared to grant, but "didactic" is nonetheless a pejorative term, as Charles Repp points out, "It is generally understood that *didacticism* refers to some sort of defect in a work of literature as such".[66] This defect cannot be a straightforward link to instruction because there are works which are not didactic—Repp cites Fyodor Dostoyevsky's *Crime and Punishment* and George Eliot's *Middlemarch*—despite having instruction as their purpose.

Sidney suggests how this negative connotation may have arisen.[67] Responding to accusations that poetry could not be both fictional and instructive, he maintains that poetry instructs by delighting. Samuel Johnson subsequently picked up on this distinction: "The end of writing is to instruct; the end of poetry is to instruct by pleasing".[68] As twentieth century scholars questioned instruction as a literary value, F. R. Leavis, D. H. Lawrence, and others prised appropriate moralism apart from disagreeable didacticism.[69] Despite Leavis's critique of Johnson's alleged requirement that the morality of a work should be explicitly stated, he excused Johnson from "the most indefensible didacticism".[70] Indefensible didacticism in literature is apparently pure instruction, and defensible didacticism, instruction by pleasing as recommended by Johnson and Sidney. Repp follows Leavis in this respect as the instruction must not only be overt, but "*too* overt" in order to qualify as didactic.[71]

Once these two categories of didacticism are differentiated, my response to the didactic thinness objection to narrative thickness becomes obvious. Works that are too overt—that is, messages which have (to employ the terms of Bradley, Brooks, and Nabokov) been *clothed*, *enveloped*, or *towed* by fiction, will not reward the demand for narrative thickness. In works which (to employ the terms of Sidney, Leavis, and Repp) didacticism is *pleasurable*, *defensible*, or *not too overt*—the demand for narrative thickness will be rewarded. This defence is reliant on the incompatibility of overtly didactic narratives, where the author's intention is to communicate a message, with narrative thickness, where the author's intention is that the work be appreciated as literature. Short of committing to a theory of literature that focused on characteristics such as complexity, ambiguity, and open-endedness as essential to literature, my position is fragile: any interpretation of an overtly didactic work which made a convincing case for the work as literary would prove fatal. [72] If one considers the canon of literature there are, however, very few works that pose this threat—with one notable exception.

J. M. Coetzee's *Elizabeth Costello* is a collection of seven short stories (one of which is in two parts) and a postscript, first published in 2003. The full title of the collection is *Elizabeth Costello: Eight Lessons*, and lessons three and four share the same title, "The Lives of Animals", with subtitles distinguishing part one from part two. Although my discussion will focus on "The Lives of Animals", I want to draw attention to four of the other titles: "Realism" (lesson one), "The Novel in Africa" (lesson two), "The Humanities in Africa" (lesson five), and "The Problem of Evil" (lesson six). All four are closer to the titles of lectures or academic papers than short stories—especially the fourth, which identifies the philosophical paradox evinced by the coexistence of evil in the world and a creator who is both omnipotent and benevolent. The combination of these titles with their presentation as lessons creates the expectation of "messages", of content that will retain its identity independently of the context of the work, and will not thus reward the demand for narrative thickness.

With regard to "The Lives of Animals", this expectation is heightened because the same short story in two parts appeared in *The Lives of Animals*, a non-fiction collection of essays published in 1999, which combined Coetzee's contribution with responses by Marjorie Garber, Peter Singer, Wendy Doniger, and Barbara Smuts. The four replies are philosophical responses to "The Philosophers and the Animals" (part one) and "The Poets and the Animals" (part two) read *qua* philosophy—as lessons or arguments. The content of the narrative appears to meet this expectation as it is concerned with a lecture (part one) and a seminar and a debate (part two) by novelist Elizabeth Costello at the fictional Appleton College. Part one is composed almost entirely of Costello's lecture, a question from the audience, and a discussion of Costello's position at a dinner held in her honour. A significant proportion of part two consists of Costello's seminar in the English department and her debate in the philosophy department. Furthermore, "The Philosophers and the Animals" includes explicit discussions of German war crimes in Poland, Thomas Nagel's 1974 philosophy paper "What Is It Like to Be a Bat?", and the practice of vegetarianism. [73] "The Poets and the Animals" includes discussions of Plato and Aquinas, Swift's *Gulliver's Travels*, and the philosophical tradition from Aristotle to Descartes. [74]

"The Lives of Animals" is therefore an apparently exemplary case of didactic literature. Whether the story appears in *The Lives of Animals* or *Elizabeth Costello*, it should be understood as a work of moral philosophy which—due to Coetzee's inventiveness or his desire to contrast the literary approach with the philosophical—has been clothed with or embedded in a fictional narrative. Indeed, in her introduction to *The Lives of Animals*, Amy Gutmann states, "In the frame of fiction, Coetzee's story of Elizabeth Costello's visit to Appleton College contains empirical and philosophical arguments that are relevant to the ethical issue of how human beings should treat animals".[75] The embedding itself seems shallow and the philosophical discussion dominates more usual narrative concerns like diegetic detail, character development, and resolution. Further evidence can be found in the depiction of Costello in *Slow Man*, where she is presented as an authorial intrusion into the novel.[76] The protagonist, Paul Rayment, suspects that Costello is writing a book about him, but Costello's presence suggests to the reader that Rayment is nothing more than a character in the book Costello is writing (and Costello a character in the book Coetzee has written). Costello may well simply be Coetzee's alter ego and David Lynn's review of *Elizabeth Costello* is typical in expressing the critical concern with the relationship between Coetzee and Costello, whether Costello speaks directly for Coetzee, and whether she should always be regarded as an authorial intrusion of sorts— that is, as a deliberately thinly-disguised characterisation of Coetzee himself.[77] If this is the case, there is even less reason to think that the demand for narrative thickness will be met because the eight lessons of *Elizabeth Costello* are literally Coetzee's lessons, messages delivered in the medium of fictional tales.

Coetzee has expressed his own view of the relationship between form and content:

> A story is not a message with a covering, a rhetorical or aesthetic covering. It is not a message plus a residue, the residue, the art with which the message is coated with the residue, forming the subject matter of rhetoric or aesthetics or literary appreciation. There is no addition in stories. They are not made up of one thing plus another thing, message plus vehicle, substructure plus superstructure. On the keyboard on which they are written, the plus key does not work. There is always a difference; and the difference is not a part, the part left behind after the subtraction. The minus key does not work either: the difference is everything.[78]

Coetzee is thus adamant that narrative form and narrative content cannot and should not be separated. Given that he has written numerous essays, his decision to write about animal rights in a short story is clearly deliberate rather than imposed. In which case, "The Lives of Animals" is not intended as *a message with an aesthetic covering* and the informed reader should expect, and will indeed find, that the demand for form-content inseparability is rewarded in the work.

The story is not only an example of Attridge's staging, but what Derrida might have called *staging of staging*. "The Philosophers and the Animals" was the first of Coetzee's Tanner Lectures on Human Values, delivered at

Princeton University on 15 October 1997, and "The Poets and the Animals", the second, which—like Costello's seminar in the story—was delivered the next day. Coetzee's lecture was thus a performance of a short story in which a novelist gave a lecture on the relationship between humans and animals. The apposition of Coetzee and Costello, reality and fiction, is reproduced in the appearance of the story and replies in *The Lives of Animals*, but an extra level of complexity attends the inclusion of the lectures in *Elizabeth Costello*, a collection of short stories linked only by the presence of the eponymous character. Here, the reader is invited to read "The Lives of Animals" *qua* literature despite knowing that Coetzee presented these stories as Tanner Lectures and published them as essays in *The Lives of Animals*. One of the reasons for this self-reflexive staging becomes apparent when the thematic content of the story is scrutinised. Aside from the explicit concern with the relationship between human and animal, there is a more subtle exploration of the relationship between literature and philosophy, the contrasting ways in which they approach the subject of the moral status of animals, and the failure of the latter.

My main concern is whether the didacticism in "The Lives of Animals" is overt and identifying "the moral of the story" is thus crucial for my inquiry. The search for such a moral, however, reveals precisely its absence. There is no immediately obvious, explicit, or readily-paraphrased message, despite the tale's trappings as a "lesson" or "lecture within a story within a lecture" and despite the narrative including discussions of, and meditations on, questions of moral philosophy. The tale is narrated by John, Costello's son, and the reader sees her entirely from his point of view. She is presented as an admirable individual—highly intelligent and fiercely principled—but not an attractive one. Notwithstanding her finer qualities, Costello seems to fail in the most basic sense of what it means to be human and has great difficulty maintaining relationships with people: Her relationship with John is strained; her relationship with his wife (Norma) is antagonistic; she has no relationship with John's father; the subsequent story, "The Humanities in Africa", reveals an uncomfortable relationship with her sister; and her final engagement at the college ends with "acrimony, hostility, bitterness".[79] What kind of person, one cannot help but ask, devotes so much time and energy to saving the lives of cattle and sheep, but not to their own family and cannot manage to get along with other human beings?

The fact that the story is told from John's point of view—rather than Costello's or Norma's—is highly significant. The reader has access to John's thoughts and he quickly emerges as a kind, reasonable, personable man. Unlike his mother, he is not an exceptional individual devoted to a higher purpose, but a successful academic (in the department of physics and astronomy), and a caring husband, father, and son. There is a juxtaposition of John's virtues with those of his mother, but what is perhaps more important is that he has no obvious vices. In short, there is every reason to think that John will provide the reader with an informed and sympathetic perspective of his mother, and that if *he* has doubts about her or her views, these should be taken seriously. On a thematic—as well as personal—level John, who is a scientist (and therefore neutral in the conflict between literature and philosophy), is situated midway between his mother (a successful novelist, suggestive of the capabilities of literature in answering ethical questions) and Norma (an unsuccessful philosopher of mind, suggestive of a discipline that is severely limited, perhaps even defunct).

The overall plot unfolds in the following scenes: John picks up Costello at the airport, Costello lectures, the lecture is discussed at dinner (in part one); John discusses his mother with Norma after dinner, Costello receives a letter objecting to her comparison of the slaughter of animals with the Holocaust, Costello leads a seminar in the English department, Costello debates with a philosopher, John discusses her with Norma again, John takes Costello back to the airport (in part two).[80] The notion that the story—Costello's arrival, academic activities, and departure—is an aesthetic covering constructed in order to deliver the philosophical message—that the form is merely decorative—is completely unfounded as the absence of a message is made explicit at the end of the second part, when Costello is speaking to John. This final scene provides both narrative closure and retrospectively infuses the story with new patterns of meaning. The following two comments of Costello's are particularly important:

1. "'It's that I no longer know where I am. I seem to move around perfectly easily among people, to have perfectly normal relations with them. Is it possible, I ask myself, that all of them are participating in a crime of stupefying proportions?'"[81]
2. "'Yet I'm not dreaming. I look into your eyes, into Norma's, into the children's, and I see only kindness, human kindness. Calm down, I tell myself, you are making a mountain out of a molehill. This is life. Everyone else comes to terms with it, why can't you? *Why can't you*?'"[82]

The reader suddenly sees not only Costello, but her philosophy, from a different perspective. In the discussion leading up to this point she has shown that she is not guilty of the vices which she admits often accompany animal rights advocates (snobbery, superficiality, naivety), she has engaged with opposing viewpoints in rational argument, even when practices discussed (like bullfighting) must physically repulse her, and she has accepted that her views (for example, the Holocaust comparison) are regarded as extreme and offensive. Here, in the last few lines of the tale, the reader realises that Costello is not a fanatic or even a crusader, that she simply possesses an

enhanced sensitivity to animal suffering which—because she is morally motivated—she cannot help but act upon. This sensitivity is presented as a
burden, and the conclusion invites a reappraisal of both Costello and her
philosophy: she becomes more sympathetic, but her views more question-
able. There are at least two features of the narrative that heighten this effect.
First, repetition: part one ends with Costello in apparent confusion, with
doubt cast upon her intellectual capacities; in part two she rallies, negotiating
a series of interrogations with skill and insight; now the doubt returns—this
time self-doubt, not about her capacities, but about the value of the sensitivity to which she confesses.

Second, all John can say in response is: "'There, there. It will soon be
over'".[83] Bearing in mind that the reader has come to trust John by this point,
to identify with him even, this is a shocking end to the story, a literary
equivalent of the "twist in the tale" common to short genre fiction. The fact
that Costello's visit is at an end (and thus already over) and the repeated
references to Costello as *old* and *tired* suggest that John is talking about
nothing other than her death, a merciful end to the suffering that is the result
of her heightened sensitivity. This interpretation is also supported by the
content of the final story in the collection, "At the Gate", which is reminiscent of Kafka's "Before the Law" (from *The Trial*), and appears to concern
Costello's death. Instead of simply arguing—in summary of Costello—that
owning a leather lamp is as morally repugnant as owning a lamp made from
human skin, Coetzee seems to be suggesting that there are some people who
see the world in this way and questioning whether this sensitivity is desirable. Despite her disingenuous comment in (1) above, Costello clearly has
difficulty maintaining normal human relationships and one can see why she
is estranged when the full impact of her sensitivity is revealed. Ultimately,
there is indeterminacy rather than resolution. Is it desirable to be a Costello in
a world of Normas? John, for one, thinks not, but Coetzee does not provide a
straightforward answer.

There is a great deal more that can be said about "The Lives of Animals"
that is relevant to my inquiry, but which I do not have space to discuss. I
selected *Elizabeth Costello* as a potential counterexample to my claim that
narrative thickness is a necessary condition of literature because the collection is apparently an overtly didactic work of literature—that is, an example
of narrative thinness. Focusing on "The Lives of Animals", I showed that
there are numerous reasons to expect a *message with an aesthetic covering*,
content which is salient to the extent that the particular mode of narration is
not necessary to the communication of that message. In sitting down to a
Tanner Lecture or picking up *The Lives of Animals* one might thus expect
that one was about to hear or read a work whose essential content could have
been expressed in another form. Subsequently, I offered evidence from Coetzee and the story to establish that this is not the case, that "The Lives of

Animals" does not admit of an alternate mode of presentation: the particular content is necessarily expressed in the particular form of the story. The demand for narrative thickness is thus rewarded and the didacticism is revealed to be of the pleasurable, defensible, or covert sort—if, indeed, it is correctly categorised as "didactic" at all. (My interpretation of the story is as a literary *exploration* of the relevant philosophical issues rather than an *instruction* therein.)

The example in fact seems to be a narrative equivalent to *De rerum natura*, and I think Lamarque's response to Kivy (discussed in §13 in chapter 3) is appropriate here. "The Lives of Animals" can be read *qua* philosophy or *qua* literature, but the reader who reads it *qua* philosophy is likely to have an impoverished experience, because part of the work's value is the way it engages with philosophical issues in a literary manner, demonstrating that literature *qua* literature can engage with ethical issues as well as—if not better than (according to Coetzee)—philosophy. The *form* as well as the content of the two parts of the story offer contrasting approaches to the lives of animals: Costello's lecture is the focus of "The Philosophers and the Animals", whereas "The Poets and the Animals" is more of a traditional narrative. Even though the inclusion of "The Lives of Animals" in *The Lives of Animals* appears to be an invitation to read the short story *qua* philosophy, to read it *qua* philosophy—to extract Costello's arguments and views—is to miss something significant about the way in which the short story, *Elizabeth Costello*, and literature in general can explore moral problems while being read *qua* literature. Doniger admits a similar view when she begins her response with the statement: "It seems somehow reductionistic to respond to these deeply moving readings as if they had been dry academic arguments".[84] Having established narrative thickness as a necessary condition of literary narratives, I can now conclude that form-content inseparability—as instantiated in either poetic thickness, narrative thickness, or both—is a necessary condition of all literary works and it is to literary thickness that I turn next.

NOTES

1. A. C. Bradley, "Poetry for Poetry's Sake," in A. C. Bradley, *Oxford Lectures on Poetry* (London: Macmillan, 1959 [1901]), 3–34: 15. Part of this quote appeared in my discussion of Weitz in §10 in chapter 3.

2. Bradley, "Poetry for Poetry's Sake," 25.

3. Nigel Fabb, "Why Is Verse Poetry?," *PN Review 36* (2009), 52–57: 55–56.

4. Fabb, "Why Is Verse Poetry?," 56.

5. Anna Christina Ribeiro, "Toward a Philosophy of Poetry," *Midwest Studies in Philosophy 33* (2009), 61–77: 66.

6. Ribeiro, "Toward a Philosophy of Poetry," 68.

7. Tzvetan Todorov, "The Typology of Detective Fiction," in T. Todorov, *The Poetics of Prose*, trans. Richard Howard (Oxford: Blackwell, 1977 [1971]), 42–52: 45.

8. Peter Brooks, *Reading for the Plot: Design and Intention in Narrative* (Cambridge, MA: Harvard University Press, 1992 [1984]), 326.

9. Hayden White, "The Value of Narrativity in the Representation of Reality," *Critical Inquiry 7* (1980), 5–27: 6.

10. White, "Value of Narrativity," 11.

11. White, "Value of Narrativity," 14.

12. Peter Goldie, *The Mess Inside: Narrative, Emotion, and the Mind* (Oxford: Oxford University Press, 2012), 14.

13. White, "Value of Narrativity," 13.

14. White, "Value of Narrativity," 20.

15. Goldie, *Mess Inside*, 22–25.

16. White, "Value of Narrativity, 13; Brooks, *Reading for the Plot*, 25.

17. White maintains that an annal has a plot due to the structure provided by the listing of the years ("Value of Narrativity," 13), but I consider both coherence and closure as necessary for plot.

18. Derek Attridge, *The Singularity of Literature* (New York: Routledge, 2004), 108.

19. Attridge, *Singularity of Literature*, 114.

20. Bradley, "Poetry for Poetry's Sake," 15.

21. David Wiggins, "On Being in the Same Place at the Same Time," *The Philosophical Review 77* (1968), 90–95: 90. The coincident objects explanation of material constitution is considered to be the standard account in metaphysics and defences include the following: Saul Kripke, "Identity and Necessity," in Milton K. Munitz, ed., *Identity and Individuation* (New York: New York University Press, 1971), 83–94; Frederick Doepke, "Spatially Coinciding Objects," in Michael C. Rea, ed., *Material Constitution: A Reader* (Lanham, MD: Rowman & Littlefield, 1997), 10–24; E. J. Lowe, "Instantiation, Identity, and Constitution," *Philosophical Studies 44* (1983), 45–59; Judith Jarvis Thomson, "Parthood and Identity Across Time," *Journal of Philosophy 80* (1983), 201–20; and Sydney Shoemaker, "Self, Body, and Coincidence," *Proceedings of the Aristotelian Society Supplementary Volume 73* (1999), 287–306.

22. Attridge, *Singularity of Literature*, 108.

23. Attridge holds that a poem, play, or novel is a *potential* literary work that is only realised as a literary work in the act-event of reader or listener engagement with the poem, play, or novel. There is thus a sense in which each reading generates a unique literary work, but there is also a sense in which the potential literary work places normative constraints on the act-event—that is, the engagement must be appropriate in order for the realisation to take place (*Singularity of Literature*, 58–59). Both Bradley and Attridge therefore identify the work with the experience of the work; Bradley's emphasis is on the author's creation, and Attridge's, on the reader's or listener's response.

24. Derek Attridge, *J. M. Coetzee and the Ethics of Reading: Literature in the Event* (London: University of Chicago Press, 2004), 9.

25. Jacques Derrida, "From *Signsponge*," in Jacques Derrida, *Acts of Literature*, ed. D. Attridge, trans. R. Rand (London: Routledge, 1992), 344–69: 359–61.

26. Attridge, *J. M. Coetzee and the Ethics of Reading*, 10.

27. Attridge, *Singularity of Literature*, 111. Part of this quote appeared in my characterisation of Attridge as an autonomist in §5 in chapter 1.

28. Attridge, *Singularity of Literature*, 109.

29. Attridge, *Singularity of Literature*, 109 & 98–99. Staging has a similar function and significance to the *dramatic* in John Gibson: "A literary narrative is in effect a sustained dramatic gesture, a way not only of presenting some content or material but of responding to it" (*Fiction and the Weave of Life* [Oxford: Oxford University Press, 2007], 117).

30. Attridge, *Singularity of Literature*, 110. Like Bradley on the relationship between resonant meaning and poetry (as noted in §13 in chapter 3), it is not clear whether Attridge is proposing staging as a sufficient condition or a necessary and sufficient condition of literature.

31. Attridge, *Singularity of Literature*, 113.

32. Attridge, *Singularity of Literature*, 119.

33. Attridge, *Singularity of Literature*, 109. *Ethicity* is the particular relationship between responsiveness and responsibility which Attridge envisages, mentioned in §5 in chapter 1.

While staging is a necessary condition of ethicity, the relation is not symmetrical and I shall not discuss ethicity in this book.

34. Attridge's conception of staging is compatible with both (1) the relation of inseparability rather than constitution, and (2) this relation being a demand rather than a discovery—especially when one considers that staging is realised in performative reading.

35. Peter Lamarque, *The Opacity of Narrative* (London: Rowman & Littlefield International, 2014), 146. The initial discussion of narrative opacity is by Peter Lamarque and Stein Haugom Olsen, who use the examples of "London" in the Sherlock Holmes stories, *Tom Jones*, and *Bleak House* (*Truth, Fiction, and Literature: A Philosophical Perspective* [Oxford: Clarendon, 2002 (1994)], 80–82) and "Canterbury" in *The Canterbury Tales* (*Truth, Fiction, and Literature*, 126–28).

36. Attridge, *Singularity of Literature*, 108.

37. W. V. O. Quine, "Reference and Modality," in W. V. O Quine, *From a Logical Point of View: Nine Logico-Philosophical Essays* (New York: Harper, 1963 [1961]), 139–59: 141.

38. Lamarque, *Opacity of Narrative*, 149.

39. Lamarque, *Opacity of Narrative*, 12.

40. Charles Dickens, *Hard Times. For These Times* (Ware, Herts: Wordsworth Classics, 2000 [1854]), 18.

41. Charles Dickens, *Oliver Twist; or, The Parish Boy's Progress* (London: Penguin, 1994 [1838]), 468–69.

42. Lamarque, *Opacity of Narrative*, 166.

43. Lamarque, *Opacity of Narrative*, 154.

44. Lamarque, *Opacity of Narrative*, 155.

45. Narrative thickness should not be confused with John Gibson's *thick narratives*. Thick narratives are narratives that provide an insight into ethical values without promoting a particular morality ("Thick Narratives," in N. Carroll & J. Gibson, eds., *Narrative, Emotion, and Insight* [University Park: Pennsylvania State University Press, 2011], 69–91).

46. Lamarque, *Opacity of Narrative*, 154–55.

47. Dickens, *Oliver Twist*, 5.

48. Dickens, *Oliver Twist*, 9.

49. Dickens, *Oliver Twist*, 20.

50. Dickens, *Oliver Twist*, 40.

51. Dickens, *Oliver Twist*, 84.

52. Dickens, *Oliver Twist*, 100.

53. Lamarque, *Opacity of Narrative*, 155. Part of this quote appeared in my comparison of Lamarque and Attridge above.

54. Stein Haugom Olsen, *The End of Literary Theory* (New York: Cambridge University Press, 1987), 197.

55. Levinson provides a delineation of *musico-historical context* which is similarly adaptable to the literary case. See: Levinson, "What a Musical Work Is," 10–11.

56. Nelson Goodman & Catherine Z. Elgin, *Reconceptions in Philosophy and Other Arts and Sciences* (London: Routledge, 1988), 61–63.

57. Nelson Goodman, *Languages of Art: An Approach to a Theory of Symbols*, 2nd edition (Indianapolis, IN: Hackett, 1976), 209.

58. Goodman, *Languages of Art*, 113.

59. Goodman, *Languages of Art*, 186.

60. Goodman, *Languages of Art*, 186–87.

61. See: Edwin McDowell, "New Edition Fixes 5,000 Errors in 'Ulysses,'" *New York Times*, 7 June, 1984, http://www.nytimes.com/books/00/01/09/specials/joyce-edition.html (accessed 28 February, 2015).

62. Vladimir Nabokov, "On a Book Entitled *Lolita*" [1956], in Vladimir Nabokov, *Lolita* (London: Penguin, 1997 [1955]), 309–15: 313.

63. Bradley, "Poetry for Poetry's Sake," 23.

64. Ernest Hemingway cited in Ben Stolzfus, "Hemingway's 'After the Storm': A Lacanian Reading," in J. J. Benson, ed., *New Critical Approaches to the Short Stories of Ernest Heming-*

way (Durham, NC: Duke University Press, 1999), 48–57: 52; Cleanth Brooks, *The Well Wrought Urn* (Orlando, FL: Harcourt, 1975 [1947]), 226.

65. Monroe Beardsley, *Aesthetics: Problems in the Philosophy of Criticism* (New York: Harcourt, Brace & World, 1958), 427.

66. Charles Repp, "What's Wrong with Didacticism?" *British Journal of Aesthetics 52* (2012), 271–86: 271.

67. Sir Philip Sidney, *A Defence of Poesy* [e-book] (Oregon: Renascence Editions), available at: University of Oregon, http://darkwing.uoregon.edu/%7Erbear/defence.html (accessed 11 July 2015).

68. Samuel Johnson, "Preface to the Edition of Shakespeare's Plays," in S. Johnson, *Samuel Johnson on Shakespeare* (London: Penguin, 1989 [1765]), 120–65: 126.

69. See: F. R. Leavis, *The Common Pursuit* (London: Chatto & Windus, 1958 [1952]), 110–11; F. R. Leavis, *Anna Karenina and Other Essays* (London: Chatto & Windus,1967), 197–218; and D. H. Lawrence, "Morality and the Novel," in E. D. McDonald, ed., *Phoenix I: The Posthumous Papers of D. H. Lawrence* (London: Heinemann, 1961), 527–32.

70. F. R. Leavis, *Anna Karenina and Other Essays* (London: Chatto & Windus,1967), 215.

71. Repp, "What's Wrong with Didacticism?" 272.

72. I am nonetheless sympathetic to the argument advanced by Richard Posner for these very traits as characteristic of literature ("Against Ethical Criticism: Part II," *Philosophy and Literature 22* [1998], 394–412).

73. J. M. Coetzee, *Elizabeth Costello* (London: Vintage, 2004 [2003]), 63–64, 75–78, & 87–90.

74. Coetzee, *Elizabeth Costello*, 98–99, 100–5, & 105–12.

75. Amy Gutmann, "Introduction," in J. M. Coetzee, *The Lives of Animals* (Princeton, NJ: Princeton University Press, 1999), 3–11: 4.

76. J. M. Coetzee, *Slow Man* (London: Vintage, 2005).

77. David Lynn, "Love and Death, and Animals Too," *The Kenyon Review, New Series 27* (2005), 124–33: 125–26.

78. J. M. Coetzee, "The Novel Today," *Upstream 6* (1988), 2–5: 4.

79. Coetzee, *Elizabeth Costello*, 112.

80. The comparison may have been inspired by one of Derrida's lectures, delivered at a conference at Cérisy three months before Coetzee's Tanner Lectures. See: Jacques Derrida, *The Animal That Therefore I Am*, ed. Marie-Louise Mallet, trans. David Wills (New York: Fordham University Press, 2008 [2006]), 26.

81. Coetzee, *Elizabeth Costello*, 114.

82. Coetzee, *Elizabeth Costello*, 115.

83. Coetzee, Elizabeth Costello, 115.

84. Wendy Doniger, "Reflections," in J. M. Coetzee, *The Lives of Animals* (Princeton, NJ: Princeton University Press, 1999) 93–106: 93.

Chapter Five

Literary Thickness

The purpose of this chapter is twofold: to define *literary thickness*, the form-content inseparability that is characteristic of literature, and to argue that an *aboutness* relation holds between work and world as a consequence thereof. In §18, I subsume poetic thickness and narrative thickness under the concept of literary thickness, which is understood as a demand made of a work rather than a property discovered therein and identified as a necessary condition of literature. Section §19 explores the implications of literary thickness for reference and truth by analysing first Michael Riffaterre's referential fallacy and then Richard Gaskin's literary cognitivism. Drawing on the work of Riffaterre, Arthur Danto, and John Searle, I propose a *substantive axis* and a *formal axis* for every work in §20. I show that these conflicting interests in literary works are reconciled in literary thickness and that works that reward the demand for thickness are works for which an *aboutness* relation holds with the world. My position on reference and truth in literature emerges as pro-reference, but anti-cognitivist.

18. LITERARY THICKNESS (I)

In §13 in chapter 3, I quoted Peter Kivy's description of literary language as a thick medium, as opposed to non-literary language, which is a thin medium (and therefore transparent). Subsequently, I agreed with Lamarque that the practice of reading poetry is the practice of imposing poetic thickness on a work. Poetic thickness is not an objective property that is discovered in a text, but a demand which is made of the work by the reader who appreciates the work *qua* poetry. Poetic thickness is not entirely reliant upon the psychology of each reader either, however, and the demand is twofold. Recall from chapter 1: §3 that the work of literature is identified by the author's intention to invoke a literary response—that is, appreciation. Malcolm Budd claims that "the experience a work offers is an experience of interacting with it in whatever way it demands if it is to be understood".[1] The demand made by the work is determined by the intention and ability of the author such that not all works that are intended to be appreciated—intended to meet the demand for poetic thickness—will succeed in this aim. A work that fails in this way is a work which merely aspires to be a poem.

Understood in these terms, Kivy's *literary language* is not a medium with essential features that ground the property of literariness, but a literary use of language—that is, an employment of language which is characterised by a match between authorial intention on the one hand and reader appreciation on the other. Similarly, *non-literary language* is not a medium that lacks a literary essence, but an employment of language which is not characterised by an authorial intention for appreciation or a reader demand for poetic or narrative thickness (or which is characterised by an authorial intention for appreciation, but fails to meet the demand for poetic or narrative thickness). A newspaper is therefore a paradigmatic example of a non-literary use of language because reports are typically neither intended for literary apprecia- tion nor read with a demand for poetic or narrative thickness. To read a newspaper *qua* poetry or *qua* literary narrative would in most, if not all, instances be entirely unrewarding; one reads a report for its content—hence the transparency of the medium. While I shall at times find it expedient to write of the thickness of literary language, this is shorthand for the match between the intention behind and reception of the particular use of language, rather than an objective property of that language.

Literary thickness should not be confused with *thick concepts*, although the ideas are related. Following Gilbert Ryle's introduction of the thick/thin distinction into philosophy, Bernard Williams initiated the contemporary de- bate in moral philosophy by distinguishing thin concepts such as "good", "right", and "ought" from thick concepts such as "brutality", "courage", and "treachery". He defines the latter as concepts "which seem to express a union of fact and value".[2] Both Ryle and Williams regard irreducibility as essential to their respective uses of "thick". For Williams, this means that thick con- cepts are not reducible to their descriptive and evaluative components. Al- though Simon Blackburn denies the existence of thick concepts, his charac- terisation of irreducible thickness is enlightening:

> A thick concept might be thought of in chemical terms. It is not that the two elements of attitude and description cannot be understood as separate at some level (obviously, in searching for thick concepts or terms, we know that we are looking for items with implications of attitude on the one hand, and description on the other). But the idea must be that the two form a compound or an amalgam, rather than a mixture.[3]

A commitment to thickness means that one "loses the concept if a particular amalgam dissolves back into its elements".[4] The pairing of attitude and description is reminiscent of the constitution of perspective by description in narrative thickness, explained in §15 in chapter 4. In fact, Blackburn's description of thick concepts in chemical terms articulates precisely the unity of form and content with which Bradley was concerned: two elements are fused by the author to create a new compound which cannot then be returned to the original elements without dissolving that compound. If the compound is dissolved into the elements, identity is lost because those elements differ from the compound.

I shall henceforth subsume both instantiations of form-content inseparability in literature, poetic thickness and narrative thickness, under a single concept (which I shall amend in §21 in chapter 6):

> LITERARY THICKNESS (I): the inseparability of literary form and literary content in the experience of a literary work such that neither form nor content can be isolated. Literary thickness is a demand which is satisfied by a work rather than a property of a text, and is characteristic of literature such that if a work is a work of literature, it will reward the demand for literary thickness.

Everything which is true of literary thickness will be true of both instantiations, which are—as noted in chapter 4: §14—complementary rather than exclusive. Literary thickness is a necessary, rather than sufficient, condition of literature.

19. REFERENCE AND TRUTH

Peter Lamarque and Stein Haugom Olsen discuss three views on reference in literature: pro-reference, non-reference, and anti-reference. They identify *aboutness* as a "modest pro-reference position", note that a work's referents are not identical with what it is about, and conclude that aboutness "is a more fundamental relation than that of reference, which can largely be subsumed by it".[5] The criterion of a work being about a real person, place, or event is that the reader is required to call upon information about the real person, place, or event in order to understand the person, place, or event in the work.[6] *Oliver Twist* and "Gerontion" are thus both *about* London. Aboutness captures something of the particular effect of literary thickness with which I am concerned, which is not compatible with either a non-reference view, such as Michael Riffaterre's referential fallacy, or a strong pro-reference view (where reference and/or truth play a role in determining literary value), such as Gaskin's literary cognitivism. It will be my claim that Lamarque and Olsen's aboutness relation is a function of literary thickness, but I shall first identify problems with both the referential fallacy and literary cognitivism before proposing my account of aboutness as a solution.[7]

In his defence of reference as a fallacy, Riffaterre states "that the representation of reality is a verbal construct in which meaning is achieved by reference from words to words, not to things".[8] Accordingly, he claims that "Azincour", "Crecy", and "Poictiers" in Wordsworth's poem "Yew-Trees" do not refer to the respective medieval battles of Agincourt, Crécy, and Poitiers. I reproduce the first eight lines of the poem here:

> There is a Yew-tree, pride of Lorton Vale,
> Which to this day stands single, in the midst
> Of its own darkness, as it stood of yore,
> Not loth to furnish weapons for the Bands
> Of Umfraville or Percy ere they marched
> To Scotland's Heaths; or Those that crossed the Sea
> And drew their sounding bows at Azincour,
> Perhaps at earlier Crecy, or Poictiers.[9]

Riffaterre maintains that:

> History, and referentiality, are thus all at the verbal level. Names anchor the description solidly in time because of their metonymic function, their ability to stand for a whole complex of representations. Suggestiveness is circular: the descriptive sentence finds its reference in a name whose referent need only be the preceding part of the sentence leading up to it.[10]

The work not only fails to refer to the world, therefore, but is entirely self-referential. A consequence of the referential fallacy is Riffaterre's view that the poem will remain as evocative once the Battle of Agincourt is forgotten.[11] In terms of Lamarque and Olsen's aboutness, Riffaterre is stating that "Yew-Trees" is not about Agincourt: one is not required to call upon information about the battle because the absence of this information does not degrade the experience of the poem. This is patently false.

Knowledge of the three decisive victories by English archers over French heavy cavalry at the battles of Crécy, Poitiers, and Agincourt may not be essential to the enjoyment of the work, but the information is required if the poem is to be understood and appreciated. From the poem alone one learns that yew trees provided weapons for the bands of archers that fought in Scotland and France. There is, however, a significant difference between understanding that English archers fought in foreign fields and understanding that they inflicted three great defeats on the French, defeats which had a major influence on military strategy and tactics at the time and upset the previously unrivalled dominance of the aristocracy in warfare. That these momentous victories were achieved with the longbow, which was made from the yew, makes the tree all the more interesting and important, and offers insight into why the poet holds it in such awe. I am not suggesting that the poem will cease to be evocative if the memory of these battles is lost—merely that it will not be *as* evocative. The poetic experience will be impoverished, even if only to a small extent.

The problem extends beyond the three battles: if "Yew-Trees" is not about Agincourt, it is not about yew trees either. Riffaterre suggests that the accuracy of Wordsworth's descriptions of the trunk and isolation of the yew are of little significance to the appreciation of the poem. Furthermore, one does not need to bring one's knowledge of yew trees to the work because "the yew is not described in relation to the tree of that name, but as an image of an existence closer to Eternity than ours—or, in Wordsworth's terms, more impervious to 'decay' than ours. It simply carries on in a new language the first part of the poem, which stated this poetic vision in terms of human life transcended".[12] Riffaterre's identification of the yew as a symbol of a superior type of existence is compelling, but he errs in claiming that the description is not related to *the tree of that name*. If the description is unrelated then "Yew-Trees" is not about yew trees, and—as Arthur Danto writes in his critique of Riffaterre—"it is difficult to locate literature in the plane of human concern at all".[13] If the relation between work and world is severed, the satisfaction derived from the poem would be restricted to the sound of the words and the morphology of the work—which, again, seems to be an impoverished reward for appreciation. The referential fallacy does not therefore provide a satisfactory account of reference in literature and I shall proceed to literary cognitivism, which appears more promising.

In chapter 1: §4, I defined "literary cognitivism" as the thesis that truth is, or can be, a value of literature *qua* literature. In Thomson-Jones's terminology, the cognitivist answers the question of whether literature can provide knowledge in a manner that is relevant to its literary value in the affirmative. Gaskin's literary cognitivism constitutes a strong pro-reference view of literature because he maintains that those works of literature that have cognitive value as part and parcel of their literary value have it in virtue of *referring to, and making true statements about, the world.* Gaskin's theory of the relationship between literature and truth emerges from his linguistic idealism, the claim that the world is propositionally structured: "The world, we may say, is composed, in the first instance, of propositions, true and false; and then, in virtue of the fact that these propositions are themselves composed of objects and properties, the world comes, mediately, to be composed of these objects and properties too".[14] There is thus no reality outside of, or which cannot be expressed by, language. This is counter-intuitive in one respect, but intuitive in another because it appears that human beings are unable to conceive of that which cannot be exhaustively described in language. Gaskin is quick to distinguish his idealism from Richard Rorty's pragmatism and Derrida's anti-realism, and realism is central to his distinction between text and work:

the former is an abstract possibility, the latter a realisation of that possibility by a particular author at a particular time and a particular place. Once this realisation occurs, the work's "literary qualities remain fixed across all possible worlds in which it exists", as well as over time.[15]

With linguistic idealism as a premise, Gaskin maintains that fiction is not only inessential to literature, but that literature is characteristically factualist—that is, aims at truth.[16] This is understood in terms of the relevance of historicity, the use of the names of real people and places, the use of general terms that refer to universals, and the status of works as incomplete structures that must be completed by the reader. In literary fictions, the author makes assertions, but the reader is invited to adopt the fictive stance—that is, to preface the assertions that appear in the content of the work with "it is fictionally the case that". These assertions will, of course, be true. For most works of literature the cognitive value of the work resides in reference to universals, which are actual components of reality. Gaskin's conclusion is that "all works of literature bear on the world by virtue of making, or implying, true statements about the world".[17] He sums up his position on the relationship between truth value and literary value as, "Falsity can thus make a difference to the value of a work, but it is not necessarily a decisive factor in determining overall aesthetic worth; it may be outweighed, or compensated for, by other factors".[18] Truth is a *pro tanto* literary merit for Gaskin. Returning to Wordsworth's "Yew-Trees", the accuracies I noted Riffaterre as mentioning—the description of the trunk and the tree's isolation—make the poem better *qua* poem. Inaccuracies, such as describing the trunk as thin or the tree as growing in groves, would apparently not matter at all to Riffaterre as long as they maintained the vision of the first part of the poem in new language, but they would reduce the poetic value of the poem for Gaskin. Questions of truth and falsity are not restricted to factual details in a work, but include its themes, such as whether yew trees actually are closer to eternity than human beings in the manner Wordsworth suggests. The plausibility of this claim—the extent to which Wordsworth's "poetic argument" convinces—contributes to the poetic value of the poem for Gaskin.

Gaskin's literary cognitivism is a particularly strong cognitivist thesis and his argument for the unpopular position that literature provides propositional knowledge is reliant upon his linguistic idealism. What I want to make clear is that even weaker cognitivist theses—such as Carroll's, which I discussed in chapter 2—entail that truth is a *pro tanto* literary merit and falsehood a *pro tanto* literary defect. If a work's cognitive value is part and parcel of its literary value, then literary value is partly constituted by cognitive value. Cognitive value is understood in a variety of terms—for example truth, (Gaskin), clarification (Carroll), and knowledge (Wilson). As I noted in chapter 1: §4, knowledge is standardly accepted as justified true belief (or justified true belief plus something)—that is, directly linked to truth. This correspondence with the world applies to both Ryle's *knowing-that* and *knowing-how* distinctions in knowledge, as well as Dorothy Walsh's third category, which Wilson describes as *knowing-what*.[19] In Gaskin, Carroll, and Wilson—as well as the vast majority of cases where literature is claimed to provide knowledge—truth is a *pro tanto* literary merit and falsehood a *pro tanto* literary defect.[20] With regard to the institutional practice of literature, which I discussed in chapter 1: §3, Lamarque and Olsen are adamant that "literary criticism is not defined by a series of speculative issues (of a psychological, sociological, philosophical, or historical nature) which are debated with reference to canonical standards of truth and reference. Nor is there a part of criticism which deals with the truth or falsity of works".[21] The cognitivist notion that falsehood is a *pro tanto* literary defect is revealed as problematic by a consideration of the brief but instructive debate about errors in literature.

If falsehood is a *pro tanto* literary defect, then errors—that is, unintended departures from fact—will be paradigmatic *pro tanto* literary defects. In his lecture on "Literature and the Matter of Fact", Christopher Ricks maintains that accuracy is always critically relevant and always pertinent to literary value, but not always equally pertinent due to considerations such as genre and kind.[22] Ricks's most interesting example is the apparently crucial flaw in Golding's *Lord of the Flies*, pointed out by T. Hampton eleven years after the novel's publication in 1954: Piggy's glasses would have had diverging not converging lenses and he would not therefore have been able to light fires with them.[23] What makes this error so significant is that both Piggy's myopia and his ability to light fires are essential to his role in the narrative. If Piggy is long-sighted rather than short-sighted, then he loses his physical vulnerability; if he is short-sighted, then he cannot also light fires and is no longer the bringer of fire. M. W. Rowe joined the debate with his critique of Lamarque and Olsen's no-truth theory of literature, and his explicit position is, "In fiction, truth is neither necessary nor sufficient for literary merit, since our interest can always be sustained by a work's wit, energy, epic sweep, pathos or humour, etc., but truth is always a virtue and falsehood always a vice".[24] Rowe reiterates the significance of literary genre and adds another interesting example. The poem "Absences" by Philip Larkin contains the line, "A wave drops like a wall: another follows".[25] Larkin is explicitly describing waves at sea not on the shore and in 1961 an oceanographer informed him that only waves breaking against the shore drop in the manner indicated. Larkin was upset by the error, expressed his hope that his work was not read by many oceanographers, and added an apologetic note to a later edition to the effect that his error seriously marred the poem but that he was unable to correct it.[26] Rowe identifies such errors as literary defects because "while we read, we have to make a conscious effort to suppress the knowledge that what they describe is impossible".[27] He refers to errors as evidence for his conclusion about the relationship between truth and literary value and shares Ricks's view that *an error is a* pro tanto *literary defect.*

The most recent contributor to the debate is Christopher Mole, who proposes four ways in which inaccuracy can reduce literary value: distraction, authority, hypocrisy, and ignorance. I shall confine my commentary to his two most convincing reasons: distraction and authority.[28] Errors can distract readers from a work by impeding the suspension of disbelief. Mole comments on Ricks's example of Pushkin describing the clink of cavalry spurs in a crowded ballroom in *Eugene Onegin*. Ricks claims that the description is not merely inaccurate, but "absurd", due to the damage the spurs would have done to the ladies' dresses.[29] Either during or shortly after writing the poem, Pushkin became aware of his error, but decided not to change it. Mole echoes Rowe: "We cannot compensate for the inaccuracy without that compensation itself being an impediment to what the poem might achieve".[30] The consequence of Pushkin's error is that to imagine the scene as he intended one must restrict one's imaginative engagement with the poem. Mole notes that errors of this sort vary greatly in the extent to which they distract readers. The second category is errors that undermine the authority of the author. Mole maintains that this matters because the appreciation of a work of literature requires trust, as "we subject ourselves to another's sensibility".[31] Imaginative engagement involves trusting the author and errors undermine the authority of the author and make readers less likely to trust him or her and therefore less likely to appreciate the work. Mole's conclusion is that if an error is not problematic in one of the ways he has indicated, it will not matter to the value of the work *qua* literature—that is, *an error is not a* pro tanto *literary defect*.

Mole's two reasons for errors being problematic in literature—distraction and authority—are ultimately reducible to distraction. Errors that matter in literature matter because they interfere with the reader's imaginative engagement with the work. The direction of causation is that the distracting error comes first—the interference with what Mole calls "imaginative realization"—and this distraction may or may not result in the further distraction of the questioning of authorial authority.[32] He states that it is not just the magnitude of the error, but the likelihood of discovery which matters, but obfuscates the essential issue: some errors matter to some readers. A more enlightening observation is that *some errors distract some readers*. Due to the different knowledge of the world different readers bring to works, their imaginative experiences of the same works is characterised by varying grains of detail. One would expect, for example, that John Bright and Chloé Obolensky—the costume designers for Martha Fiennes's 1999 film, *Onegin*—would have experienced richer and more specific imaginings of the crowded ballroom than most contemporary readers. And the more detail one imagines, the more likely the spurs are to distract. There will be some readers for whom neither Pushkin's spurs nor Larkin's wave are distracting, some who find one but not the other distracting, and others who find neither distracting. Larkin recognised this diversity in responses when he expressed his desire that few oceanographers had read his poem. Errors matter because they distract readers and some errors are likely to distract more readers than others because of the knowledge those readers bring to the appreciation of literature. No general principles can be established for identifying which types of error are likely to be defective because each reader's imaginative engagement will be determined in part by the individual's psychology.

If this seems implausible, consider the magnitude of Golding's error. A large minority—if not the vast majority—of his readers would have been familiar with the various ways in which lenses are employed to assist vision. If ever there was an example upon which to construct a general principle for what type of error is a literary defect, this seems to be it: the error is not only crucial to the plot, but reliant upon exactly the opposite of what is true in the world and furthermore likely to be discovered by a substantial proportion of readers. As deserving of his Nobel Prize in Literature as Golding was, this is a *very* silly mistake for an author to make. Yet what proportion of the millions of readers of *Lord of the Flies* since 1954 (1) realised the error and (2) having realised the error, found it an impediment to their imaginative engagement with the work? The literary and popular success of the novel speaks for itself. Similarly, the fact that one can become a Nobel literature laureate despite making a juvenile error in one of one's major works, says something about literature and literary value that Ricks, Rowe, and Gaskin fail to grasp. If only some errors matter, and these to only some people, then errors cannot be *pro tanto* literary defects. According to the cognitivist, however, errors should be paradigmatic literary defects because—as *unintended* departures from fact—they do not serve a purpose within the work and are therefore, in Gaskin's terms, less likely to be *outweighed or compensated for by* literary merits. If errors are not *pro tanto* literary defects, then falsity is not a *pro tanto* literary defect and truth is not a *pro tanto* literary merit. This is not, as Olsen notes, to deny that verisimilitude is ever relevant to literary appreciation—only that truth is always (even if only to a *pro tanto* extent) a literary merit.[33]

I take the evidence of errors to be a decisive objection to Gaskin's literary cognitivism, which is explicit that truth is a *pro tanto* literary merit at both the factual and thematic levels. If this is the case, then I have demonstrated why Gaskin does not offer a satisfactory account of the relationship between literature and truth. Other literary cognitivists could, however, accept the evidence above, but restrict their respective claims about literary knowledge to the thematic level—that is, claim that truth is only a *pro tanto* literary merit at the thematic level. Where the empirical evidence seems to favour the view that falsity is not a *pro tanto* defect at the factual level, it seems to favour the converse at the thematic level. While there are numerous canonical works that embody obvious truths, there are very few that embody obvious falsehoods. Rowe employs the example of a hypothetical novel with the theme that treating children cruelly benefits them:

> How could we possibly be interested in seeing such ideas enacted, explored, developed and imaginatively entertained? We shall not find such controversies about *literary* works, not because truth is irrelevant to literary evaluation, but because truth is so important that obviously idiotic ideas automatically debar the books which express them from the category of literature. [34]

Cognitive value is part and parcel of literary value for Rowe and a work with a theme that is so obviously false cannot be valuable *qua* literature. Rowe's point could also be made about moral as opposed to cognitive value. When one considers the literary canon, there is a paucity of works that embody a morally reprehensible perspective. Recall my claim in chapter 1: §4 that neither *Lolita* nor *Paradise Lost* offer immoral perspectives on their respective subjects. Similarly, if one considers many of the themes of canonical works, it seems highly unlikely that a work of equivalent literary value could embody a contradictory theme: for example, *civil wars are not characterised by hatred and savagery* (*For Whom the Bell Tolls*) or *animal suffering on a grand scale is morally insignificant* ("The Lives of Animals").

I have two responses to Rowe, both of which explain why the overwhelming empirical evidence for the truth and virtue of literary themes does not provide evidence that truth is a *pro tanto* literary merit at the thematic level. The first response is taken from Lamarque's reply to Rowe's inquiry into whether a literary work could sustain the theme *human hopes are never thwarted*. He claims that Rowe's question is flawed for several reasons, three of which are relevant to my analysis:

1. "To start with a statement and ask what kind of work it might characterize and what value such a work might have distorts the whole process of literary interpretation, which always begins with a specific work and reaches a judgment of value, if at all, on a plurality of measures".
2. "It is common for different works to develop diametrically opposed thematic visions. Love destroys, love liberates; hope springs eternal, hopelessness prevails".
3. "The themes explored in the great literary works (of all cultures) are drawn from a relatively small pool of concerns that are of perennial interest to reflective human beings. . . . Literary works seldom add to this pool, though they can provide fresh perspectives on each item". [35]

The fact that there appear to be no canonical literary works that embody obvious thematic falsehoods must indeed be explained by the anti-cognitivist and Lamarque provides the explanation in (3). Olsen offers support for (3) when he states of literary interpretation that the "interpretative terms on the high levels . . . belong to a fairly limited class of terms which cluster around a set of 'interesting' concepts concerning 'eternal human problems'".[36]

It should also be noted that while there seem to be no uncontested examples of canonical works embodying glaring thematic falsehoods, there are at least some works for which such interpretations are not only plausible, but compelling. I mentioned the amoral perspectives of a number of surrealist and existentialist works in §4 in chapter 1, but Lamarque points to what may be a less controversial case: "Martha Nussbaum characterizes a theme of Euripides' *Hecuba* as 'nothing human is ever worthy of trust: there are no guarantees at all, short of revenge or death.' As a thematic statement this captures well an implicit motif in this dark and troubling play. But as a generalization about human nature its truth is highly dubious".[37] Lamarque asks whether this falsity affects the play's literary value and claims that it does not, because pessimists and optimists alike can value the work for its dark vision of the human condition. He concludes, "The example shows that a thematic statement might be true about a work but broadly false about the world at large. It also shows that worldly truth is not always relevant to literary value".[38] Lesson (2) above fails to answer Rowe's critique in full, but it suggests that the direct relationship between truth and literary merit which he, Ricks, and Gaskin hold is at least not as straightforward as any of them maintain. Employing hypothetical novels with themes that directly oppose the classics is indeed disingenuous, for the reason Lamarque states in (1), but if such examples are permitted, then Rowe would have to consider the possibility I sketch below, which constitutes my second response.

The True Knights is a hypothetical novel that enacts a glaring falsehood which is also extremely morally reprehensible: *The Ku Klux Klan were heroic defenders of liberty*. Imagine that this novel closely parallels the narrative of D. W. Griffith's *The Birth of a Nation* and was published in the same year as the film was released, 1915.[39] Unlike the film, the novel is not overtly didactic and is frequently compared to contemporaries such as Joseph Conrad's *Under Western Eyes* and Booth Tarkington's *The Magnificent Ambersons*. Like the film, the novel presents the following view of the reconstruction of the Confederacy: that the Union government punished the Confederates for the assassination of Abraham Lincoln by garrisoning the Southern states with black soldiers; that these soldiers treated the white population harshly in reprisal for slavery; and that the only way for the Confederates to protect their human rights was to form a defence league. The novel thus justifies the formation of the KKK and advocates the retention of white supremacist practices.

Could a novel enacting such falsehoods have literary value? I think it could. For all its obvious failings, *The True Knights* deals with a subject of human interest—the treatment of the defeated by the victors in the aftermath of a war— a subject that is all the more poignant in the aftermath of a civil war. At the very least, the novel raises an important issue: Given the circumstances of the reconstruction of the Confederacy, there was a tension between uniting the American states and ensuring the former citizens of the Confederacy accepted that their former practices had to change. *The True Knights* makes one realise why, for example, well-motivated steps towards achieving racial equality and integration may have caused racial violence and the creation of extremist organisations such as the KKK. There are close parallels with the Truth and Reconciliation Commission in post-apartheid South Africa, but the subject extends beyond particular times and places to universal questions of transitional justice, post-war reconstruction, and the ethical question of how to treat one's former enemies, especially when those enemies are fellow citizens of the same nation state. The problem with *The True Knights* is, of course, that it gives the wrong—false and morally wrong— solutions to the dilemmas it raises. One would be saddened that such a talented author lacked a moral compass, but there is no reason to prevent the handling of the dilemma being serious and mature, explored in a rich and subtle moral pattern, and deserving of praise *qua* literature (in a similar manner to that in which the film is praised *qua* cinema).[40] My conclusion is that truth is not a *pro tanto* literary merit at either the factual or thematic levels and that literary cognitivism is therefore flawed. In the final section of this chapter, I offer my own account of the relationship between work and world, which is pro-reference, but anti-cognitivist.

20. ABOUTNESS

My quote from Danto in §19 above follows his claim that philosophers appear to be solely concerned with vertical references and literary theorists horizontal references.[41] This is a response to Riffaterre, who maintains,

> In cognitive language, a "vertical" semantic axis supports every word and links it to things or to commonplace concepts about things. The truth test of a cognitive message is whether or not it conforms to these commonplaces. In a poem, the descriptive sentence is a chain of derivations. Each word is generated by positive or negative conformity with the preceding one—that is, either by synonymy or by antonymy—and the sequence is thus tautological or oxymoric [*sic*]. . . . The truth test of such a sequence cannot be whether or not each component corresponds to a referent, but whether or not the sequence is well constructed, that is, exemplary in establishing word-to-word relationships of similarity or dissimilarity, duplicating the grammatical sequence with a string of semantic associations. The description has verisimilitude because it in fact

confirms again and again the same statement in various codes. The relation of literary description to its subject matter is not the relation of language to its nonverbal context, but that of meta-language to language. [42]

Riffaterre does not mention a horizontal axis, but the concept is implicit: in cognitive language, the vertical axis links word to world by means of reference; in poetic language, the horizontal axis links word to word by means of cross-reference and meaning relations. If these "languages" are understood as different types of interest taken by a reader in a text or work (types that may or may not be rewarded), as proposed in §18 above, then these axes are measures of the different demands made by readers. If I am reading *Oliver Twist qua* guide to Victorian London, I am concerned with the vertical axis, but if I am reading *Oliver Twist qua* literature then—according to Riffaterre—I am concerned with the horizontal axis—that is, solely with the relations amongst the words in the work.

Riffaterre's axis—or *axes* in my interpretation—recalls John Searle on "parasitic forms of discourse". [43] Searle argues that parasitic discourses, a category which includes fictional utterances, refer. A fictional entity exists in the fiction, but the self-referentiality of fictional discourse does not alter meaning:

> If we think of the meaning conventions of linguistic elements as being (at least in part) vertical conventions, tying sentences to the world, then it is best to think of the tacit conventions of fictional discourse as being lateral or horizontal conventions lifting, as it were, the discourse away from the world. But it is essential to realize that even in "Little Red Riding Hood", "red" means red. [44]

Searle's concern in this passage is with pretended illocutionary acts, and his interest in the way in which words relate to the world differs from mine. Furthermore, it seems unlikely that Riffaterre would deny that "tree" means tree in "Yew-Trees" (despite the fact that "Yew-Trees" is not about yew trees). What I want to appropriate from Searle is the notion of a horizontal axis that *lifts language away from the world*.

The idea is that focus on the horizontal axis of a work—its internal relations, including structure, morphology, syntax, metre, and tropes—lifts the work away from the world. The reason for the opening of this distance is that the types of interest represented by each axis not only differ, but also conflict: reference is directed towards external relations with the world and cross-reference towards internal relations within the work. An analysis of the juxtaposition of the two central plots of *Oliver Twist*—Oliver's escape from poverty and his reclamation of his birthright—which are both consecutive and simultaneous, involves attending to the horizontal axis to an extent that would detract from mapping the geography of Dickens's London. In contrast, attending to the metre and tropes in a newspaper report would detract from attending to the content of the report, its substantive salience regarding peo-ple, places, and events in the world. The point is that one cannot perform a formal analysis of *Oliver Twist* and engage with the novel *qua* guide to Victorian London in a single reading. The two types of interest one brings to the work—an interest in plot structure and an interest in historical geogra-phy—are entirely different.

One might object to the definition of the "vertical axis" in terms of the relation between word and world; in Riffaterre's terms, the link between words and either *things* or *concepts about things*. Despite his adventures in London, Oliver Twist is a fictional character and there are works—such as J. R. R. Tolkien's *The Hobbit* and Margaret Atwood's *The Handmaid's Tale*—where there is very little, if any, obvious resemblance between the world of the work and the real world. In chapter 1: §3, I accepted that literature is characteristically fictional and I understand the relation between fictional people, places, and events and the world in terms of reference to universals, in a similar manner to Gaskin. The notion is from Aristotle's famous obser-vation on the superiority of poetry over history:

> The difference between the historian and the poet is not that the one writes in prose and the other in verse; the work of Herodotus might be put into verse, and in this metrical form it would be no less a kind of history than it is without metre. The difference is that the one tells of what has happened, the other of the kinds of things that might happen. For this reason poetry is something more philosophical and more worthy of serious attention than history; for poetry speaks more of universals, history of particulars. By "universals" I mean the kinds of thing a certain type of person will probably or necessarily say or do in a given situation; and this is the aim of poetry, although it gives individual names to its characters. "Particulars" are what, say, Alcibiades did, or what happened to him. [45]

The relation between the words "Oliver Twist" in Dickens's work and the real world is therefore between the fictional particular—the character—and the universal that the particular instantiates, for example "an orphan in Victo-rian England" or just "an orphan".[46] This relation is not restricted to proper names, as general terms also refer to universals. The relation of particular to universal applies not only to words and their various combinations within the work, but also to the work as a whole considered in terms of its theme. *Oliver Twist*, "The Lives of Animals", *Hard Times*, and the *Iliad* thus instantiate universals such as "the inhumanity of human beings towards each other", "the inhumanity of human beings towards animals", "the dehumanising ef-fect of industrialisation", and "the fragility of human existence". These uni-versals are, as noted in §19 above, typically concerns *that are of perennial interest* or *eternal human problems*—that is, have significance for human beings. Literature, like all art, is not only by people for people, but also about people and things that are important to people.

The two axes I have identified can be defined as follows:

> *SUBSTANTIVE AXIS*: a measure of the extent to which the interest a reader brings to a work or text is concerned with the relations between the words in the work or text and what those words represent in the world. This interest will focus on the content of a work or text—the *what* that is represented.
> *FORMAL AXIS*: a measure of the extent to which the interest a reader brings to a work or text is concerned with the relations among the words in the work or text, including the relations of parts of the work or text to other parts and to the unified whole. This interest will focus on the form of a work or text—the *how* of representation.

If the demand for literary thickness is necessarily satisfied by literary works—as I maintained in §18 above—then both the substantive and formal axes are salient. When one demands literary thickness one is not concerned with the formal axis alone, but with both the formal and substantive axes. These axes represent two different types of interest in a work, however, a conflict in which the formal axis lifts the substantive axis away from the world, drawing focus away from the external relations of reference to the internal relations of cross-reference; and in which the substantive axis lowers the formal axis towards the world, drawing focus away from the internal relations of cross-reference to the external relations of reference. This conflict suggests that one of the axes will have to be of primary significance and the other of secondary—for example, one would expect the formal axis to be of primary importance in reading *Oliver Twist*, but of secondary importance in reading a newspaper report. But this dichotomy is very similar to Riffaterre's distinction between cognitive language and poetic language, and is precisely a *thin* interest in literature because it separates form and content. Literary thickness should therefore be understood as an interest in the integration of the two axes—that is, an interest in *formed content*. Works that reward the demand for thickness are works which reward interest in this integration and for which an aboutness relation holds with the world.

Recall from §19 above that Lamarque and Olsen identify aboutness as a *pro-reference* position. Literary works refer by means of both particulars and universals and the salience of this reference is reflected in the substantive axis. Aboutness is also, however, a *modest* pro-reference position. In literary works, the internal relations amongst the words and parts are also salient and this salience is reflected in the formal axis, an interest that is in conflict with the (external) referential relations. The integration of these two axes involved in literary thickness produces an aboutness relation with the world where works refer, but where the accuracy of their reference is not part and parcel of their value *qua* literature. The criterion for a work being about a real person, place, or event is the substantive link requiring the employment of information about the real person, place, or event in order to understand the person, place, or event in the work. "Gerontion" and *Oliver Twist* are therefore, as noted in §19 above, both about London, but "London" is not used in its full extension in either case. There may be disparities between Eliot's London and interwar London or between Dickens's London and Victorian London, but these substantive inaccuracies are not *pro tanto* literary defects and may even be literary merits. This is why aboutness understood in terms of literary thickness entails literary anti-cognitivism.[47] To demand literary thickness is to attend to *formed content* and formed content is content—particulars or universals—which has been shaped so as to serve a specific role within the literary work such that it may no longer accurately represent the particular or universal.

In summary, aboutness is explained by literary thickness because of the effect of the reciprocal relationship of form and content. Aboutness in turn explains the relationship between work and world that holds for literature. Aboutness retains the link between work and world that Riffaterre's account severs, but does not require Gaskin's problematic commitment to truth as a *pro tanto* literary merit. I shall have more to say about the anti-cognitivist commitment of literary thickness in my discussion of the relationship between literary thickness on the one hand and final and instrumental value on the other, in chapter 6: §23. The next chapter begins, however, with a more detailed explanation of literary thickness, followed by an argument that literary thickness is characteristic of literary appreciation.

NOTES

1. Malcolm Budd, *Values of Art* (London: Penguin, 1995), 4.
2. Bernard Williams, *Ethics and the Limits of Philosophy* (London: Routledge, 2011 [1985]), 143–44. See also: Gilbert Ryle, "The Thinking of Thoughts: What Is 'Le Penseur' Doing?," in G. Ryle, *Volume II: Collected Essays 1929–1969* (London: Hutchinson & Co., 1971 [1968]), 480–96.
3. Simon Blackburn, "Through Thick and Thin," *Proceedings of the Aristotelian Society, Supplementary Volumes 66* (1992), 285–99: 298.
4. Blackburn, "Through Thick and Thin," 299.
5. Peter Lamarque & Stein Haugom Olsen, *Truth, Fiction, and Literature: A Philosophical Perspective* (Oxford: Clarendon, 2002 [1994]), 108 & 119.
6. Lamarque & Olsen, *Truth, Fiction, and Literature*, 121.
7. Lamarque and Olsen describe the anti-reference view as "being associated both with the pragmatist's rejection of truth as correspondence and with the conception of language as a 'game' rather than a 'picture' of reality", citing Richard Rorty and C. G. Prado as examples (*Truth, Fiction, and Literature*, 107–8). I shall not discuss anti-reference views.
8. Michael Riffaterre, "Interpretation and Descriptive Poetry: A Reading of Wordsworth's 'Yew-Trees'," *New Literary History 4* (1973), 229–56: 230.
9. "Yew-Trees" was composed in 1807 and first published in *Poems of the Imagination* in 1815. My quotation is from *Poems of the Imagination* as it appeared in *Poems by William Wordsworth: Including Lyrical Ballads, and the Miscellaneous Pieces of the Author* in 1815

(*Volume I*. [e-book] [London: Longman, Hurst, Rees, Orme, and Brown], 297–337, available at: Community Books, https://archive.org/details/poemsbywilliamwo02word [accessed 28 December 2015]). In the version Riffaterre employs, the following words are not capitalised: "Bands", "Heaths", "Those", and "Sea". There is also a colon rather than a comma at the end of line three (see Riffaterre, "Interpretation and Descriptive Poetry," 230–31). The differences affect neither Riffaterre's thesis nor my commentary thereon.

10. Riffaterre, "Interpretation and Descriptive Poetry," 233.

11. Riffaterre, "Interpretation and Descriptive Poetry," 232.

12. Riffaterre, "Interpretation and Descriptive Poetry," 237.

13. Arthur Danto, "Philosophy and/as/of Literature," in G. L. Hagberg, & W. Jost, eds., *A Companion to the Philosophy of Literature* (Oxford: Blackwell, 2010 [1984]), 52–67: 61.

14. Richard Gaskin, *Language, Truth, and Literature: A Defence of Literary Humanism* (Oxford: Oxford University Press, 2013), 11.

15. Gaskin, *Language, Truth, and Literature*, 75.

16. Gaskin, *Language, Truth, and Literature*, 38.

17. Gaskin, *Language, Truth, and Literature*, 65.

18. Gaskin, *Language, Truth, and Literature*, 153.

19. Gilbert Ryle, *The Concept of Mind: 60th Anniversary Edition* (Abingdon, UK: Routledge, 2009 [1949]), 14–48; Catherine Wilson, "Literature and Knowledge," *Philosophy 58* (1983), 489–96: 491–92. See also: Dorothy Walsh, *Literature and Knowledge* (Middletown, CT: Wesleyan University Press, 1969). Walsh describes the correspondence with which I am concerned as *authenticity*.

20. I have qualified this claim as a result of the very few exceptions, which include Gibson and Tzachi Zamir. Zamir argues that literature provides justified beliefs which constitute moral knowledge because truth is a "redundant" notion in ethics (*Double Vision: Moral Philosophy and Shakespearean Drama* [Princeton, NJ: Princeton University Press, 2007], 15). This is, of course, a controversial claim which I do not have space to discuss here.

21. Lamarque & Olsen, *Truth, Fiction, and Literature*, 332.

22. Christopher Ricks, "Literature and the Matter of Fact," in C. Ricks, *Essays in Appreciation* (Oxford: Clarendon Press, 1996), 280–310: 283 & 303. Ricks does not actually specify *unintended* factual inaccuracies, but his numerous examples demonstrate that these are his concern.

23. Ricks, "Literature and the Matter of Fact," 306; and T. Hampton, "An Error in 'Lord of the Flies,'" *Notes and Queries 12* (1965), 275.

24. M. W. Rowe, "Lamarque and Olsen on Literature and Truth," *The Philosophical Quarterly 47* (1997), 322–41: 335.

25. Philip Larkin, *The Less Deceived* (London: The Marvell Press, 1977 [1955]), 40.

26. Rowe, "Lamarque and Olsen on Literature and Truth," 334–35.

27. Rowe, "Lamarque and Olsen on Literature and Truth," 335.

28. Christopher Mole, "The Matter of Fact in Literature," *International Journal of Philosophical Studies 17* (2009), 489–508. Aside from considerations of space, Mole deals with hypocrisy and ignorance together, briefly, and both are reducible to the problem with authorial authority.

29. Ricks, "Literature and the Matter of Fact," 302.

30. Mole, "The Matter of Fact in Literature," 499.

31. Mole, "The Matter of Fact in Literature," 502.

32. Mole, "The Matter of Fact in Literature," 501.

33. Olsen, *End of Literary Theory*, 74.

34. Rowe, "Lamarque and Olsen on Literature and Truth," 337.

35. Peter Lamarque, "Cognitive Values in the Arts: Marking the Boundaries," in M. Kieran, ed., *Contemporary Debates in Aesthetics and the Philosophy of Art* (Oxford: Blackwell, 2006), 127–39: 138 & 139.

36. Stein Haugom Olsen, *The Structure of Literary Understanding* (Cambridge: Cambridge University Press, 1978), 114.

37. Peter Lamarque, *The Philosophy of Literature* (Malden, MA: Blackwell, 2009), 237.

38. Lamarque, *Philosophy of Literature*, 237.

39. *The Birth of a Nation* is in fact based on a novel, *The Clansman: An Historical Romance of the Ku Klux Klan*, which author Thomas F. Dixon, Jr. adapted into a play titled *The Clansman* (both published in 1905). In contrast to the film, neither the novel nor the play has entered the artistic canon, which is why I employ an invention. I have used *The True Knights* as an example previously. See: Rafe McGregor, "Moderate Autonomism Revisited," *Ethical Perspectives 20* (2013), 403–26: 421–22.

40. The critical terminology I have employed here is from Leavis's various works of criticism. See: F. R. Leavis, *The Great Tradition: George Eliot, Henry James, Joseph Conrad* (London: Chatto & Windus, 1960 [1948]), passim.

41. Danto, "Philosophy and/as/of Literature," 61.

42. Riffaterre, "Interpretation and Descriptive Poetry," 235–36.

43. John R. Searle, *Speech Acts* (Cambridge: Cambridge University Press, 1969), 79.

44. Searle, *Speech Acts*, 79.

45. Aristotle, *Poetics*, trans. P. Murray & T. S. Dorsch, in P. Murray, ed., *Classical Literary Criticism* (London: Penguin, 2004), 57–97: IX, 1451a42–b12.

46. Gaskin's discussion of the character of Hamlet as a universal is enlightening in this regard (*Language, Truth, and Literature*, 60–61).

47. My conception of aboutness as a product of literary thickness is neither identical with Lamarque and Olsen's original nor sufficiently different to justify a neologism. The reconception is also compatible with their theory of literature, which is a no-truth theory and therefore also anti-cognitivist.

Chapter Six

Literary Value

The purpose of this chapter is to present my completed argument for the autonomy of literature. In §21, I develop the conception of literary thickness from the previous chapter and argue that it is characteristic of literary appreciation. Section §22 proposes an experiential account of literary value that draws on the work of Malcolm Budd and Derek Attridge. Literary value is explained in terms of literary satisfaction, which arises from the simultaneity and interplay of the sensory, imaginative, affective, and intellective aspects of the work. I consider, in §23, the relation between the three different types of interests in literary works articulated thus far with two of the types of value defined previously, demonstrating the following pair of necessary relations: (1) the substantive axis and instrumental value. and (2) the formal axis/ literary thickness and final value. I set out the premises and conclusion of my argument for the final value of literature in §24, establishing literary autonomy by means of the argument from literary thickness.

21. LITERARY THICKNESS (II)

I concluded chapter 5 on the promissory note of explaining literary thickness in detail and I shall do so by contrasting it with the substantive and formal axes discussed in §20 in chapter 5. My comparison will focus on two descriptions of André Marty, a man who was born in Perpignan in 1886, died in a village near Toulouse in 1956, and is best known for the role he played in the Spanish Civil War. The first passage is from Antony Beevor's historical work, *The Spanish Civil War*, and the second from Hemingway's *For Whom the Bell Tolls*. Beevor describes the arrival of volunteers for the International Brigades at Albacete late in 1936:

The recruits were lined up on the parade ground for an address by André Marty, the Brigades' controller who had earlier brought the French volunteers over the border during the fighting at Irún. Marty, a squat man, with a white moustache, drooping jowl and outsized beret, had made his name as a signals operator in the 1919 mutiny of the French Black Sea Fleet. The heroic legend woven around him in Party mythology made him one of the most powerful figures in the Comintern. Almost nobody dared challenge his authority. At that time he was starting to develop a conspiracy complex that rivalled Stalin's. Influenced by the show trials in Moscow, he became convinced that "Fascist-Trotskyist" spies were everywhere, and that it was his duty to exterminate them. Marty later admitted that he had ordered the shooting of about 500 Brigaders, nearly one-tenth of the total killed in the war. Many claim that Marty's figure is modest.[1]

The interest in the work is typically thin because form and content can be separated. The content—information about people, places, and events—can be separated from the form—the way in which Beevor presents them. The information in the text could be communicated in a different way without loss of identity. "Marty", "the parade ground", and "the show trials in Moscow" are not presented under an aspect, but transparently. "Marty" is Marty (i.e., "Marty" in its fully extensional use), not *Marty-in-Beevor's*-The-Spanish-Civil-War (i.e., Marty under the aspect Beevor's *The Spanish Civil War* licenses one to imagine). The people, places, and events can be described exhaustively without recourse to aspect. *The Spanish Civil War* is not intended for literary appreciation and my primary interest as a reader is with the substantive axis: I want to know if Marty really looked and acted as Beevor states, and because Beevor is a reputable historian I accept his description as true.

Beevor's description of Marty contrasts with the character who makes a brief and sinister appearance in *For Whom the Bell Tolls*, even though it appears that Hemingway's portrayal of Marty is factually accurate:

He recognized his bushy eyebrows, his watery eyes, his chin and the double chin under it, and he knew him for one of France's great revolutionary figures who had led the mutiny of the French Navy in the Black Sea. Gomez knew this man's high political place in the International Brigades and he knew this man would know where Golz's headquarters were and be able to direct him there. He did not know what this man had become with time, disappointment, bitterness both domestic and political, and thwarted ambition and that to question him was one of the most dangerous things that any man could do. Knowing nothing of this he stepped forward into the path of this man, saluted with his clenched fist and said, "Comrade Marty, we are the bearers of a dispatch for General Golz. Can you direct us to his headquarters? It is urgent".

The tall, heavy old man looked at Gomez with his out-thrust head and considered him carefully with his watery eyes. Even here at the front in the light of a bare electric bulb, he having just come in from driving in an open car on a brisk night, his gray face had a look of decay. His face looked as though it were modelled from the waste material you find under the claws of a very old lion.[2]

For Whom the Bell Tolls does not authorise one to imagine "the man at the centre of *l'affaire Marty-Tillon*" when one reads "Marty".[3] "Marty" in Beevor is Marty; "Marty" in Hemingway is *Marty-in*-For-Whom-the-Bell-Tolls. Descriptions of real people, places, and events do not license one to invoke just any information about those people, places, and events in one's imaginative engagement with the novel because one's interest in the work is typically *qua* literature—that is, recognises the salience of both the substantive and formal axes and thus requires the demand for literary thickness. It would, however, be an error to state that *For Whom the Bell Tolls* is not *about* Marty. If one were concerned only with the formal axis, as Riffaterre seems to be, then one could indeed claim that the novel was not about Marty. A defender of Riffaterre might even argue that knowledge of the real Marty adds nothing to the experience of the work, which is self-sufficient to the extent that the wonderful description of his face as "*modelled from the waste material you find under the claws of a very old lion*" provides one with all the information one requires to appreciate the character.

While this is certainly an evocative employment of language that not only describes Marty's appearance, but also offers an insight into his personality, the reader's experience of the novel is augmented by knowledge of the real Marty. The information from Beevor—an interest in the substantive axis— enhances the aspect under which Marty appears in *For Whom the Bell Tolls*. Hemingway offers a sketch of the relevant historical information, but the additional facts one finds in Beevor flesh out this representation and provide the informed reader with a richer and more rewarding experience. The words "*he stepped forward into the path of this man*" are that much more chilling with Beevor's facts to hand than they are without, relying only upon Hemingway's brief biographical description. Furthermore, the situation directly parallels the problem I identified with the referential fallacy in §19 in chapter 5: If *For Whom The Bell Tolls* is not about Marty, then it is not about the Spanish Civil War either. But being about the Spanish Civil War in particular, with themes and conceptions that extend beyond that conflict to civil wars in general, seems precisely part of what makes the novel valuable *qua* novel. My primary interest in *For Whom the Bell Tolls* is not therefore in the formal axis, but in the integration of the two axes—that is, in Marty as a character in the novel, or *Marty-in*-For-Whom-the-Bell-Tolls.

Fundamental to the author's intention—and therefore the literary stance—is the idea that the appearance of a person, place, or event in a literary work serves a function within that work. It is not only the appearance of a person, place, or event that has one or more purposes, however, but also the way in which the person, place, or event is presented. The question of *why* thus applies to both the *what* and the *how*. The content of a work is formed just so for a reason; the specific integration of form and content is in each case deliberate. In chapter 4: §14, I mentioned that selectivity is a feature of all representations of sequences of events, both narrative and non-narrative. In narratives where the form is salient in addition to the content, this selectivity takes on an additional significance. Aristotle comments on the relationship between selectivity and function when he praises Homer for his unity of plot in the *Odyssey*: "the plot of a play, being the representation of an action, must present it as a unified whole; and its various incidents must be so arranged that if any one of them is differently placed or taken away the effect of wholeness will be seriously disrupted".[4] If Homer could not present all of Odysseus's story, why did he select the parts of that story which appear in the *Odyssey*? Aristotle's answer is that he selected the parts that are essential to the plot of the work, those which serve a particular function (or more likely *functions*) within the work as a unified whole.

The significance of the relationship between selectivity and function in narrative has resulted in the mystery novel being singled out as paradigmatic of all novels. In his deconstructed detective story, *City of Glass*, Paul Auster begins (or perhaps concludes) a line of thought that leads back to Todorov's distinction between *fabula* and *sjužet*:

> Even before he became William Wilson, Quinn had been a devoted reader of mystery novels. He knew that most of them were poorly written, that most could not stand up to even the vaguest sort of examination, but still, it was the form that appealed to him, and it was the rare, unspeakably bad mystery that he would refuse to read. Whereas his taste in other books was rigorous, demanding to the point of narrow-mindedness, with these works he showed almost no discrimination whatsoever. When he was in the right mood, he had little trouble reading ten or twelve of them in a row. It was a kind of hunger that took hold of him, a craving for a special food, and he would not stop until he had eaten his fill.
>
> What he liked about these books was their sense of plenitude and economy. In the good mystery there is nothing wasted, no sentence, no word that is not significant. And even if it is not significant, it has the potential to be so—which amounts to the same thing. The world of the book comes to life, seething with possibilities, with secrets and contradictions. Since everything seen or said, even the slightest, most trivial thing, can bear a connection to the outcome of the story, nothing must be overlooked. Everything becomes essence, the centre of the book shifts with each event that propels it forward. The centre, then, is everywhere, and no circumference can be drawn until the book has come to its end.[5]

Quinn's peculiar hunger is explained by the fact that he is a writer (using William Wilson as his pen name) and is therefore particularly sensitive to the plenitude and economy described.

William Lavender regards Auster as responding to Peter Brooks's discussion of the Sherlock Holmes tale, "The Adventure of the Musgrave Ritual", as paradigmatic of the mystery genre.[6] In the short story, Holmes regales Watson with one of his early cases, where he had to reconstruct and repeat the movements of a criminal who was searching for treasure.[7] Brooks holds that Holmes's method exemplifies an essential feature of detective fiction, "that the detective repeat, go over again, the ground that has been covered by his predecessor, the criminal".[8] He refers to Todorov's discussion of detective stories in terms of *fabula* as "the story of the crime" and *sjužet* as "the story of the investigation", and maintains that Todorov "thus makes the detective story the narrative of narratives".[9] In Attridge's terminology, the detective story *stages* the plot of all narratives, the relationship between the sequence of events and the mode of presentation of those events. If Lavender is correct, then Auster is making a similar claim about detective novels, that they stage the relationship between selectivity and function in all novels— where "*there is nothing wasted, no sentence, no word that is not significant*".[10]

Lamarque states that narratives not only list facts, but shape them into a "kind of 'gestalt' of impressions and attitudes".[11] The narrative presents its content from a point of view and its particular integration of form and content will contribute to the gestalt that constitutes the work. Referring to Olsen, Lamarque calls this the "principle of functionality": "broadly the idea that what is there (in the poem) is there for a purpose, things are not just accidentally as they are".[12] The principle applies to both poetic and narrative thickness, but is more prominent in the former: "Reading poetry demands a sharper attention to detail than is characteristic of other kinds of reading, not surprisingly as the form of expression—the actual choice of words—is assigned unusual salience; that follows from the Principle of Functionality".[13] I shall make a slight amendment to the principle as follows:

> *PRINCIPLE OF FUNCTIONALITY*: the idea that what is in the work is there for a purpose—that is, things are not just accidentally as they are. The principle holds for all works of literature. Every sentence, arguably every word, is assumed to have a function in the work as a unified whole, within the interplay of themes and the developing picture of people, places, and events that comprise the work's content.

To demand literary thickness is to attend to the operation of this principle in the text, to the combination of the *what* and the *how* of the work in terms of the *why*. In appreciating *For Whom the Bell Tolls*, therefore, one understands that Hemingway made a decision to include Marty as a character in his novel. He also decided that Marty would be presented in a particular way. The complexity of these choices is revealed in what is perhaps the simplest part of this process, Hemingway's decision to offer a brief physical description of Marty. Given a desire for verisimilitude, the options seem fairly limited, and yet contrast Hemingway's description with Beevor's. Hemingway mentions Marty's eyebrows, eyes, and chin while Beevor mentions his physique, moustache, cheeks, and headgear. The descriptions are both entirely different and completely compatible. This array of choices would have increased exponentially when Hemingway decided which parts of Marty's biography and which aspects of his personality to include in the narrative. Had Hemingway the information to hand at the time of writing, for example, would he have mentioned that Marty was the cause of ten percent of the casualties suffered by his own troops? I suspect not, because the phrase "*to question him was one of the most dangerous things that any man could do*" is more expressive than pure statistics—although, as noted above, the possession of the statistics augments the description in the novel in this instance. All these decisions about the *what* (or the *who* in this case) and the *how* are guided by the *why*.

Hemingway's presentation of Marty under a particular aspect at a particular point in the narrative is designed to achieve a particular purpose—or *purposes*, in this case: at the level of the novel's plot, Marty frustrates the delivery of Robert Jordan's message, which is aimed at preventing the Republicans from launching an offensive for which the Nationalists are prepared; at the dramatic level, Marty's appearance and intervention heightens the tension in the novel, the suspense as to whether the doomed offensive will or will not take place; at the thematic level, Marty heightens the sense of danger and distrust that permeates the entire novel, of people turning against their own in a civil conflict and betrayal by allies being as likely a cause of harm as enemy action. There are thus at least three answers to the *why*, and to appreciate literature is to be concerned with the relationships between not only form and content, but also form, content, and function. Both the author's intention and the reader's response—where that response is appreciation—are thus guided by the principle of functionality.

It is difficult to deny the role of this principle without threatening the very concept of literature. In fact, the principle of functionality appears to hold not only for literature, but also for all art forms and artworks, and seems to have a necessary rather than contingent relation to art. The reason for this is the link to intentionality, as identified by Scruton: "Art provides a medium transparent to human intention, a medium for which the question, Why? can be asked of every observable feature, even if it may sometimes prove impossible to answer".[14]

Even in non-essentialist theories of art, there is an assumption that the work is an intentional creation. In the case of ready-mades like Duchamp's

Fountain, the urinal was—in Dickie's terminology—intentionally *presented to an artworld public* and the same applies to ready-mades appropriated from nature. Intentionality explains why the drawings of chimpanzees are not art and why a painted canvas that was indistinguishable from Pollock's *Autumn Rhythm* would not be considered a work of art if it was the result of canvas and paint falling from a truck. Art is bound up with the intention of an artist (or appropriator of ready-mades) and intentionality is bound up with the idea that every element of a work serves a function.[15]

The principle of functionality is crucial to both authorial intention and literary appreciation and the demand for literary thickness constitutes the match between the intended and recognised functions of the elements in the work—that is, not just the *what* and the *how*, but *why* the content is formed in a particular way in the work. Literary thickness unites the author's intention with the reader's response by means of the principle of functionality and is therefore characteristic of literary appreciation. Given the significance of the principle of functionality to literary thickness I shall revise the conception I defined in §18 in chapter 5 as follows:

> *LITERARY THICKNESS (II)*: an interest in a literary work that focuses on the integration of the formal and substantive axes—that is, the inseparability of form and content in the experience of that work. Literary thickness is characteristic of literary appreciation in attending to the combination of form and content in terms of function and characteristic of literature such that if a work is a work of literature, it will reward the demand for literary thickness.

In the remainder of this book, I shall employ "literary thickness" as an abbreviation for "literary thickness (II)".

22. EXPERIENTIAL VALUE

In chapter 1: §2, I defined final value in terms of non-derivative value such that ϕ is finally valuable if and only if ϕ is valuable in a way that is non-derivative. I also noted that my account of the value of a literary work *qua* literature is that it is both final and experiential. I have emphasised the importance of the experience of the literary work throughout my argument, discussing the experience of a poem in §12 in chapter 3 and the experience of a literary narrative in §15 in chapter 4. My conception of literary value is based on Budd's account, but two points should be noted at the outset. First, Budd uses the term "artistic value" for the value of a work of art *qua* art—that is, the literary value of literary works. Second, Budd specifies that he does not employ "intrinsic" to mean internal or non-relational, but the opposite of instrumental—that is, "for its own sake" or *final* (non-derivative) in my terms.[16]

Budd states:

> My claim is that the value of a work of art as a work of art is intrinsic to the
> work in the sense that it is (determined by) the intrinsic value of the experience
> the work offers (so that if it offers more than one experience, it has more than
> one artistic value or an artistic value composed of these different artistic val-
> ues). It should be remembered that the experience a work of art offers is an
> experience *of the work itself*, and the valuable qualities of a work are qualities
> *of the work*, not of the experience it offers. It is the nature of the work that
> endows the work with whatever artistic value it possesses; this nature is what
> is experienced in undergoing the experience the work offers; and the work's
> artistic value is the intrinsic value of this experience. So a work of art is
> valuable as art if it is such that the experience it offers is intrinsically valuable;
> and it is valuable to the degree that this experience is intrinsically valuable. [17]

Budd is explicit that offering an experience which is finally valuable is a
sufficient condition for a work having artistic value, but his discussion implies that a finally valuable experience is a sufficient *and* necessary condition
for artistic value. I shall adopt this stronger line and claim: *a work of literature has literary value if and only if the experience it offers is finally valuable, and is valuable to the degree that this experience is finally valuable.*
Offering a finally valuable literary experience is therefore a necessary and
sufficient condition for a work's having literary value.

Budd stipulates that the work of art must be experienced with understanding and that the experience of the work is a type rather than any person's
actual experience. [18] He then summarises artistic value as:

1. intrinsic,
2. sentiment-dependent,
3. intersubjective,
4. anthropocentric, and
5. incommensurable. [19]

Given that "intrinsic" means *final*, I agree with (1). Budd takes "sentiment-
dependent" to "include all the ways in which something can be found intrinsically rewarding". [20] I do not wish to commit to this view, but I am committed to the view that literary value is response-dependent, because it is the
value of the literary experience of a work. Despite my adoption of Lamarque's reconceptualisation of form-content inseparability as an imposed
demand rather than an objective property, I emphasised that the respective
demands for poetic (chapter 3: §12), narrative (chapter 4: §15), and literary
thickness (chapter 5: §18) are not rewarded by all works intended to invoke a
literary response. As such, literary judgement is not based entirely upon the
preference of the judge and is objective rather than subjective because one

evaluation may be more or less appropriate than another. This particular combination of objectivity and response-dependence is neatly formulated in Budd's characterisation of artistic value as *intersubjective*. I shall therefore accept (3) but not (2).

I also agree that literary value is *anthropocentric* and in chapter 7: §26, I shall demonstrate that literature is profoundly concerned with human values. Regarding incommensurability, Budd states that artistic value "is not a measurable quality", by which he means that when one work is evaluated as better than another, the difference cannot be measured on a quantitative scale.[21] Budd's account of value does not therefore authorise me to claim that *For Whom the Bell Tolls* has five percent more literary value than *Oliver Twist* or assign the former 3.9 out of 5 stars (its current rating at *goodreads.com*). I agree with Budd, but "incommensurable" is misleading as it denotes the absence of a standard for comparison in addition to the absence of a common measure. The literary value of different works can be compared, but not quantified, and I shall employ the term *unquantifiable* instead of "incommensurable". My characterisation of literary value is therefore that it is: (1) final, (2) intersubjective, (3) anthropocentric, and (4) unquantifiable.

Thus far I have identified literary value with the value of the experience of a literary work and enumerated four characteristics of the experiential value. I have not, however, provided an indication of what the experience is like or suggested why such experiences are worth having. In chapter 1: §4, I noted that both autonomists and heteronomists agree that pleasure as a literary value is correctly characterised as final rather than instrumental and that my proposed identification of literary value with pleasure does not necessarily trivialise the former. I also stated my intention to present my own account of the particular pleasure afforded by literature, but Gaskin is sceptical about precisely this possibility. Although he is a literary cognitivist, as discussed in chapter 5: §19, he defines a literary work in terms of literary pleasure and then states that the "appeal to 'literary' pleasure indeed imports a circularity, but there is no independent way of specifying the peculiar pleasure that literature provides for consumers".[22] Gaskin is overly pessimistic, however, as at least some light can be thrown on literary pleasure.

Alan Goldman provides a useful starting point for this illumination. He maintains that the type of pleasure peculiar to reading novels is

> the satisfaction that John Rawls subsumed under what he called the Aristotelian Principle, although Aristotle never described it explicitly, the satisfaction derived from the full and vigorous exercise of our human faculties or capacities. The physical equivalent is intense exertion in a competitive sport, but here we are speaking of the full and interactive exercise of our mental capacities: perceptual, imaginative, emotional, and cognitive. For a work of art to engage these capacities simultaneously and interactively is the mark of aesthetic value, as I argued in an earlier book with that title.[23]

> Pleasure here lies in appreciating aesthetic value. Aesthetic value lies in the capacity of a work to engage us in this broad and full way, not simply in the more superficial pleasure derived immediately from its surface sensuous or formal qualities. I take it that literary value is simply the value of literary works of art as such, the aesthetic or artistic value of works of literature. It therefore demands the same broad analysis in terms of full engagement. [24]

There are three points that I want to adopt and two with which I disagree.

First, I shall retain Goldman's initial description of "satisfaction" rather than "pleasure". There is very little difference in the extension of the two terms, but the difference in connotation (pleasure as enjoyment, satisfaction as complete fulfilment), however minor, is important if some type of gratification is to be defended as the characteristically literary value. Second, the mental capacities identified by Goldman are broadly correct. Perceptual engagement with a literary work may appear erroneous, but Goldman refers to the "rhythms and textures of the language" and "grasp of the larger structural patterns" in novels, in addition to the more obvious sensuous and musical qualities of poetry. [25] I shall take the experience of a literary work to include a perceptual aspect, but shall call this "sensory" in order to avoid the ambiguity of "perception", which denotes both sensory awareness and reflective understanding. Third, what is also important about Goldman's account is the emphasis he lays on the simultaneity and interactivity of the mental capacities when experiencing a literary work. The simultaneity and interactivity are part of what makes literary satisfaction so rewarding and part of what makes literary satisfaction so difficult to specify. Like Gaskin, Goldman is also a literary cognitivist and he argues that some novels are valuable as novels in virtue of the truth value of their philosophical theses. I noted in chapter 5: §20 that my account of literary appreciation (as characterised by the demand for literary thickness) is incompatible with literary cognitivism. I shall therefore drop Goldman's "cognitive" in favour of "intellective" to describe the relevant mental capacity, which I explain below. [26] Finally, Goldman is also emphatic about the ability of the literary experience to engage *all* the mental capacities. I do not want to claim that sensory perception, imagination, emotion, and the intellect exhaust human mental capacity, nor that the literary experience does not involve the engagement of any other proposed capacities. My claim is simply that literary experience consists of at least the four aspects identified, that these aspects occur simultaneously, and that they interact with each other.

Attridge describes the significance of pleasure to the experience of literature as follows:

> The literary work thus has available to it all the resources of meaningful language—it can describe, prove, evoke, cajole, warn, persuade, promise, or narrate in the most concrete and convincing manner—without suffering the

limitations imposed on purely instrumental language by the purposes which it must serve. (The one requirement that remains, perhaps, is the need to produce pleasure, and this pleasure, in so far as it is literary is brought about precisely by the performative, or more accurately the performing and performed, dimension of literature).[27]

In discussing staging in §15 in chapter 4, I identified a performative reading as *an experience of a literary work that activates its linguistic power by involving the simultaneous experience of its conceptual, emotional, and physical qualities.* A performative reading is the experience of a literary work as a literary work, an experience that produces the pleasure Attridge describes above. This pleasure "derives, in part, from this experience of new possibilities opening up, and from the revelation of language's hitherto unsuspected power to produce this effect. Hence the importance of what we inadequately call *form*: the writer's skilful handling of the properties of language to make possible the literary event".[28] Attridge thus links literary pleasure with authorial creativity.

Despite the link between performance and pleasure, however, the satisfaction produced by the literary experience is not always pleasing or joyful. Aaron Smuts subsumes both the paradoxes of tragedy and horror under the title of "the paradox of painful art", which is the apparent contradiction inherent in the desire to experience works of art that arouse painful emotions.[29] The paradox has a lengthy history, from Aristotle's brief mention of "catharsis" to Hume's discussion of the pleasure taken in "sorrow, terror, anxiety, and other passions", and I make no attempt to offer a solution here.[30] It is not just tragic or horrific works which produce a tension in the reader, but potentially all literature, as Attridge suggests when he states that the literary experience "involves the emergence within the reader's set of assumptions, routines, and expectations of an element of foreignness, something unanticipated, not immediately graspable, at a tangent to ingrained habits of thought and feeling".[31] The experience of the foreign, the unanticipated, and the ungraspable can be a source of confusion or irritation rather than joy and the literary experience is often simultaneously pleasing and discomforting.[32]

In chapter 1: §4 I stated that *literary satisfaction is an essentially intellectual pleasure.* Since Kant's initial identification of the source of the particular pleasure associated with the perception of beauty as the harmonious free play of the cognitive faculties, the particular pleasure associated with the appreciation of art has been characterised as cognitive. It is, indeed, difficult to deny Olsen's claim that literary works demand *intelligence, intellectual rigour, self-discipline, and sensitivity both to detail and to language.* With regard to the cognitive engagement with literature, Attridge adopts a position that comments on what I called the "substantive axis" in §20 in chapter 5.

Take the referential properties of a text: I may enjoy and learn from my encounter with the concepts, feelings, historical or imagined entities, and so on, to be found in any text, including a literary text (which always functions in ways other than the literary). But when, in conjunction with other modalities of reading, I respond to a text *as literature* (and it may or may not impose this choice upon me), my pleasure and profit come from the experience of an event of referring, from a staging of referentiality, not from any knowledge I acquire.[33]

The *"event of referring"* and *"staging of referentiality"* indicate that what is important in the experience of "Yew-Trees" and *For Whom the Bell Tolls* as literature is not the historical accuracy, but the function of the history in the works, the way in which the historical information and the manner in which it is presented contribute to the work as a unified whole. This is what I wish to convey with the *intellective* aspect of the literary experience, which involves exploring, interpreting, and comprehending the work itself rather than focusing on what can be learnt about the particulars or universals to which the work refers. Understanding the numerous elements of form and content in literary works, the manner in which they interact, and the role they play in the unity of the work, is—in the experience of a work with literary value—a sophisticated intellectual exercise, one that is often more difficult than extracting facts about the world from the work. I have employed the term "intellective" in order to avoid confusion with the cognitive aspect of literary experience—the learning about particulars and universals—that is usually part of literary experience, but is always contingent rather than necessary.

Thus far I have had very little to say about literary interpretation. I shall neither offer a theory of interpretation nor engage with the numerous critical and philosophical debates concerned with the practice, but I must clarify the role interpretation plays in my conception of literary value.[34] I defined "appreciation" as the grasping of the literary value of a literary work in chapter 1: §2 and argued for the demand for literary thickness as characteristic thereof in §21 above. "Interpretation" is the means by which literary value is identified, recognised, or grasped. Goldman notes that interpretation combines description and evaluation, and he distinguishes between the interpretation of an element of an artwork and the interpretation of the whole artwork. In the former, the focus is on understanding meaning, and in the latter, on recognising artistic value.[35] My interest in literary interpretation is in the latter—the description and evaluation of the work as a whole, as the way in which works are appreciated. I think that the combination of interpretation and appreciation is precisely what Attridge means when he writes of a *performative reading*. It is significant that he discusses neither interpretation nor appreciation explicitly in *The Singularity of Literature*, and the event of literature—the "literary experience" in my account—is the reader's performance of interpretation, the means by which he or she appreciates the work.

As noted in chapter 4: §15, I do not endorse Attridge's conception of the reader as having a role in the creation of the literary work, but the notion of a performative reading is useful in conveying that both interpretation and appreciation are active, rather than passive, processes. The activation of the linguistic power of the work involving the simultaneous experience of its sensory, imaginative, affective, and intellective qualities requires intense concentration on the part of the reader. The extent of this concentration also distinguishes literary satisfaction from the kind of entertainment value usually (but not always) associated with works of genre fiction.

In summary, the value of a work of literature is: (1) experiential, (2) final, (3) intersubjective, (4) anthropocentric, and (5) unquantifiable. Literature is valuable as the source of literary satisfaction, which is the satisfaction taken in the simultaneity and interactivity of the sensory, imaginative, affective, and intellective aspects of the literary experience. This satisfaction is partly derived from the revelation of the creative power of language. The appreciation of a literary work is the identification, exploration, and comprehension of the value of the work as literature, and appreciation is grounded in and promoted by the demand for literary thickness, which unites the authorial intention with the reader's response by means of the principle of functionality. Before I can proceed to my argument for the autonomy of literature, I must deal with an immediate and obvious objection to this account of literary value.

Budd's location of artistic value in artistic experience has resulted in numerous objections, beginning with the three Levinson offered in his critical notice of *Values of Art: Pictures, Poetry and Music*.[36] Noël Carroll's critique has been the most incisive, however, and his "Aesthetic Experience: A Question of Content"—originally published in 2004 and reprinted in *Art in Three Dimensions*—presents a critique of the *axiological approach* to aesthetic experience, which distinguishes the experience "in terms of the kind of value it is thought to secure, typically intrinsic value or value for its own sake".[37] Although Budd characterises artistic value in terms of artistic experience—rather than experience in terms of value—Carroll's objection is pertinent because it poses a problem for the relationship between final and experiential value: "If one values the artwork because it affords an experience valued for its own sake, then, without further qualification, the artwork would not appear to be valued for its own sake, but rather to be valued instrumentally as something that makes an intrinsically valuable experience available to the percipient".[38] The idea is that valuing an object for the experience it produces is a paradigmatic instance of instrumental value, like valuing an analgesic pill for the experience of pain relief it produces. Carroll does not develop the point, so I shall augment his objection with a complementary argument from Nicholas Stang.

Stang describes Budd's final value thesis as an "experiential view" and defines *artistic value* as "the value that works of art *as such* have"—that is, the literary value with which I am concerned.[39] He accepts that a pleasurable experience is finally valuable, notes the difference between the final/instrumental and intrinsic/extrinsic distinctions, and maintains that the extrinsic character of the property of having artistic value does not preclude artistic value itself from being final. Stang's claim is that the experiential account of value falsifies the final value thesis and his argument is:

1. If an object possesses a value in virtue of its contribution to a finally valuable whole, then the former object is not valuable for its own sake in virtue of its contribution to the finally valuable whole. The object may be finally valuable, but not in virtue of its contributing to the finally valuable whole.

2. If experiential theories of artistic value are correct, then a work possesses artistic value in virtue of its contribution to a finally valuable experience of that work.

3. ∴ If experiential theories of artistic value are correct, works are not valuable for their own sake in virtue of their contribution to the value of experiences of them.

4. ∴ If experiential theories of artistic value are correct, works of art are not valuable for their own sake in virtue of their artistic value. In other words, artistic value is not valuable for its own sake.[40]

The key term is *contribution* and Stang uses the example of the contribution a dramatic rest makes to a Beethoven sonata. While the experience of the work is finally valuable, the rest is only valuable in terms of its contribution to the work. Stang makes no commitment to the value of the rest being characterised as instrumental, as he refuses to assume that an object that is not finally valuable is necessarily instrumentally valuable.[41] His conclusion is that in Budd's account, artistic value is not final, and his argument therefore applies to my account of literary value.

While Budd does not explicitly acknowledge the point that Carroll raises, there is indeed a tension between the *finality* of artistic value and its location in the *experience* of the work. In one of the passages quoted above, Budd states that "the [artistically] valuable qualities of a work are qualities *of the work*, not of the experience it offers", and that this value is "intrinsic [final] to the work in the sense that it is (determined by) the intrinsic [final] value of the experience the work offers".[42] Literary value is thus both the value *of the work* and the value *of the experience* of the work—and there seems little difficulty in prising the two apart. Carroll does not distinguish between intrinsic value and final value, and if Budd were employing "intrinsic" in contrast to "extrinsic" then Carroll's objection would be fatal: a value cannot be both non-relational and experiential.[43] Budd is, however, clear that he is not employing "intrinsic" in this manner:

> By the intrinsic value of an item I do not mean a value that depends solely on the intrinsic nature of the item—a value that depends solely on its internal properties (its qualities and inner relations)—as contrasted with an extrinsic value—a value that depends, wholly or in part, on its external properties (its relations to other things). My conception of intrinsic value opposes it, not to extrinsic value, but to instrumental value, and I do not assume that something's intrinsic value is dependent solely on its intrinsic nature.[44]

If literary satisfaction is a final value—and even critics of the final value thesis like Carroll and Stang accept pleasure as finally valuable—then Carroll's objection collapses. The value of satisfaction is identical with the value of the experience of satisfaction. If there is no one currently experiencing the work, its final value is the power to produce satisfaction in a reader. Literary value is response—and therefore *experience*—dependent and thus both relational and final.

Stang's argument against the final value thesis is also flawed. A condensed version of his first two premises reads:

1. If an object possesses a value in virtue of its contribution to a finally valuable whole, then the former object is not valuable for its own sake.
2. If experiential theories of artistic value are correct, then a work possesses artistic value in virtue of its contribution to a finally valuable experience of that work.

There is a conflation between *whole* in (1) and *experience* in (2). Budd is clear that the artistic value of the work *is* the value of the artistic experience of the work. The experience is not the experience of the work plus something; it is simply identical with the experience of the work. A work does not therefore possess literary value in virtue of its *contribution* to a finally valuable experience, it possesses literary value by providing a finally valuable experience. The work is not part of the experience—it is all there is to experience. In chapter 1: §2, I employed the example of an analgesic pill and identified two potential types of pleasure, taste and pain relief, characterising the former as final (non-derivative) and the latter as instrumental (derivative). The objection raised by Carroll and Stang can be understood as claiming that the value of the experience of a literary work is akin to the value of the experience of pain relief produced by the pill or valuing the pill for its contribution to pain relief. My argument is that the value of the experience of a literary work is akin to the value of the experience of the taste of the pill, which is all there is to experience initially. In these terms, the cognitive and moral values of a literary experience are akin to the pain relief because the literary work can make a contribution to knowledge and it is to this classification that I turn next.

23. THICKNESS AND VALUE

Thus far, I have argued that the demand for literary thickness is necessarily rewarded by literary works and identified three different types of interest that can be taken in a literary work: the substantive axis, the formal axis, and literary thickness. I characterised literary appreciation in terms of literary thickness and literary satisfaction in terms of the sensory, imaginative, affective, and intellective aspects of the literary experience. There is one more step to take before setting out my argument for the autonomy of literature and that is to clarify the relations between the different interests in literary works and the different types of value. After defining final value as non-derivative in chapter 1: §2, I defined literary autonomy as the thesis that literary value is identical with literary satisfaction, independent of cognitive and moral values, and finally, rather than instrumentally, valuable in chapter 1: §5. In chapter 1: §4, I noted that while my claim that pleasure is a final value of literature is not controversial, my claim that cognitive and moral value are instrumental values of literature is. Using the example of the analgesic pill, I suggested that the cognitive value of *For Whom Bell Tolls* and the moral value of "The Lives of Animals" could be classified as derivative. In Stang's terminology, one might say that the experience of the works both afford the reader literary satisfaction and make a contribution to the reader's education. My claim is that these contributions to the reader's education— that is, the cognitive values of a literary work (whether understood in terms of truth, clarification, or knowledge) and the moral values of a literary work (whether understood in terms of truth or not)—are instrumentally rather than finally valuable. As mentioned in §6 in chapter 2, Carroll agrees with this classification, advancing an explicitly instrumentalist conception of artistic value, but I shall offer further reasons for those who are unconvinced.

The substantive axis is an interest in the relations between work and world in which the accuracy of representation at both the factual and thematic levels is of primary significance. As such, the substantive axis will be adopted in the judgement of the instrumental values—cognitive, religious, moral, and political—I identified in chapter 1: §4 as being of interest to philosophers. I defined literary cognitivism as the thesis that *truth is, or can be, a value of literature* qua *literature*. To judge *For Whom the Bell Tolls* for its cognitive value at the factual level is to evaluate the historical characters (such as Marty) appearing in the novel in terms of their resemblance to reality and the fictional characters (such as Jordan, the protagonist) for the veracity of the universals that they instantiate. One might, for example, compare Jordan to one or more of the actual American volunteers for the Republican cause—perhaps Robert Hale Merriman, who was also an academic and also killed in action. If Hemingway's Jordan is sufficiently like the real volunteers such that he would not seem out of place in Beevor's history, then the novel can be judged as factually accurate. At the thematic level, one could compare the hatred and savagery Hemingway depicts with the actual conduct of the war—for example Marty's penchant for executing his own men. If Hemingway's representation is authentic, then the novel can be judged as embodying a true theme. In each case one is comparing the literary fiction with the reality and judging the fiction exclusively in terms of the reality.

Although moral irrealists and non-cognitivists eschew truth as their criterion of moral evaluation, their substantive interest in the moral value of a literary work is nonetheless an interest in the relation between work and world that is focused on accuracy. In my example of *The True Knights* in § 19 in chapter 5, I stated that the hypothetical novel offers false and morally reprehensible answers to the questions it raises, but even if one considers the immoral answers neither false nor true, they are still judged against a moral standard that they fail to meet. Significantly, that standard is set in the world rather than in the novel and the fiction is judged entirely in terms of the reality. The difference between a moral realist/cognitivist and an irrealist/non-cognitivist judging the moral value of "The Lives of Animals" is that the former pair regards the theme as truth evaluable, and the latter pair, as non-truth evaluable. Notwithstanding, both pairs rely upon veracity, accuracy, or correspondence with the world. Whether one considers the cognitive or moral value of a work, therefore, the value is judged in terms of the accuracy of representation.[45] In other words, the cognitive and moral values of a literary work are *derived from* the work's correspondence with the world. There is thus a necessary relation between the substantive axis, which includes cognitive and moral evaluations of works, and derivative (instrumental) value.

In contrast, the demand for literary thickness recognises the salience of both the substantive and formal axes—that is, the relation between work and world *and* the relations within the work. As explained in chapter 5: §20, interest in the relation between work and world is integrated with interest in internal coherence and power of presentation—an integration that often demands a balance between factual accuracy and imaginative inventiveness. The literary value of *For Whom the Bell Tolls* is not thus measured in terms of, for example, the accuracy of the representation of Marty, but—as noted in §21 above— in terms of the function of Marty in the work and the way in which the historical information and its mode of presentation contribute to the work as a unified whole. The historical verisimilitude is not, however, irrelevant to the appreciation of the novel and the realistic presentation of Marty as powerful, bitter, and irrational is vital to the role he serves in the novel. An inaccurate description of Marty as tall and emaciated would not necessarily be a literary defect, although a description of him as amiable and eager to assist would, because the character would no longer serve the narrative, dramatic, and thematic functions identified. Substantive inaccuracies may detract from literary value, but are not *pro tanto* literary defects, which is why aboutness is incompatible with literary cognitivism. Truth, whether understood in propositional or non-propositional terms, is not part and parcel of the literary value realised by the demand for literary thickness.

A similar point can be made regarding moral value, whether or not one regards virtue and vice as truth evaluable. If one is appreciating "The Lives of Animals" *qua* literature, one's primary concern is with the function of animal suffering in the work and the way in which the philosophical content and its mode of presentation contribute to the work as a whole. In §17 in chapter 4, I quoted Wendy Doniger's claim that it is *reductionistic* to respond to Coetzee's work as a philosophical argument. One could analyse the narrative, reconstruct the premises and conclusion Coetzee presents, and then assess the argument for soundness, but in doing so one would no longer be appreciating the work as literature. One could also isolate the theme—*animal suffering on a grand scale is morally significant*, assess it in terms of one's preferred moral theory, and judge the short story in terms of the extent to which the theme meets the demands of that theory. This may be more appropriate than reducing the work to a philosophical argument, but nonetheless constitutes a failure to appreciate the work as literature. If "The Lives of Animals" invites one to view the human treatment of animals as a holocaust and if this is immoral in minimising the suffering of the victims of the Holocaust, then the immorality is not necessarily a literary defect. Moral mismatches are also—like historical mismatches—substantive inaccuracies and, as noted, substantive inaccuracies are not *pro tanto* defects. The portrayal of animal suffering as trivial would detract from the value of the work because the theme would no longer unite elements such as those I described: (absent) message, point of view, and narrative closure. The substantive axis matters, but it is tempered by the formal axis. As such, the demand for literary thickness is incompatible with moral value being part and parcel of the work's literary value.

The literary satisfaction I described in §22 above does not have either cognitive or moral value as a constituent part, but is entirely reliant upon the non-derivative value of the particular type of pleasure that accompanies the experience of reading a literary work *qua* literature. The demand for literary thickness therefore has a necessary relation to final value. This relation to final value is shared by the formal axis, the interest in the relations within the work in which the coherence of the various linguistic elements in the work's design or structure into a satisfying whole is of primary significance. An evaluation of a literary work in terms of form alone will judge the accuracy of the factual and thematic representations in the work as either irrelevant or of minimal relevance to the value of the work *qua* work. A consequence of this view is that it severs the literary work and literary appreciation from the world, which was my primary objection to Riffaterre's referential fallacy in chapter 5: §19. Aside from this objection, I have emphasised, from my initial discussion of formalism in chapter 1: §4, that I consider both literary form and literary content as salient. The salience of the substantive axis is why my perspective on literature is correctly classified as realist, why (in spite of my concluding comments on freedom in §24 below) the argument from literary thickness is a defence of literary humanism, and why I cannot accept literary formalism. Both the demand for literary thickness and the formal axis have a necessary relation to final value, but only the demand for literary thickness is characteristic of literary appreciation.

24. THE ARGUMENT FROM LITERARY THICKNESS

I began my thesis by arguing for two conceptions of form-content insepara-bility: poetic thickness and narrative thickness. I then showed that the two conceptions could be subsumed under the concept of literary thickness, which I identified as a necessary condition of literature. I proposed that literary thickness, understood as a demand made of a work rather than a property discovered therein, combined two conflicting interests that can be taken in a work: the substantive axis and the formal axis. I demonstrated that the conflicting interests could be integrated in the demand for literary thick-ness and that literary thickness was characteristic of literary appreciation. I then explained literary value in terms of the non-derivative value of the experience of a literary work—that is, literary satisfaction. I have established a relation between literary thickness and literary satisfaction and argued that the literary value of a literary work is independent of the work's cognitive, moral, and other instrumental values, and that literature is therefore autono-mous. The argument can be set out as follows:

1. In literary works both the substantive and formal axes are salient.
2. If both the substantive and formal axes are salient, then literary appre-ciation is characterised by literary thickness—the demand for form-content inseparability.
3. Therefore the appreciation of literary works is characterised by literary thickness.
4. Literary value is the value of the experience of literary appreciation.
5. If the experience of literary appreciation is characterised by literary thickness, then literary value is final.
6. Therefore literary value is final.

In the terms I set out in chapter 1: §5, the argument establishes the autonomy of literature: *the value of a work of literature* qua *literature is the value of the experience afforded by the work and the experience afforded by the work is valuable to the degree that this experience is finally valuable—that is, produces literary satisfaction.*

Before proceeding to the final chapter, which responds to the objections presented in chapter 2, I offer a brief comment on the significance of my conception of literary value. In §22 above, I quoted Attridge as stating, "*The literary work thus has available to it all the resources of meaningful language . . . without suffering the limitations imposed on purely instrumental language by the purposes which it must serve.*" John Gibson expresses a similar view: "Of all the uses of language we have developed, the literary has some claim to being the most liberated. It speaks in freedom from the truth and the facts, and it is largely unconstrained by the very world that our other, less elevated uses of language struggle to represent".[46] So does Catherine Belsey: "As one instance of culture, one form of representation, fiction sets the signifier free of any supposed moorings in reality or utility. It has no obligation to refer to the world or to obey any laws but its own, and even those laws, it appears, are there to be broken".[47] *Contra* Belsey, the relation between work and world is referential and literature is to that extent (at least) moored in reality.

All three quotes nonetheless identify what I believe is the most important feature of literature: *the literary use of language is free from limitation, free from the truth and the facts, and free from any laws but its own.* I am not suggesting that this freedom is a sufficient condition of literature, but I am suggesting that it is a necessary condition. Freedom from limitation is why the literary use of language is special, why it matters the most, and why it provides such intense and prolonged pleasure. I know no way of demonstrating that this freedom is essential to literature other than to point to the thousands of examples provided by the canon and the argument from literary thickness requires no such commitment to its value. Freedom from limitation is explicitly freedom from truth and implicitly freedom from virtue, however, which is why a commitment to its value does require that literary value is independent of cognitive value and moral value. It is in the service of this end that this monograph has been written.

NOTES

1. Antony Beevor, *The Spanish Civil War* (London: Cassell & Co., 2001 [1982]), 184.

2. Ernest Hemingway, *For Whom the Bell Tolls* (London: Grafton Books, 1976 [1940]), 364–65.

3. This was the scandal that resulted in Marty's being expelled from the *Parti communiste français* in 1952. This example is a repetition of my points about "London" in "Gerontion" (chapter 3: §12) and *Oliver Twist* (chapter 4: §15). Lamarque provides a useful guide to what

information one is licensed to invoke when he identifies that which is "roughly speaking . . . contemporaneous" with the work itself (Peter Lamarque, *The Opacity of Narrative* [London: Rowman & Littlefield International, 2014], 145–46).

4. Aristotle, *Poetics*, trans. P. Murray & T. S. Dorsch, in P. Murray, ed., *Classical Literary Criticism* (London: Penguin, 2004), 57–97: VIII: 1451a33–36.

5. Paul Auster, *The New York Trilogy* (London: Faber & Faber, 2011 [1987]), 7–8.

6. William Lavender, "The Novel of Critical Engagement and Paul Auster's 'City of Glass,'" *Contemporary Literature 34* (1993), 219–39: 219. See also: Arthur Conan Doyle, "The Adventure of the Musgrave Ritual," *The Strand Magazine: An Illustrated Monthly 5* (1893), 479–90.

7. Holmes's story is an embedded narrative, which offers further evidence for Lavender's claim about Auster's drawing on Brooks.

8. Peter Brooks, *Reading for the Plot: Design and Intention in Narrative* (Cambridge, MA: Harvard University Press, 1992 [1984]), 24.

9. Brooks, *Reading for the Plot*, 24–25. See also: Tzvetan Todorov, "The Typology of Detective Fiction," in T. Todorov, *The Poetics of Prose*, trans. Richard Howard (Oxford: Blackwell, 1977 [1971]), 42–52: 45.

10. Interestingly, Alan Goldman makes an unrelated argument for the unique significance of the mystery novel in literature. See: Alan H. Goldman, *Philosophy and the Novel* (Oxford: Oxford University Press, 2013), 82–106.

11. Lamarque, *Opacity of Narrative*, 160.

12. Peter Lamarque, "The Elusiveness of Poetic Meaning," *Ratio 22* (2009), 398–420: 412. See: Stein Haugom Olsen, *The Structure of Literary Understanding* (Cambridge: Cambridge University Press, 1978), 94–95.

13. Lamarque, "Elusiveness of Poetic Meaning," 412. I suggested several relevant differences between poetry and narrative literature in §14 in chapter 4.

14. Roger Scruton, "Photography and Representation," *Critical Inquiry 7* (1981), 577–603: 593.

15. Note that in appreciating a work one can assume that every element has a function without assuming that the artist had an explicit intention regarding that function.

16. Malcolm Budd, *Values of Art* (London: Penguin, 1995), 4–5. See also: Malcolm Budd, "Aesthetic Essence," in M. Budd, *Aesthetic Essays* (Oxford: Oxford University Press, 2008), 31–47: 46.

17. Budd, *Values of Art*, 4–5.

18. Budd, *Values of Art*, 11–12 & 4.

19. Budd, *Values of Art*, 43.

20. Budd, *Values of Art*, 38–39.

21. Budd, *Values of Art*, 42.

22. Richard Gaskin, *Language, Truth, and Literature: A Defence of Literary Humanism* (Oxford: Oxford University Press, 2013), 33.

23. Alan H. Goldman, *Aesthetic Value* (Boulder, CO: Westview Press, 1995). More recently, Goldman has defended aesthetic value as experiential in: "The Experiential Account of Aesthetic Value," *The Journal of Aesthetics and Art Criticism 64* (2006), 333–42.

24. Goldman, *Philosophy and the Novel*, 3.

25. Goldman, *Philosophy and the Novel*, 5.

26. I shall not discuss either the imaginative or affective aspects of literary satisfaction as neither are controversial. The imagination has been explicitly linked to art since Hutcheson's prototype aesthetic theory and the connection was explored by both Hume and Kant later in the eighteenth century. The expression of emotion has been linked to art since the Sturm und Drang movement in the mid-eighteenth century, and was explicated by Friedrich Schlegel, Goethe, G. E. Lessing, and J. G. Herder—and later Wordsworth and Coleridge. For contemporary treatments of the respective subjects, see: Roger Scruton, *Art and Imagination: A Study in the Philosophy of Mind* (London: Methuen, 1974); and Derek Matravers, *Art and Emotion* (Oxford: Oxford University Press, 1998).

27. Derek Attridge, *The Singularity of Literature* (New York: Routledge, 2004), 119.

28. Derek Attridge, "The Singular Events of Literature," *British Journal of Aesthetics 50* (2010), 81–84: 83. Attridge's performative reading recalls J. L. Austin's *performative utterances*. Austin states, "The term 'performative' will be used in a variety of cognate ways and constructions, much as the term 'imperative' is. The name is derived, of course, from 'perform,' the usual verb with the noun 'action': it indicates that the issuing of the utterance is the performing of an action—it is not normally thought of as just saying something" (*How to Do Things with Words* [London: Oxford University Press, 1962], 6–7). The extent to which Attridge has drawn on Austin is not entirely clear as although he mentions the significance of Austin to both the analytic and continental approaches to literature ("The Singular Events of Literature," 81), Austin's name appears only once in *The Singularity of Literature*, in the bibliography (164). In the absence of an explicit connection, I shall continue to employ "performative reading" without recourse to Austin.

29. Aaron Smuts, "The Paradox of Painful Art," *Journal of Aesthetic Education 41* (2007), 59–76: 60.

30. Aristotle, *Poetics*, VI: 1449b26–30; David Hume, "Of Tragedy," in D. Hume, *David Hume: Essays, Moral, Political, and Literary* (Indianapolis, IN: Liberty Fund, 1987 [1757]), 216–25: 216.

31. Attridge, "Singular Events of Literature," 83.

32. I reiterate this point in my brief discussion of *Lolita* in §26 in chapter 7.

33. Attridge, *Singularity of Literature*, 95–96.

34. Beardsley's discussion of the role of authorial intention in interpretation is just one such example. For a comprehensive overview of the intentionalist debate and the other debates relevant to literary interpretation, see: Peter Lamarque, *The Philosophy of Literature* (Malden, MA: Blackwell, 2009), 115–31 & 148–68.

35. Goldman, *Philosophy and the Novel*, 29.

36. See: Jerrold Levinson, "Art, Value, and Philosophy," *Mind 105* (1996), 667–82.

37. Noël Carroll, *Art in Three Dimensions* (Oxford: Oxford University Press, 2012 [2010]), 90.

38. Carroll, *Art in Three Dimensions*, 91.

39. Nicholas F. Stang, "Artworks Are Not Valuable for Their Own Sake," *The Journal of Aesthetics and Art Criticism 70* (2012), 271–80: 271.

40. Stang, "Artworks Are Not Valuable for Their Own Sake," 273.

41. Stang, "Artworks Are Not Valuable for Their Own Sake," 272.

42. Budd, *Values of Art*, 4–5.

43. Carroll refers to *final value* as "value for its own sake" (*Art in Three Dimensions*, 90).

44. Budd, *Values of Art*, 5.

45. Understood in these terms, the cognitive and moral values of a literary work could conflict. For example, Hemingway could have deliberately misrepresented facts about the Spanish Civil War for the purpose of developing the theme of hatred and savagery. The reader with a substantive interest in the work might judge the factual inaccuracies as reducing the work's cognitive value and the greater thematic richness as increasing the work's moral value.

46. John Gibson, *Fiction and the Weave of Life* (Oxford: Oxford University Press, 2007), 50.

47. Catherine Belsey, *A Future for Criticism* (Malden, MA: Wiley-Blackwell, 2011), 126.

Chapter Seven

Literary Autonomy

The purpose of this chapter is to explain why my account of literary value is rationally more justifiable than that of my main opponents, identified as Noël Carroll and Martha Nussbaum in chapter 2. Section §25 responds to both of Carroll's objections, first demonstrating that the virtue wheels which he regards as exemplifying clarificationism can both clarify and obscure moral concepts, and then that the close relation he proposes between realist novels and mimetic value is flawed. My claim, upon which I expand in §26, is that Carroll fails to establish cognitive value as partly constitutive of literary value and that he furthermore sets up a false dichotomy between literary formalism and literary instrumentalism. In §27 I respond to both of Nussbaum's objections, first showing that she fails to admit the complexity of the relationship between moral value and literary value and then that she fails to offer evidence for her empirical claim. I provide a critique of Nussbaum's instrumentalism in §28, concluding with a brief comment on my contribution to the defence of literary humanism.

25. VICE AND MIMESIS

In §7 in chapter 2, I identified *clarificationism* as an objection to my thesis on the basis that the primary—but not the only—value of literary works *qua* literature is the conceptual clarification they provide—that is, their cognitive value. The virtue wheels deployed in works such as *Great Expectations* and *Howards End* are paradigmatic examples of clarificationism because they refine the virtue concepts of readers in terms of parenting in the former and imaginativeness in the latter. Before responding to the challenge presented by virtue wheels, I want to note two of Carroll's claims with which I disagree but which I am not going to dispute here. The first is that literary narratives are sufficiently like thought experiments to be regarded as enthymematic arguments. My view on the thick interest one brings to a literary narrative *qua* literary narrative precludes me from accepting this claim. The sense in which a literary narrative is like a thought experiment is the sense in which one's interest in it is *qua* philosophy. These two types of interest—*qua* literature and *qua* philosophy—are very different, as explained in my comment on "The Lives of Animals" in §23 in chapter 6. The second is the empirical evidence that Carroll mentions, the discussion of the components of virtue wheels by actual audiences. Carroll's failure to refer to any studies aside, this discussion—should its existence be established—would offer as much evidence for my response as for Carroll's position.

In chapter 1: §4, I defined literary cognitivism in terms of truth, and then in chapter 5: §19, I argued that truth is a *pro tanto* literary merit for Carroll and Catherine Wilson as well as Richard Gaskin. In chapter 1: §4, I also identified my concern with virtue and vice in literature as with the vision or perspective embodied by the work, noting that different works embody pro- or anti- attitudes towards the same subject. With regard to Carroll's virtue wheels, a single work clarifies a virtue concept by including a range of characters who instantiate the virtue and its corresponding vice to different extents. Carroll's examples follow a predictable course, works in which one is invited to adopt a pro-attitude towards characters in whom the virtue is instantiated and an anti-attitude towards characters who lack the virtue or in whom the vice is instantiated. The attitudes one is invited to adopt reflect the virtue wheel itself, varying from strong approval of the most virtuous characters to strong disapproval of the most vicious characters. *Great Expectations* thus invites approval of Joe and Matthew Pocket, disapproval of Mrs Gargery and Miss Havisham, and something in between for Magwitch and Molly. This is how readers acquire clarification of their virtue concepts—by responding to the characters in the manner endorsed by Dickens's narrative, and refining their understanding such that they have a better (i.e., more accurate) grasp of the concept in question. One's capacity to recognise virtuous parents and vicious parents is enhanced by the engagement with *Great Expectations* because the narrative invites one to regard Joe's virtue with admiration and his wife's vice with contempt.

In chapter 5: §19, I agreed with Peter Lamarque's criticism of Rowe's strategy of employing contradictory literary themes, so I shall avoid using it here—that is, asking *what if* Great Expectations *invited admiration for Mrs Gargery's parenting and contempt for Joe's parenting*? In the same section, I used the example of a hypothetical novel, *The True Knights*, whose narrative runs parallel to *The Birth of a Nation*. If the novel made use of the same characters as the film, it might easily deploy a virtue wheel of its own with regard to the concept of racial equality (or, more simply, "egalitarianism"). The novel could present a particularly complex virtue wheel because of the salience of racial identity to the instantiation of the virtue and vice in individuals, a complexity which is enhanced by the presence of mixed race characters. The virtue wheel for the concept of racial equality would include: Ben Cameron (white, opposes), Flora Cameron (white, opposes), Mammy (black, opposes), Austin Stoneman (white, supports), Silas Lynch (mixed race, supports), and Gus (black, supports). There are various other characters, such as Elsie Stoneman and Lydia Brown, whose attitudes lie in between support and opposition, which is to be expected from a nuanced treatment of a virtue concept. The problem with *The True Knights* is, as I noted, that it provides the wrong answers to the serious and interesting questions it raises. Similarly, the virtue wheel described above invites admiration for the Camerons and their loyal black servants and contempt for white abolitionists and non-whites who wish to assert their equality. The virtue wheel in *The True Knights* would not therefore be an example of clarificationism for Carroll because the presentation of racial equality as a vice works to obscure the virtue concept rather than clarify and refine it. The *vice wheel* is thus a cognitive—and therefore, according to Carroll, a *literary*—defect in the work.

Thus far I have not stated anything with which Carroll would disagree. The problem I envisage for him is not that his conception of virtue wheels fails, but that it is successful. In his attempt to address a potential objection from Lamarque and Stein Haugom Olsen, Carroll makes a compelling argument for virtue wheels as a "formal or organizational" merit of a literary or cinematic work.[1] I agree that the virtue wheels in *Great Expectations* and *Howards End* are devices which enhance the literary value of the works. Carroll is, however, committed to maintaining that the vice wheel of *The True Knights* is not a literary merit because whatever role it plays in structuring the novel, it obscures the virtue concept and is thus a cognitive and literary defect. Carroll's presentation of virtue wheels is nonetheless convincing and it is difficult to see how the vice wheel fails to improve the work in some way, providing as it does *"a studied array of characters who both correspond and contrast with each other along the dimension of a certain virtue or package of virtues"*. The novel is flawed in presenting racial equality as a vice, but the way in which it communicates this cognitive and moral defect appears to have merit. If the novel were well-written enough, there is no reason it should not deploy an even more effective vice wheel than the virtue wheels in *Great Expectations* and *Howards End*. Carroll's detailed analysis of virtue wheels has shown that there is more to the wheel than the accuracy of the representation of the virtue concept—that is, it is not just the (true) content, but also the (intricate) form which constitutes the literary merit. What he cannot account for is vice wheels—that is, cases where the virtue wheel is both a literary merit and a cognitive defect.

If my counterexample seems implausible, based on a hypothetical novel which is in turn based on a film that is now considered overtly didactic amongst its many other flaws, there are numerous examples that could be drawn from works whose literary merit is exemplary. In chapter 1: §4, I mentioned surrealist and existentialist works as embodying nihilist or amoral perspectives. In Miller's surrealist autobiography, *Tropic of Cancer*, the supporting cast of male characters are not fully developed and function to some extent as mirrors reflecting various aspects of, and possibilities for, the protagonist. The Miller character, Van Norden, Boris, Collins, Carl, and Fillmore constitute a vice wheel with regard to misogyny. The novel can readily be interpreted as inviting one to regard Van Norden, who continually refers to women synecdochically (by their genitals), as amusing; Fillmore, who marries a woman he has impregnated, as pathetic; and Collins, the only homosexual character, as living a carefree and happy existence free from the problems women create. Vice wheels are not, however, restricted to high modernist literature. Consider James Ellroy's L.A. Quartet, comprising *The Black Dahlia*, *The Big Nowhere*, *L.A. Confidential*, and *White Jazz*. In each of these novels, the subject of the virtue wheel is virtue itself, specifically the question of how to retain one's virtue as a law enforcement officer in a society that is oppressive, corrupt, racist, and homophobic (Los Angeles in the 1950s). Ellroy deploys virtue wheels in each novel—particularly the final three, which share several characters—contrasting two to three protagonists and several minor characters in terms of their virtues and vices as law enforcement officers. The virtue wheel in *White Jazz* is especially rich and the attitudes one is invited to adopt towards David Klein, Edmund Exley, and Dudley Smith, the three main characters who survive the rigours of the narrative, are sophisticated and subtle. All three are marred with flaws and vices too numerous to catalogue and yet some degree of admiration is plainly prescribed for Klein. Ellroy's series may not disguise vice as virtue, but it complicates rather than clarifies the concept in question.

Vice wheels—understood as virtue wheels that obscure rather than clarify the moral concepts with which they are concerned—are thus a feature of several (if not many) works of literature. In both of the examples briefly discussed above—*Tropic of Cancer* and *White Jazz*—the structure provided by the vice wheel is an unlikely candidate for a literary defect. In fact, the formal device appears to make the respective works *better* novels and is thus a merit (of some sort). In each case, the vice wheel increases the value of the work in one way, but decreases it in another. My theory of literary autonomy can account for this dichotomy, because literary value is regarded as independent of cognitive and moral value. Where cleverly executed, vice wheels therefore increase a work's literary value, but decrease its cognitive and moral values. In contrast, Carroll's clarificationism cannot account for works that are both vicious and valued *qua* literature because the immorality they endorse is a literary, cognitive, and moral defect in the work.[2] Vice wheels thus expose clarificationism as fallacious.

Following my explanation of clarificationism in §7 in chapter 2, I interpreted Carroll's discussion of realist novels as a direct objection to my argument for autonomy: realist novels are a category of literary works for which (1) the accuracy of psychological and social representation is part and parcel of literary value, but which also (2) reward the demand for literary thickness. I have been clear throughout this monograph that both form and content are salient in literary works. When I set out the respective interests in form and content in terms of the formal and substantive axes in chapter 5: §20, I was similarly clear that both axes are relevant to the value of a work *qua* literature. In the same section I claimed that the two axes are integrated in the demand for literary thickness, which reconciles the opposing interests and constitutes a pro-reference, but anti-cognitivist position on literature. The pro-reference position follows straightforwardly from the salience of the substantive axis: reference links word and work to world. The anti-cognitivism is a result of the significance I ascribed to the principle of functionality in §21 in chapter 6. In literary appreciation, it is not only the *how* (form) and the *what* (content) which is important, but also the *why*—that is, the function the formed content serves in the work. In order to grasp the literary value of a work on my account one must therefore attend primarily to the function of the person, place, or event in the work with the result that inaccurate reference is not a *pro tanto* literary defect. To employ alternative terms, the demand for literary thickness combines the coherence and correspondence values of a work, but prioritises the former over the latter. This priority is why I adopted Lamarque and Olsen's *aboutness* terminology to describe the relation between work and world. Carroll's objection can be restated as: *in realist novels (at least), psychological and social inaccuracies are (at least)* pro tanto *literary defects.* The relation between work and world is thus stronger than I have maintained and if I retain literary thickness as characteristic of literary appreciation, it should be as a pro-reference cognitive position—that is, recognise that cognitive value (understood in terms of psychological and social knowledge) is partly constitutive of literary value.

In the context of what I called the "value interaction debate" in chapter 1: §4, Matthew Kieran has expressed concern about the use of counterexamples and his scepticism is worth quoting in full:

> However, counter-examples as such cannot do the work of philosophical argument. One of the problems with the current debate is that too often the appeal to examples is relied on in place of argument. Yet competing characterisations and explanations can be offered. The trouble with over-reliance on examples is that they can be cut different ways to suit distinct positions.[3]

Counterexamples cannot perform the work of philosophical arguments and I am therefore reluctant to load my responses with them. I have, however, provided arguments for literary thickness as a necessary condition of literary works, for literary thickness as characteristic of literary appreciation, and for the autonomy of literature in chapters 3 through 6. The counterexamples I employ should therefore be seen as offering evidence for the arguments already provided rather than being presented *in lieu* of philosophical argument. I noted that Carroll defined realist artworks as *artworks that represent the social and psychological dimensions of human affairs in such a way that the works are intended to impart knowledge or understanding*. If cognitive value really is part and parcel of literary value in this straightforward manner, then a lack of realism or mimesis would be a literary defect in realist narratives.

Dickens is a paradigmatic realist novelist yet his oeuvre provides numerous counterexamples to Carroll's thesis. In fact, the very basis of his realism—the extent to which Victorian society was accurately represented in his novels—is contested.[4] Given Carroll's definition of a realist artwork in terms of being intended to impart knowledge, D. W. Jefferson's commentary on *Hard Times* is revealing: "It is certainly written with great vigour and economy, the discipline of the weekly instalments being evident in the sharp decisive handling of episodes, but the central contentions so confidently urged will not bear critical inspection, and it must be condemned for its distortion of truth".[5] The subject of Jefferson's critical interest is stated in the first sentence of his essay, "*Hard Times* has the air initially of being a novel of precise social relevance", and he is not explicit as to whether he regards the imprecision he exposes as a defect *qua* literature.[6] If Jefferson's claim is correct, however, then Carroll is committed to the view that *Hard Times* fails *qua* realist novel because the *distortion of truth* is incompatible with the imparting of knowledge.[7] The commitment extends beyond a particular interpretation of *Hard Times* because if, as various critics suggest, Dickens exaggerated the harsh treatment of orphans in *Oliver Twist* or the Byzantine machinations of the Court of Chancery in *Bleak House*, then the lack of accuracy in his novels may be extensive, if not ubiquitous.

Malcolm Pittock maintains that there is a second problem with Dickens's realism:

> It is, moreover, arguable that the Grundyish inhibitions of the early and mid-Victorian period were inimical to the creation of the greatest fiction anyway; but Dickens made matters worse by being more inhibited than he needed to be. Aunt Esther in *Mary Barton* may not be a very convincing prostitute, but Mrs Gaskell could allow herself to show how a prostitute's dependence on alcohol could effectively rule out any prospect of change in her way of life. And that touch of social reality makes Aunt Esther memorable in a way that none of Dickens's prostitutes, as prostitutes, are.[8]

According to Pittock, Dickens's accurate representation of social ills such as prostitution was restricted by his own inhibitions as a writer in addition to the legal and conventional censorship of the era. It thus seems likely that Dickens embellished some aspects of the social and psychological reality of Victorian England for dramatic and thematic purposes and downplayed others in order to avoid violating personal and public norms. Were it to be proved that Dickens had, for example, misrepresented reality in *Oliver Twist* by exaggerating the plight of orphans, Carroll would be committed to the view that the work is correspondingly flawed *qua* realist novel. But to evaluate *Oliver Twist* in this way is to evince a thin interest in the work, to separate the content from the formed content that constitutes the work. If Dickens did exaggerate, the exaggeration appears to exemplify the staging—or dramatizing– of the cruelty faced by orphans and, in this instance, increases rather than decreases the value of the novel *qua* novel.

Many more counterexamples to Carroll could be drawn from Dickens, but I shall consider the case of a very early realist novel instead. Setting aside the character of Alexander Selkirk, upon whom Robinson Crusoe may have been based, Coetzee's *Foe* presents a much more likely—and therefore realistic— portrait of Crusoe's character than Defoe in the original novel. Coetzee's Cruso is suffering from a variety of physical and psychological ailments caused by his enforced residence on the uninhabited island and the following description by the narrator, Susan Barton, is indicative of both:

> Sometimes Cruso kept me awake with the sounds he made in his sleep, chiefly the grinding of his teeth. For so far had his teeth decayed that it had grown a habit with him to grind them together constantly, those that were left, to still the ache. Indeed, it was no pretty sight to see him take his food in his unwashed hands and gnaw at it on the left side, where it hurt him less. But Bahia, and the life I had lived there, had taught me not to be dainty. [9]

This portrait provides a stark contrast with Defoe's Crusoe, who—aside from his illness in his first year and a few moments of despair—essentially retains his health, energy, and optimism for twenty-four years of solitude before rescuing Friday in the twenty-fifth. Selkirk spent a little more than four years on his own and he would have been a remarkable man indeed if he could have sustained both his physical and mental health for more than two decades of isolation. Nonetheless, it would be difficult to make a convincing argument that Coetzee's reimagining of Defoe's work shows the latter as defective *qua* literature due to the mimetic failure revealed. In addition, despite its realistic portrayal of Cruso, *Foe* is not itself a realist novel (the notoriously impenetrable ending is probably the most obvious evidence for this claim), which indicates the complexity of the relationship between mimesis and literary value. As with my first response, the problem for Carroll's objection is not just that there appear to be counterexamples, but that the existence of these counterexamples indicates a more serious issue: if virtue wheels are literary merits in virtue of refining moral concepts, then vice wheels should be literary defects; if accurate mimesis is a literary merit in virtue of its truth value, then failed mimesis should be a literary defect. The practice of literature, including in particular literary criticism, simply fails to support either claim.

26. LITERATURE IN TWO DIMENSIONS

In §25 above, I responded the two specific objections to my position set out in chapter 2: §7. In this section, I shall show why, despite the merits that I mentioned in chapter 2: §6, Carroll's "literature in three dimensions" does not constitute a threat to literary autonomy more generally. I begin by making my agreement with Carroll on four points clear. First, it would be foolish to deny that art originated in non-artistic practices and was—perhaps for a very long period of time—indistinguishable from these practices. Second, it would be almost as foolish to deny that art continues to be a significant source of enculturation. I think Carroll overstates the case concerning the separation of the artworld from society (and aestheticians from other philosophers), but even if I am wrong, I propose no such separation myself. Third, I have been explicit throughout my thesis that I neither wish to deny the existence of instrumental values of art nor—in the case of cognitive, religious, ethical, and political values—their significance. There are many circumstances where a work's ethical value will be more important than its artistic value; in fact, a work's ethical value may *always* be more important than its artistic value (except when the work is being evaluated *qua* art). Finally, the weight of history does indeed lend force to the association of art with instrumental values and Carroll is correct to place the burden of proof upon those who seek to identify the characteristically artistic value as final.

With regard to literature, I believe this is precisely what I have done: presented an argument for literary value as final, rather than instrumental. The argument is reliant upon my identification of two opposing axes: the substantive and the formal. The substantive axis retains the link between work and world by means of reference—which makes "Gerontion" and *Oliver Twist* about London, "Yew-Trees" about the yew, and "The Lives of Animals" about vegetarianism. The problem is not connecting work and world—this function is already served by the substantive axis—but integrating this substantive interest in the external relations of the work with the formal interest in the internal relations of the work. To employ Searle's terminology again, "human" still means human in *Oliver Twist*; the question is how to reconcile the semantic interest in "human" with the interest in the role that "human" plays in establishing an atmosphere of inhumanity in the first part of the novel. The answer is, of course, the demand for literary thickness, which is characteristic of literary appreciation.

Bradley, as quoted in chapter 1: §5, is doubly erroneous: not only is one not required to *ignore the beliefs, aims, and conditions which belong to you in the world of reality* when appreciating literature, but one *cannot*. I do not, would not want to, and could not, abandon my belief in the evil of paedophilia, for example, when I read *Lolita*. Furthermore, it is this very belief that creates the dramatic tension in the novel (as soon as I become aware that the protagonist and narrator is an unrepentant paedophile). Nabokov knew that— I would like to say *all*, but realistically—*most* of his readers would be horrified by Humbert Humbert's thoughts and his selection of a vice that most people cannot tolerate or forgive is essential to the work. If I were willing to set my ethics aside and imagine a world where paedophilia was morally acceptable, *Lolita* would fail *qua* literary work. Nabokov's composition is so skilful that one is gripped by the story and fascinated by the promised finale *despite* reading descriptions which make one's skin crawl.[10] This "satisfying horror", with its sensory, imaginative, affective, and intellective aspects, is facilitated by the fact that the perspective Nabokov offers on Humbert Humbert is one of disapproval, that one is invited to regard him as contemptible. Like all literary works, therefore, *Lolita* requires one to bring the world to the work even if the world in the work is a little—or a lot—different from that world. Depending upon whether one reads Bradley as holding an anti-realist or a realist perspective on poetry, Carroll's objection may or may not succeed, but it fails against my thesis.

My main dispute with Carroll is that he includes *art for art's sake* and *artistic autonomy* with formalism and aesthetic theory in the category of one-dimensional views of art. In other words, he suggests that anyone who does not consider either cognitive value or moral value (or both) part and parcel of literary value is a formalist. As such he, like many other instrumentalists, sets up a false dichotomy of either one or three-dimensional art—faced with which, art in three dimensions is evidently the preferable option. The dichotomy is false because, in the case of literature at least, there is a second option. In my argument, which could be called *literature in two dimensions*, both form and content are salient to literary value, and my approach therefore retains the one-dimensional view of form as significant and the three-dimensional view's link between work and world. I have thus provided a "third way" between instrumentalism and formalism, an approach to literature that negotiates a safe passage between the Scylla of formalism and the Charybdis of instrumentalism. *Contra* Carroll, the realist can acknowledge the value of literary form while retaining his or her humanist intuitions. In my account, literature can be valued for the particular satisfaction that appreciation affords without ignoring the content of the work or divorcing the work from the world. In consequence, literature is not required to be a vehicle for education or to make a contribution to knowledge in order to be valued, and the moral defects of *Tropic of Cancer* and *White Jazz* make them neither less nor more valuable *qua* literature than the morally exemplary *Hard Times* and "The Lives of Animals".

27. MORAL MERITS AND EMPIRICAL EVIDENCE

In §9 in chapter 2, I summarised Nussbaum's first objection to my thesis as: *a moral merit in a realist novel is a literary merit*. I am not denying that a moral merit is one of the many ways in which a novel can be judged as being valuable, merely that a moral merit is a literary merit, so a more accurate way to express Nussbaum's position is this: *a moral merit in a realist novel is (also) a literary merit* (and therefore part and parcel of literary value). The first point to note is that, as with Carroll in chapter 2: §7, realist novels are presented as problematic for the literary autonomist. I dealt with the objection in Carroll by arguing that mimetic failures—Dickens's distortions of truth and Crusoe's cheery disposition—are not necessarily literary defects and may even enhance the literary value of a work. A similar strategy will not work here because Nussbaum has restricted her thesis to a subcategory of realist novels that are morally meritorious and any discussion of works which embody flawed moral perspectives will move beyond that subcategory. I shall, instead, begin by stating my agreement with Nussbaum: there are numerous literary works, including her subcategory of realist novels, where moral content is particularly relevant to literary value. In fact, given that all narratives are concerned with agency—not only that of the narrator but also in virtue of their combination of character, action, and connectedness—and that all agency is subject to moral appraisal, there appears to be an essential link between narrative representation and moral value.

The problem for Nussbaum is that this relation is not as simple as she suggests. In §17 in chapter 4, I quoted Repp as stating, "*It is generally understood that didacticism refers to some sort of defect in a work of literature.*" I claimed that works which instantiate this defect—where messages are *clothed, enveloped, or towed by fiction*—will not reward the demand for literary thickness. I identified "The Lives of Animals" as being a potential example of didactic thinness and although I demonstrated that it was not, I also demonstrated that there was—at the very least—a tension between didacticism and literary value (evinced in the difference between reading the work *qua* philosophy and *qua* literature). Marcia Muelder Eaton holds that sentimentalism is also generally understood to refer to a defect in a work of literature. She identifies the earliest unambiguous employment of the term as being in 1749, claims that by 1785 it had already assumed a derogatory connotation, and states that "'sentimental' is used most often in straightforward negative assessment, both ethical and aesthetic".[11] Eaton cites Richards's discussion of sentimentality in *Practical Criticism* as an example of an early and extensive analysis of sentimentality as an aesthetic defect.[12] I shall not discuss her argument for sentimentalism as a moral defect, but it is worth noting that she regards it as a vice of excess rather than deficiency. The relation between sentimentalism and appropriate affect is thus akin to the relation between rashness and courage rather than cowardice and courage. As such, sentimentalism in literary works is usually a feature of a morally meritorious, rather than a morally defective, intention on the part of the author. In fact, the two literary defects of didacticism and sentimentalism are frequently instantiated in the same works and these are often works with a virtuous moral message.

In §25 above, I quoted Kieran's scepticism of proffering examples *in lieu* of philosophical arguments, including his claim that one theory's example can be another theory's counterexample, which is particularly apt with regard to *Hard Times*. Dickens has frequently been accused of both didacticism and sentimentality in his works and, despite Leavis's argument to the contrary, much of this criticism has focused on *Hard Times*.[13] The following four examples are representative:

1. "Is it not as foolish to estimate his melodramatic and sentimental stock-in-trade gravely, as it would be to undertake a refutation of the jokes of the clown in a Christmas pantomime?"[14]
2. Following discussion of Dickens's didacticism, flat characterisation, and sentimentalism, David H. Hirsch states that *Hard Times* is "one of his dullest and least successful works".[15]
3. "If one begins to question *Hard Times,* the structure which sustains the didactic message also begins to buckle".[16]
4. "*Hard Times* illustrates, in fact, the frequent banality of literary moralizing".[17]

I am not denying that *Hard Times* is a work of literature, or that it rewards the demand for literary thickness, but I am suggesting that it is a borderline case. The novel is riddled with instances of didacticism and sentimentality, from the exclamations Dickens directs at his readers throughout, to the straw man of Gradgrind's school at the beginning of book one, Louisa's confrontation with Gradgrind at the end of book two, and Stephen's death in book three. If my criticism seems harsh, a comparison of the contrasting manner in which *Hard Times* and *Oliver Twist* treat similar themes is instructive in revealing the difference between the two types of didacticism discussed in §17 in chapter 4.

My point is that there is a strong argument that the moral merits of *Hard Times*—for example, its promotion of egalitarianism and compassion—are literary defects due to the didactic and sentimental way in which the novel enacts its liberal democratic vision. The complexity of the relation between moral merits and literary value is revealed in a more obvious example, Harriet Beecher Stowe's *Uncle Tom's Cabin; or, Life Among the Lowly*. The moral merit of Stowe's abolitionist novel is beyond question, but so is the extent to which the work instantiates the literary defects of didacticism and sentimentalism. The following four comments are both representative and free from controversy:

1. "As is well known, American literary history has almost always been uneasy with *Uncle Tom's Cabin*, as it has been with sentimentality in general".[18]
2. "*Uncle Tom's Cabin* has not survived as literature—the only interest that it holds for us is historical—even though its author's opposition to slavery now commands universal assent".[19]
3. "Unfortunately, in the history of art there are many instances of works like *Uncle Tom's Cabin*; works which hit us over the head with the right moral message while betraying their overall mediocrity in terms of style and engagement".[20]
4. John Havard identifies Stowe as making a direct and explicit call for social change and the novel as "implementing a sentimental, typological jeremiad against slavery".[21]

It seems, therefore, that there are cases where a moral merit can be a literary merit or a literary defect, but in fact the issue is still more complex. The question is not whether a moral merit is a literary merit or defect, but rather the extent to which the moral content of a work is relevant to its literary value.

I suggested above that due to the necessary relation between narrative representation and moral value there will be many instances where moral content is relevant to literary value and this is certainly the case in realist novels. The contribution the moral content makes to the literary value of a work is not a function of the virtue or vice of the perspective a work embodies, however, but a function of the way in which that content is integrated with the novel's form. In Nussbaum's terminology, the responsiveness to moral particulars is integrated with the play back and forth between the particular and the universal characteristic of realist form. She gestures towards the significance of literary satisfaction, which I associated with the demand for literary thickness in chapter 6: §22, in the following passage:

> This brings me to one further feature of the novel: its capacity to give pleasure. Its moral operations are not independent of its aesthetic excellence. It binds us to the workers because it causes us to take pleasure in their company. A

tedious novel would not have the same moral power, or rather, the precision of attention that makes for interest is itself a moral feature. This is no incidental aspect of *Hard Times*, but one that it prominently stresses.[22]

Nussbaum and I obviously disagree on whether *Hard Times* is tedious, but we would likely both agree that *Uncle Tom's Cabin* is a novel whose moral power is inhibited by its aesthetic defects and *Oliver Twist* a novel whose moral power is enhanced by its aesthetic merits. Assessing the moral operations and moral power of a novel in terms of the pleasure produced by the thick combination of content and form in the work is, however, a completely different type of evaluation to assessing the virtue of liberal democratic or abolitionist moral perspectives.

As I noted in my discussion of "The Lives of Animals" in chapter 6: §23, the moral virtue of the theme—*humans are inflicting a holocaust on animals*—is less significant to appreciation than the way in which the theme is integrated with the form selected for the story. *Uncle Tom's Cabin* serves as an example that Nussbaum's theory conflates two evaluations: the novel's moral value is beyond criticism, but its numerous flaws as a work of literature detract from its moral power. M. M. Eaton and Thomson-Jones regard this particular type of failure—the loss of moral impact as a result of aesthetic flaws that distract readers or trivialise the moral content—as a *moral* flaw. I prefer to call the failure a literary flaw because the loss of moral impact is a result of a defect in the integration of content and form, but the nomenclature is not particularly important. What is important is that this type of defect is distinct from the type of defect—an immoral perspective—which Nussbaum has in mind in her discussion of the moral merits of realist novels. Virtuous and vicious moral content can both form part of the thickness of a literary work and virtuous and vicious moral content can both be enacted in a didactic, sentimental, or otherwise non-literary manner. Nussbaum is thus correct to state that examples of literary works which embody immoral perspectives are not counterexamples to her theory of the moral merits of realist novels, but she is nonetheless merging two distinct types of evaluation of a work of literature. The liberal democratic vision of *Hard Times* is a moral merit, but the relation between that moral merit and literary merit is determined by the way in which the moral content is integrated with the realist form. The novel thus exemplifies moral but not literary merit: two separate evaluations are being made employing different criteria in each case. A moral merit is not therefore a literary merit in realist novels and moral value is not therefore part and parcel of literary value.

In chapter 2: §9, I summarised Nussbaum's second objection to my thesis as: *reading realist novels responsibly and receptively will* ceteris paribus *improve one's moral judgement*. The experience of reading these novels in this way is thus a means to moral improvement. I noted that I would take her claim as empirical rather than behavioural due to the extensive problems associated with establishing the effects of reading literature on ethical behaviour, mentioned in chapter 1: §4. If Nussbaum is making an empirical claim, however, then it is precisely the type of claim for which empirical evidence could—and should—be provided.[23] In my summary of the moral improvement Nussbaum envisages, I quoted the following statements about the experience of reading realist novels:

1. The experience "develops moral capacities without which citizens will not succeed in making reality out of the normative conclusions of any moral or political theory";[24] and
2. The experiences "strengthen the propensity so to conduct oneself in other instances".[25]

These are very strong assertions to make about the value of realist novels. (1) states that reading such novels is a prerequisite for, and necessary condition of, understanding moral and political philosophy. Setting aside the second token of "conduct" in (2), Nussbaum is stating that reading the relevant novels is itself a moral exercise, the literary experience a kind of moral gymnasium in which one's moral muscles are strengthened regardless of whether and how that strength is subsequently employed. The proffering of these substantial claims without any supporting evidence is, I think, the kind of philosophical flaw to which Geoffrey Galt Harpham alludes when he compares the quality of Nussbaum's philosophy with Derrida's (noted in chapter 2: §8). Nussbaum is no more justified in stating that reading realist novels improves the moral judgement of readers sympathetic to liberal democratic ideals than I would be in stating that reading existentialist novels worsens the moral judgement of readers sympathetic to amoralism. If either statement is to rise about the trivial or banal, evidence must be provided and, *in lieu* of any evidence, neither statement should be accepted.

Nussbaum claims that the experience of reading realist novels is a moral experience and I agree completely. Realist novels are narratives and I mentioned above that there is a necessary relation between narrative representation—specifically the dual concern with agency instantiated—and moral perception and judgement. Narratives are, as I noted in §14 in chapter 4, stories and stories are necessarily told by an agent, even if one is unable to discover the identity of that agent. Similarly, stories contain characters who make decisions and perform actions (or refuse to make decisions and do nothing). In any complex narrative, including short stories such as "The Lives of Animals" and all of Nussbaum's realist novels, the author and the characters he or she depicts are subject to moral evaluation. The essential connection is between narrative representation and the moral *sphere*, however, not between narrative representation and (positive) moral value. In other words, narratives are necessarily moral, but moral as opposed to amoral rather than moral as opposed to immoral. It is of the essence of narrative representation that it is subject to moral judgement—and that the experience of a narrative is to this extent a moral experience—but that judgement may be positive, negative, or ambiguous. The experience of reading realist novels is thus indeed a moral experience, but so is the experience of reading "The Lives of Animals", *Tropic of Cancer*, *Waiting for Godot*, and *White Jazz*. Given that the moral experience can be so varied, any connection to moral improvement requires evidence—evidence which Nussbaum fails to provide.

28. LITERARY HUMANISM

Nussbaum's literary education proposes literature as a means to a moral end and attempts to establish a link between literary value and moral value. In a similar vein, Olsen identifies the thematic concepts of perennial interest in which literature trades as shared by philosophy and religion. He proposes a "special connection" between literature, philosophy, and religion, but restricts this connection to the common subject matter.[26] Literature, philosophy, and religion all address eternal human problems, but they do so in different ways and with distinct purposes. Olsen rejects "the *dulce et utile*" approach to literature I identified in chapter 1: §4 and his phrasing draws attention to what I consider an irony in Nussbaum: *Poetic Justice* criticises the reductive utilitarianism of Gradgrind, but reduces the value of *Hard Times* to its "usefulness" as anti-utilitarian philosophy, a usefulness which is enhanced by the "sweetness" noted in §27 above, and which can be put to further political and legal uses. Unlike Carroll, Nussbaum resists the instrumentalist label because she does not regard the characteristic value of literary works as being derived from their moral value; moral value is instead partly constitutive of non-derivative literary value. There is nonetheless a strong case for the claim that Nussbaum's instrumentalism is more robust than Carroll's. First, she makes the empirical claim discussed in §27 that Carroll, Wilson, and other literary cognitivists explicitly avoid. Second, her approach to literary value has a greater theoretical focus on instrumental values than Carroll's. *Poetic Justice*, for example, originated in a university course on "literature for lawyers", the subject of which was literature's "contribution to the law in particular, to public reason generally".[27] In her criticism of Posner's choice of canonical examples, Nussbaum regards T. S. Eliot and William Butler Yeats as having less literary significance than V. S. Naipaul and Rohinton Mistry.[28] She may be correct, but there is a strong implication that the only literary works she thinks should be taken seriously are those which embody a liberal, democratic perspective and are therefore useful as instruments of moral and political education.

Nussbaum's instrumentalism is most explicit in her defence of the humanities, which she values principally as a means to the political end of liberal democracy. In his review of *Not for Profit: Why Democracy Needs the Humanities* (first published in 2010), Matthew Reisz asks if Nussbaum's approach runs the risk of disguising propaganda as teaching: "'I don't say the humanities have only one use,' replies Nussbaum. 'I'm focusing on their role in inculcating citizenship. You can also investigate works for their contribution to literary history, for their own sake as aesthetic objects'".[29] Nussbaum's defence of the humanities replicates the structure of her defence of literary education: literature and the humanities are primarily valuable for their unique contribution to philosophy and liberal democracy respectively and this unique contribution is supplemented by secondary aesthetic and other values. Reisz's conclusion is, "Perhaps because she believes so much is at stake, Nussbaum takes a strikingly instrumental view of the value of the humanities in schools and universities".[30] I think the same can be said for her view of the value of the institution of literature. As I have maintained throughout my thesis, I do not wish to deny the numerous instrumental values of literature nor the significance of those values. But instrumental accounts of literary value are reductive, marginalising literature's capacity to afford satisfaction as the means by which the useful end for which literature is valued is achieved. Nussbaum's literary education thus minimises what I believe to be most important about literature: the freedom from limitation that is the essence of the literary use of language and the literary satisfaction that forms the basis of the literary use of language's *sui generic* value.

My thesis has proceeded by presenting two distinct arguments for form-content inseparability, one for poetry and the other for literary narratives, in order to establish literary thickness as a necessary condition of literature. I argued that the demand for literary thickness reconciled the two opposing types of interest—formal and substantive—that readers take in literary works and that it is characteristic of literary appreciation. Having identified literary value as the value afforded by the literary experience, I demonstrated that the demand for literary thickness has a necessary relation to final, rather than instrumental, value. Finally, I addressed two objections to my thesis, both of which I construed as characterising literary value as instrumental. In my responses, I showed that neither cognitive value nor moral value is part and parcel of literary value and that my argument for literary autonomy therefore stands.

I began this monograph by stating my intention to first continue and then complete Bradley's project. My argument may be more or less convincing, but it is neither circular nor open to accusations of anti-realism about literary value—the most obvious flaws in Bradley. I have also extended his thesis beyond poetry to the literary use of language without committing to his controversial claims about all art. In completing Bradley's project I have negotiated my way between Attridge's literary theory and Lamarque's literary aesthetics. Taking Attridge's most recent work into account, I conclude that he remains sceptical about the value of the form-content distinction and committed to the ontological view of the text as a potential literary work realised in the event, neither of which are suited to my purpose. While Lamarque offers compelling defences of Bradley on poetic value and on the realist perspective of literary value, he has little to say about the literary experience and literary satisfaction. My account of literary value is experiential and I have argued that the demand for literary thickness not only clarifies the relation between work and world, but is crucial in characterising the literary experience and explaining the satisfaction it affords.

In nuce I have, at the very least, shed light on the confusion Leopold Bloom experiences when he considers the failure of the works of Shakespeare to provide him with instruction:

> Concluding by inspection but erroneously that his silent companion was engaged in mental composition he reflected on the pleasures derived from literature of instruction rather than of amusement as he himself had applied to the works of William Shakespeare more than once for the solution of difficult problems in imaginary or real life.
>
> Had he found their solution?
>
> In spite of careful and repeated reading of certain classical passages, aided by a glossary, he had derived imperfect conviction from the text, the answers not bearing in all points.[31]

NOTES

1. Noël Carroll, *Art in Three Dimensions* (Oxford: Oxford University Press, 2012 [2010]), 232.
2. Daniel Jacobson and Matthew Kieran have both made similar criticisms of literary moralism. See, for example: Daniel Jacobson, "In Praise of Immoral Art," *Philosophical Topics 25* (1997), 155–99; and Matthew Kieran, "Forbidden Knowledge: The Challenge of Immoralism," in J. Bermudez & S. Gardner, eds., *Art and Morality* (London: Routledge, 2003), 56–73.
3. Kieran, "Forbidden Knowledge," 60.
4. See, for example: John Gross & Gabriel Pearson, eds., *Dickens and the Twentieth Century* (Toronto: University of Toronto Press, 1962); Philip Collins, ed., *Charles Dickens: The Critical Heritage* (Abingdon, UK: Routledge, 1997); and Michael Wheeler, *English Fiction of the Victorian Period: 1830–1890* (Abingdon, UK: Routledge, 2013).
5. D. W. Jefferson, "Mr Gradgrind's Facts," *Essays in Criticism 35* (1985), 197–212: 210–11.
6. Jefferson, "Mr Gradgrind's Facts," 197.
7. I am in fact sceptical about the literary value of *Hard Times*, but for different reasons, which I discuss in §27 in this chapter.
8. Malcolm Pittock, "Taking Dickens to Task: *Hard Times* Once More," *The Cambridge Quarterly 27* (1998), 107–28.
9. J. M. Coetzee, *Foe* (London: Penguin, 2010 [1986]), 19.
10. I noted the existence of such a phenomenon in my mention of the paradox of painful art in chapter 6: §22.

11. Marcia Muelder Eaton, "Laughing at the Death of Little Nell: Sentimental Art and Sentimental People," *American Philosophical Quarterly 26* (1989), 269–82: 270.

12. Eaton, "Laughing at the Death of Little Nell," 271–72.

13. F. R. Leavis, *The Great Tradition: George Eliot, Henry James, Joseph Conrad* (London: Chatto & Windus, 1960 [1948]), 227–48.

14. James Fitzjames Stephen, *Saturday Review*, in P. Collins, ed., *Charles Dickens: The Critical Heritage*. Abingdon, UK: Routledge, 1997 [1857]), 344–49: 345.

15. David A. Hirsch, "'Hard Times'" and F. R. Leavis," *Criticism 6* (1964), 1–16: 16.

16. Pittock, "Taking Dickens to Task," 112.

17. Richard Posner, "Against Ethical Criticism: Part II," *Philosophy and Literature 22* (1998), 394–412: 410 fn.23.

18. Winfried Fluck, "The Power and Failure of Representation in Harriet Beecher Stowe's *Uncle Tom's Cabin*," *New Literary History 23* (1992), 319–38: 319.

19. Richard Posner, "Against Ethical Criticism," *Philosophy and Literature 21* (1997), 1–27: 7.

20. Katherine Thomson-Jones, "Aesthetic and Ethical Mediocrity in Art," *Philosophical Papers 31* (2002), 199–215: 203.

21. John C. Havard, "Fighting Slavery by 'Presenting Facts in Detail': Realism, Typology, and Temporality in *Uncle Tom's Cabin*," *American Literary Realism 44* (2012), 249–66: 259.

22. Martha Nussbaum, *Poetic Justice: The Literary Imagination and Public Life* (Boston: Beacon Press, 1995), 35.

23. The problems with attempts to determine the effects of reading literature are not restricted to behavioural, as opposed to psychological or cognitive, changes. A recent empirical study purporting to show that reading literature improves understanding of the mental states of others serves as an unwitting example of the difficulty in selecting an appropriate methodology. See: David Comer Kidd & Emanuele Castano, "Reading Literary Fiction Improves Theory of Mind," *Science 342* (18 October, 2013), doi:10.1126/science.1239918 (accessed 31 December, 2015). Gregory Currie provides an excellent overview of the impediments researchers face. See: "Does Fiction Civilize Us?" *New York Times*, 6 February, 2013, 12.

24. Nussbaum, *Poetic Justice*, 12.

25. Martha Nussbaum, "Exactly and Responsibly: A Defense of Ethical Criticism," *Philosophy and Literature 22* (1998), 343–65: 355.

26. Stein Haugom Olsen, *The End of Literary Theory* (New York: Cambridge University Press, 1987), 190.

27. Nussbaum, *Poetic Justice*, xv.

28. Nussbaum, "Exactly and Responsibly," 360–61.

29. Matthew Reisz, "World Crisis in Humanities, Not Many Hurt," *Times Higher Education*, 21 October 2010, http://www.timeshighereducation.co.uk/413900.article (accessed 30 December 2015).

30. Reisz, "World Crisis in Humanities".

31. James Joyce, *Ulysses* (London: The Bodley Head, 2008 [1922] [reprint of 1986 edition]), 17.383–91.

Bibliography

Anderson, James C. & Dean, Jeffrey T., 1998. Moderate Autonomism. *British Journal of Aesthetics*, 38 (2), 150–66.

Aristotle. *Poetics*. Translated by P. Murray & T. S. Dorsch, 2000. In: Murray, P., ed., 2004. *Classical Literary Criticism*. London: Penguin, 57–97.

Attridge, Derek, 1999. Innovation, Literature, Ethics: Relating to the Other. *PMLA*, 114 (1), 20–31.

———, 2004. *J. M. Coetzee and the Ethics of Reading: Literature in the Event*. London: University of Chicago Press.

———, 2004. *The Singularity of Literature*. New York: Routledge.

———, 2010. The Singular Events of Literature. *British Journal of Aesthetics*, 50 (1), 81–84.

———, 2015. *The Work of Literature*. Oxford: Oxford University Press.

Auster, Paul, 2011 [1987]. *The New York Trilogy*. London: Faber & Faber.

Austin, J. L., 1962. *How to Do Things with Words*. London: Oxford University Press.

Beardsley, Monroe C., 1958. *Aesthetics: Problems in the Philosophy of Criticism*. New York: Harcourt, Brace & World.

Beardsley, Monroe & Wimsatt, W. K., 1949. The Affective Fallacy. *The Sewanee Review*, 57, 31–55.

Beevor, Antony, 2001 [1982]. *The Spanish Civil War*. London: Cassell & Co.

Bell, Clive, 1913. *Art*. New York: Frederick A. Stokes.

Belsey, Catherine, 2011. *A Future for Criticism*. Malden, MA: Wiley-Blackwell.

Biss, Mavis, 2014. Moral Imagination, Perception, and Judgment. *The Southern Journal of Philosophy*, 52 (1), 1–21.

Blackburn, Simon, 1992. Through Thick and Thin. *Proceedings of the Aristotelian Society, Supplementary Volumes*, 66, 285–99.

Bradley, A. C., 1901. Poetry for Poetry's Sake. In: Bradley, A. C., 1959 [1901]. *Oxford Lectures on Poetry*. London: Macmillan, 3–34.

Brewer, Bill, 1999. *Perception and Reason*. Oxford: Oxford University Press.

Brooks, Cleanth, 1975 [1947]. *The Well Wrought Urn*. Orlando, FL: Harcourt.

Brooks, Peter, 1992 [1984]. *Reading for the Plot: Design and Intention in Narrative*. Cambridge, MA: Harvard University Press.

Budd, Malcolm, 1995. *Values of Art*. London: Penguin.

———, 2008. Aesthetic Essence. In: Budd, M., 2008. *Aesthetic Essays*. Oxford: Oxford University Press, 31–47.

Carey, Peter, 2001 [2000]. *True History of the Kelly Gang*. London: Faber & Faber.

Carroll, Noël, 1996. Moderate Moralism. *British Journal of Aesthetics*, 36 (3), 223–38.

———, 1998. Art, Narrative, and Moral Understanding. In: Levinson, J., ed., 1998. *Aesthetics and Ethics: Essays at the Intersection*. Cambridge: Cambridge University Press, 126–60.

———, 2012 [2010]. *Art in Three Dimensions*. Oxford: Oxford University Press.

Coetzee, J. M., 1988. The Novel Today. *Upstream*, 6 (1), 2–5.

———, 2004 [2003]. *Elizabeth Costello*. London: Vintage.

———, 2005. *Slow Man*. London: Vintage.

———, 2010 [1986]. *Foe*. London: Penguin.

Collins, Philip, ed., 1997. *Charles Dickens: The Critical Heritage*. Abingdon, UK: Routledge.

Cooper, J. M., ed., 1997. *Plato: Complete Works*. Indianapolis, IN: Hackett.

Currie, Gregory, 2013. Does Fiction Civilize Us? *New York Times*, 6 February, 12.

Danto, Arthur C., 1984. Philosophy and/as/of Literature. In: Hagberg, G. L. & Jost, W., eds., 2010. *A Companion to the Philosophy of Literature*. Oxford: Blackwell, 52–67.

Derrida, Jacques, 1975. From *Signsponge*. Translated by Richard Rand, 1984. In: Derrida, Jacques, 1992. *Acts of Literature*. Edited by D. Attridge. London: Routledge, 344–69.

———, 2008 [2006]. *The Animal That Therefore I Am*. Edited by Marie-Louise Mallet, translated by David Wills. New York: Fordham University Press.

Dickens, Charles, 1994 [1838]. *Oliver Twist; or, The Parish Boy's Progress*. London: Penguin.

———, 2000 [1854]. *Hard Times. For These Times*. Ware, Herts: Wordsworth Classics.

Dickie, George, 1969. Defining Art. *American Philosophical Quarterly*, 6 (3), 253–56.

———, 1984. *The Art Circle*. New York: Haven.

———, 2000. Art and Value. *British Journal of Aesthetics*, 40 (2), 228–41.

Doepke, Frederick, 1982. Spatially Coinciding Objects. In Rea, Michael C., ed., 1997. *Material Constitution: A Reader*. Lanham, MD: Rowman & Littlefield, 10–24.

Doniger, Wendy, 1999. Reflections. In: Coetzee, J. M., 1999. *The Lives of Animals*. Princeton, NJ: Princeton University Press, 93–106.

Dorsey, Dale, 2012. Can Instrumental Value Be Intrinsic? *Pacific Philosophical Quarterly*, 93 (2), 137–57.

Doyle, Arthur Conan, 1893. The Adventure of the Musgrave Ritual. *The Strand Magazine: An Illustrated Monthly*, 5, 479–90.

Eaton, A. W., 2003. Where Ethics and Aesthetics Meet: Titian's *Rape of Europa*. *Hypatia*, 18 (4), 159–88.

Eaton, Marcia Muelder, 1989. Laughing at the Death of Little Nell: Sentimental Art and Sentimental People. *American Philosophical Quarterly*, 26 (4), 269–82.

Eggert, Paul, 2007. The Bushranger's Voice: Peter Carey's "True History of the Kelly Gang" (2000) and Ned Kelly's "Jerilderie Letter" (1879). *College Literature*, 34 (3), 120–39.

Eldridge, Richard, 1985. Form and Content: An Aesthetic Theory of Art. *British Journal of Aesthetics*, 25 (4), 303–16.

Eliot, T. S., 1979 [1969]. *The Complete Poems and Plays of T. S. Eliot*. London: Book Club Associates.

Evans, Gareth, 1982. *The Varieties of Reference*. Oxford: Oxford University Press.

Fabb, Nigel, 2009. Why Is Verse Poetry? *PN Review*, 36 (1), 52–57.

Fessenbecker, Patrick, 2013. In Defense of Paraphrase. *New Literary History*, 44 (1), 117–39.

Fishman, Solomon, 1956. Meaning and Structure in Poetry. *The Journal of Aesthetics and Art Criticism*, 14 (4), 453–61.

Fluck, Winfried, 1992. The Power and Failure of Representation in Harriet Beecher Stowe's *Uncle Tom's Cabin*. *New Literary History*, 23 (2), 319–38.

Frye, Northrop, 1957. *Anatomy of Criticism: Four Essays by Northrop Frye*. Princeton, NJ: Princeton University Press.

Gaskin, Richard, 2013. *Language, Truth, and Literature: A Defence of Literary Humanism*. Oxford: Oxford University Press.

Gaut, Berys, 2011. Telling Stories: Narration, Emotion, and Insight in *Memento*. In: Carroll, N. & Gibson, J., eds., 2011. *Narrative, Emotion, and Insight*. University Park: Pennsylvania State University Press, 23–44.

Geach, P. T. & Black, M., eds., 1970 [1892]. *Translations from the Philosophical Writings of Gottlob Frege*. Translated by Peter Geach. Oxford: Blackwell.

Gibson, John, 2007. *Fiction and the Weave of Life*. Oxford: Oxford University Press.

———, 2008. Cognitivism and the Arts. *Philosophy Compass*, 3 (4), 573–89.

———, 2011. The Question of Poetic Meaning. *Nonsite*, 4, 1 December. Available at: http://nonsite.org/article/the-question-of-poetic-meaning [Accessed 24 December 2015].

———, 2011. Thick Narratives. In: Carroll, N. & Gibson, J., eds., 2011. *Narrative, Emotion, and Insight*. University Park: Pennsylvania State University Press, 69–91.

Goldie, Peter, 2012. *The Mess Inside: Narrative, Emotion, and the Mind*. Oxford: Oxford University Press.

Goldman, Alan H., 1995. *Aesthetic Value*. Boulder, CO: Westview Press.

———, 2006. The Experiential Account of Aesthetic Value. *The Journal of Aesthetics and Art Criticism*, 64 (3), 333–42.

———, 2013. *Philosophy and the Novel*. Oxford: Oxford University Press.

Goodman, Nelson, 1976. *Languages of Art: An Approach to a Theory of Symbols*. 2nd edition. Indianapolis, IN: Hackett.

Goodman, Nelson & Elgin, Catherine Z., 1988. *Reconceptions in Philosophy and Other Arts and Sciences*. London: Routledge.

Gross, John & Pearson, Gabriel, eds., 1962. *Dickens and the Twentieth Century*. Toronto: University of Toronto Press.

Gutmann, Amy, 1999. Introduction. In: Coetzee, J. M., 1999. *The Lives of Animals*. Princeton, NJ: Princeton University Press, 3–11.

Hampton, T., 1965. An Error in "Lord of the Flies." *Notes and Queries*, 12 (7), 275.

Harold, James, 2011. Autonomism Reconsidered. *British Journal of Aesthetics*, 51 (2), 137–47.

Harpham, Geoffrey Galt, 2002. The Hunger of Martha Nussbaum. *Representations*, 77, 52–81.

Havard, John C., 2012. Fighting Slavery by "Presenting Facts in Detail": Realism, Typology, and Temporality in *Uncle Tom's Cabin*. *American Literary Realism*, 44 (3), 249–66.

Heidegger, Martin, 1962 [1927]. *Being and Time*. Translated by John Macquarrie & Edward Robinson. New York: Harper & Row.

Hemingway, Ernest, 1976 [1940]. *For Whom the Bell Tolls*. London: Grafton Books.

Hirsch, David A., 1964. "Hard Times" and F. R. Leavis. *Criticism*, 6 (1), 1–16.

Hume, David, 1757. Of Tragedy. In: Hume, D., 1987. *David Hume: Essays, Moral, Political, and Literary*. Indianapolis, IN: Liberty Fund, 216–25.

Hutcheson, Francis, 2008 [1726]. *An Inquiry into the Original of Our Ideas of Beauty and Virtue*. Indianapolis, IN: Liberty Fund.

Iseminger, Gary, 2004. *The Aesthetic Function of Art*. Ithaca, NY: Cornell University Press.

Jacobson, Daniel, 1997. In Praise of Immoral Art. *Philosophical Topics*, 25 (1), 155–99.

Jefferson, D. W., 1985. Mr Gradgrind's Facts. *Essays in Criticism*, 35 (3), 197–212.

Johnson, Samuel, 1765. Preface to the Edition of Shakespeare's Plays. In: Johnson, S., 1989. *Samuel Johnson on Shakespeare*. London: Penguin, 120–65.

Jolley, Kelly Dean, 2008. (Kivy on) The Form-Content Identity Thesis. *British Journal of Aesthetics*, 48 (2): 193–204.

Joyce, James, 2008 [1922]. *Ulysses*. London: The Bodley Head (reprint of 1986 edition).

Julius, Anthony, 2003. *T. S. Eliot, Anti-Semitism, and Literary Form*. London: Thames & Hudson.

Kant, Immanuel, 2001 [1790]. *Critique of the Power of Judgment*. Translated by Paul Guyer and Eric Matthews, 2000. Cambridge: Cambridge University Press.

Kidd, David Comer & Castano, Emanuele, 2013. Reading Literary Fiction Improves Theory of Mind. *Science*, 342 (6156, 18 October), doi: 10.1126/science.1239918 [Accessed 31 December, 2015].

Kieran, Matthew, 2003. Forbidden Knowledge: The Challenge of Immoralism. In: Bermudez, J. & Gardner, S., eds., 2003. *Art and Morality*. London: Routledge, 56–73.

Kivy, Peter, 1997. *Philosophies of Arts: An Essay in Differences*. New York: Cambridge University Press.

———, 2011. *Once-Told Tales: An Essay in Literary Aesthetics*. Chichester, UK: Wiley-Blackwell.

———, 2011. Paraphrasing Poetry (For Profit and Pleasure). *The Journal of Aesthetics and Art Criticism*, 69 (4), 367–77.

Korsgaard, Christine, 1983. Two Distinctions in Goodness. *The Philosophical Review*, 92 (2), 169–95.

Kripke, Saul, 1971. Identity and Necessity. In: Munitz, Milton K., ed., 1971. *Identity and Individuation*. New York: New York University Press, 83–94.

Lamarque, Peter, 2006. Cognitive Values in the Arts: Marking the Boundaries. In: Kieran, M., 2006. *Contemporary Debates in Aesthetics and the Philosophy of Art*. Oxford: Blackwell, 127–39.

———, 2009. The Elusiveness of Poetic Meaning. *Ratio*, 22 (4), 398–420.

———, 2009. *The Philosophy of Literature*. Malden, MA: Blackwell.

———, 2014. *The Opacity of Narrative*. London: Rowman & Littlefield International.

Lamarque, Peter & Olsen, Stein Haugom, 2002 [1994]. *Truth, Fiction, and Literature: A Philosophical Perspective*. Oxford: Clarendon.

Larkin, Philip, 1977 [1955]. *The Less Deceived*. London: The Marvell Press.

Lavender, William, 1993. The Novel of Critical Engagement and Paul Auster's "City of Glass". *Contemporary Literature*, 34 (2), 219–39.

Leavis, F. R., 1958 [1952]. *The Common Pursuit*. London: Chatto & Windus.

———, 1960 [1948]. *The Great Tradition: George Eliot, Henry James, Joseph Conrad*. London: Chatto & Windus.

———, 1967. *Anna Karenina and Other Essays*. London: Chatto & Windus.

Leighton, Angela, 2008 [2007]. *On Form: Poetry, Aestheticism, and the Legacy of a Word*. Oxford: Oxford University Press.

Levinson, Jerrold, 1980. What a Musical Work Is. *The Journal of Philosophy*, 77 (1), 5–28.

———, 1996. Art, Value, and Philosophy. *Mind*, 105 (420), 667–82.

Lopes, Dominic McIver, 2011. The Myth of (Non-Aesthetic) Artistic Value. *The Philosophical Quarterly*, 61 (244), 518–36.

Lowe, E. J., 1983. Instantiation, Identity, and Constitution. *Philosophical Studies*, 44 (1), 45–59.

Lynn, David H., 2005. Love and Death, and Animals Too. *The Kenyon Review, New Series*, 27 (1), 124–33.

Magnell, Thomas, 1993. Evaluations as Assessments, Part I: Properties and Their Signifiers. *The Journal of Value Inquiry*, 27 (1), 1–11.

Matravers, Derek, 1998. *Art and Emotion*. Oxford: Oxford University Press.

McDermott, Alex, 2001. *The Jerilderie Letter*. Melbourne: The Text Publishing Company.

McDowell, Edwin, 1984. New Edition Fixes 5,000 Errors in "Ulysses." *New York Times*, 7 June. Available at: http://www.nytimes.com/books/00/01/09/specials/joyce-edition.html [Accessed 28 February 2015].

McDowell, John, 1994. *Mind and World*. Cambridge, MA: Harvard University Press.

McGregor, Rafe, 2013. Moderate Autonomism Revisited. *Ethical Perspectives*, 20 (3), 403–26.

———, 2014. A Critique of the Value Interaction Debate. *British Journal of Aesthetics*, 54 (4), 449–66.

———, 2014. Poetic Thickness. *British Journal of Aesthetics*, 54 (1), 49–64.

———, 2015. Literary Thickness. *British Journal of Aesthetics*, 55 (3), 343–60.

———, 2015. Narrative Thickness. *Estetika: The Central European Journal of Aesthetics*, 52 (1), 3–22.

Milton, John, 1645. *Poems of Mr. John Milton*. [e-book] London: Humphrey Mosley. Available at: Community Books, https://archive.org/details/PoemsOfMr.JohnMilton1645 [Accessed 30 December 2015].

Mole, Christopher, 2009. The Matter of Fact in Literature. *International Journal of Philosophical Studies*, 17 (4), 489–508.

Moore, G. E., 1922. *Philosophical Studies*. New York: Harcourt, Brace & Co.

Nabokov, Vladimir, 1956. On a Book Entitled *Lolita*. In: Nabokov, Vladimir, 1997 [1955]. *Lolita*. London: Penguin, 309–15.

Noë, Alva, 1999. Thought and Experience. *American Philosophical Quarterly*, 36 (3), 257–65.

Nussbaum, Martha C., 1990. *Love's Knowledge: Essays on Philosophy and Literature*. New York: Oxford University Press.

———, 1995. *Poetic Justice: The Literary Imagination and Public Life*. Boston: Beacon Press.

————, 1998. Exactly and Responsibly: A Defense of Ethical Criticism. *Philosophy and Literature*, 22 (2), 343–65.

Olsen, Stein Haugom, 1978. *The Structure of Literary Understanding*. Cambridge: Cambridge University Press.

————, 1987. *The End of Literary Theory*. New York: Cambridge University Press.

Pater, Walter, 1922 [1888]. *The Renaissance: Studies in Art and Poetry*. London: Macmillan.

Peacocke, Christopher, 1992. *A Study of Concepts*. Cambridge, MA: MIT Press.

Pittock, Malcolm, 1998. Taking Dickens to Task: *Hard Times* Once More. *The Cambridge Quarterly* 27 (2), 107–28.

Posner, Richard A., 1997. Against Ethical Criticism. *Philosophy and Literature*, 21 (1), 1–27.

————, 1998. Against Ethical Criticism: Part II. *Philosophy and Literature*, 22 (2), 394–412.

Quine, W. V. O., 1961. Reference and modality. In: Quine, W. V. O., 1963 [1961]. *From a Logical Point of View: Nine Logico-Philosophical Essays*. New York: Harper, 139–59.

Rabinowicz, Wlodek & Rønnow-Rasmussen, Toni, 1999. A Distinction in Value: Intrinsic and for Its Own Sake. *Proceedings of the Aristotelian Society*, 100 (1), 33–51.

Reisz, Matthew, 2010. World Crisis in Humanities, Not Many Hurt. *Times Higher Education*, 21 October. Available at: http://www.timeshighereducation.co.uk/413900.article [Accessed 30 December 2015].

Repp, Charles, 2012. What's Wrong with Didacticism? *British Journal of Aesthetics*, 52 (3), 271–86.

Ribeiro, Anna Christina, 2009. Toward a Philosophy of Poetry. *Midwest Studies in Philosophy*, 33 (1), 61–77.

Richards, I. A., 1930 [1924]. *Principles of Literary Criticism*. London: Kegan Paul, Trench, Trübner & Co.

————, 1978 [1929]. *Practical Criticism: A Study of Literary Judgment*. London: Routledge.

Ricks, Christopher, 1996. Literature and the Matter of Fact. In: Ricks, C., 1996. *Essays in Appreciation*. Oxford: Clarendon Press, 280–310.

Riffaterre, Michael, 1973. Interpretation and Descriptive Poetry: A Reading of Wordsworth's "Yew-Trees". *New Literary History*, 4 (2), 229–56.

Rowe, M. W., 1997. Lamarque and Olsen on Literature and Truth. *The Philosophical Quarterly*, 47 (188), 322–41.

Ryle, Gilbert, 2009 [1949]. *The Concept of Mind: 60th Anniversary Edition*. Abingdon, UK: Routledge.

————, 1968. The Thinking of Thoughts: What Is "Le Penseur" Doing? In: Ryle, G., 1971. *Volume II: Collected Essays 1929–1969*. London: Hutchinson & Co., 480–96.

Schiller, Friedrich, 1967 [1794]. *On the Aesthetic Education of Man: In a Series of Letters*. Translated by Elizabeth M. Wilkinson & L. A. Willoughby. Oxford: Clarendon Press.

Scruton, Roger, 1974. *Art and Imagination: A Study in the Philosophy of Mind*. London: Methuen.

————, 1981. Photography and Representation. *Critical Inquiry*, 7 (3), 577–603.

Searle, John R., 1969. *Speech Acts*. Cambridge: Cambridge University Press.

Shaftesbury, Third Earl of (Anthony Ashley-Cooper), 2001 [1714]. *Characteristicks of Men, Manners, Opinions, Times, Volumes I–III*. Indianapolis, IN: Liberty Fund.

Shoemaker, Sydney, 1999. Self, Body, and Coincidence. *Proceedings of the Aristotelian Society Supplementary Volume*, 73 (73), 287–306.

Sidgwick, Henry, 1981 [1874]. *The Methods of Ethics*. Cambridge: Hackett.

Sidney, Sir Philip, 1595. *A Defence of Poesy*. [e-book] Oregon: Renascence Editions. Available at: University of Oregon, http://darkwing.uoregon.edu/%7Erbear/defence.html [Accessed 11 July 2015].

Singer, Peter, 1999. Reflections. In: Coetzee, J. M., 1999. *The Lives of Animals*. Princeton, NJ: Princeton University Press, 85–91.

Smith, Adam, 1982 [1759]. *The Theory of Moral Sentiments*. Indianapolis, IN: Liberty Fund.

Smuts, Aaron, 2007. The Paradox of Painful Art. *Journal of Aesthetic Education*, 41 (3), 59–76.

Stang, Nicholas F., 2012. Artworks Are Not Valuable for Their Own Sake. *The Journal of Aesthetics and Art Criticism*, 70 (3), 271–80.

Stephen, James Fitzjames, 1857. *Saturday Review*. In: Collins, Philip, ed., 1997 [1986]. *Charles Dickens: The Critical Heritage*. Abingdon, UK: Routledge, 344–49.

Stolzfus, Ben, 1999. Hemingway's "After the Storm": A Lacanian Reading. In: Benson, J. J., ed., 1999. *New Critical Approaches to the Short Stories of Ernest Hemingway*. Durham, NC: Duke University Press, 48–57.

Suppes, Patrick, 2009. Rhythm and Meaning in Poetry. *Midwest Studies in Philosophy*, 33 (1), 159–66.

Thomson, Judith Jarvis, 1983. Parthood and Identity Across Time. *Journal of Philosophy*, 80 (4), 201–20.

Thomson-Jones, Katherine, 2002. Aesthetic and Ethical Mediocrity in Art. *Philosophical Papers*, 31 (2), 199–215.

———, 2005. Inseparable Insight: Reconciling Cognitivism and Formalism in Aesthetics. *The Journal of Aesthetics and Art Criticism*, 63 (4), 375–84.

Todorov, Tzvetan, 1966. The Typology of Detective Fiction. In: Todorov, T., 1977 [1971]. *The Poetics of Prose*. Translated by Richard Howard. Oxford: Blackwell, 42–52.

Tye, Michael, 1995. *Ten Problems of Consciousness*. Cambridge, MA: MIT Press.

Walsh, Dorothy, 1969. *Literature and Knowledge*. Middletown, CT: Wesleyan University Press.

Weitz, Morris, 1964 [1950]. *Philosophy of the Arts*. New York: Russell & Russell.

Wheeler, Michael, 2013. *English Fiction of the Victorian Period: 1830–1890*. Abingdon, UK: Routledge.

White, Hayden, 1980. The Value of Narrativity in the Representation of Reality. *Critical Inquiry*, 7 (1), 5–27.

Wiggins, David, 1968. On Being in the Same Place at the Same Time. *The Philosophical Review*, 77 (1), 90–95.

Wilde, Oscar, 1992 [1890]. *The Picture of Dorian Gray*. Ware, Herts: Wordsworth Classics.

Williams, Bernard, 2011 [1985]. *Ethics and the Limits of Philosophy*. London: Routledge.

Wilson, Catherine, 1983. Literature and Knowledge. *Philosophy*, 58 (226), 489–96.

Wimsatt, W. K., 1954. *The Verbal Icon: Studies in the Meaning of Poetry*. Lexington: University Press of Kentucky.

Wordsworth, William, 1815. *Poems of the Imagination*. In: Wordsworth, William: *Poems by William Wordsworth: Including Lyrical Ballads, and the Miscellaneous Pieces of the Author. Volume I*. [e-book] London: Longman, Hurst, Rees, Orme, and Brown, 297–337. Available at: Community Books, https://archive.org/details/poemsbywilliamwo02word [Accessed 28 December 2015].

Wroe, Nicholas, 2001. Fiction's Great Outlaw, *The Guardian*, 6 January. Available at: http://www.guardian.co.uk/books/2001/jan/06/fiction.petercarey [Accessed 22 December 2015].

Zamir, Tzachi, 2007. *Double Vision: Moral Philosophy and Shakespearean Drama*. Princeton, NJ: Princeton University Press.

Index

Aristotle, 39, 40, 49, 64, 84, 106, 114, 119, 121
Attridge, Derek, xi, 11, 17, 21, 23, 28n68, 48, 69, 75, 82, 90n23, 111, 132n28, 148; singularity, 72–73, 78; staging, 73–75, 85, 90n29, 90n30, 90n33, 91n34, 115, 139; value, 120–122, 130
the argument from literary thickness, viii–ix, 129–130
Auster, Paul, 114–115, 131n7
autonomy of literature, 21

Beardsley, Monroe C., 14, 21, 22, 83, 132n34
Beevor, Antony, 111–112, 113, 115, 126
Bell, Clive, 21, 22, 29
Belsey, Catherine, 16, 130
Biss, Mavis, 40
Blackburn, Simon, 94–95
Bradley, A.C., 21, 22, 47, 48, 54, 57, 64, 66n21, 82, 83, 90n23, 95; anti-realism 23, 141; form-content unity, 48, 49, 50–52, 53, 56, 58–60, 61–62, 65, 66n27, 69–70, 72–74, 75, 78, 90n30, 95; "Poetry for Poetry's Sake" lecture, ix, 50, 148
Brooks, Cleanth, 22, 82, 83
Brooks, Peter, 71, 72, 115, 131n7
Budd, Malcolm, 15, 66n22, 93, 111, 117–119, 123–124, 124–125, 125

Carey, Peter, 1; *True History of the Kelly Gang*, 1–6, 25n7
Carroll, Noël, viii, ix, 14, 18, 19, 22, 24, 25, 29, 29–33, 33–36, 98, 123, 124–125, 126, 132n43, 133, 133–139, 140–141, 142, 147
Coetzee, J.M., 69, 92n80; *Foe*, 139; "The Lives of Animals", 15, 20, 84–89, 102, 106, 126, 127, 128, 133, 140, 141, 142, 145, 146

Danto, Arthur C., 93, 97, 104
Derrida, Jacques, 21, 22, 37, 45n27, 73, 85, 92n80, 97, 146
Dickens, Charles, 25, 29, 38, 42, 43, 78, 138–139, 142; *Bleak House* , 78, 79, 138; *Great Expectations* , 34, 133, 134, 135; *Hard Times* , 76, 138, 141, 143, 145, 147, 149n7; *Oliver Twist* , 76–77, 79, 95, 105, 106, 107, 119, 140
Dickie, George, 12, 21, 31, 80, 116
Doniger, Wendy, 84, 89, 128
Dorsey, Dale, 8, 10

Eaton, A.W., 19
Eaton, Marcia Muelder, 142, 145
Eldridge, Richard, 21, 22
Elgin, Catherine Z., 18, 80
Eliot, T. S., 67n52, 147; "Gerontion", 55–56, 77, 95, 107, 140
extrinsic value, 9

157

Fabb, Nigel, 62, 70
Final Value, 10
Fishman, Solomon, 54, 67n53
formal axis, 107
Frye, Northrop, 57

Gaskin, Richard, 18, 24, 48, 65n8, 93, 95,
    97–98, 101, 103, 106, 108, 110n46,
    119, 120, 134
Gaut, Berys, 48
Gibson, John, xi, 18, 21, 22, 48, 67n42,
    67n53, 90n29, 91n45, 109n20, 130
Goldie, Peter, 71, 72
Goldman, Alan H., 24, 119–120, 122,
    131n10, 131n23
Goodman, Nelson, 107–81
Gutmann, Amy, 84

Harpham, Geoffrey Galt, 37, 146
Havard, John C., 144
Heidegger, Martin, 54, 59, 66n41
Hemingway, Ernest, 82, 132n45; *For
    Whom the Bell Tolls*, 15, 20, 102, 111,
    112–113, 115–116, 119, 122, 126, 127
Hirsch, David A., 143
Homer, 114
Hume, David, 121, 131n26
Hutcheson, Francis, 16, 21, 30, 131n26

instrumental value, 10
intrinsic value, 9

Jefferson, D. W., 138
Johnson, Samuel, 16, 24, 83
Joyce, James, vii; *Ulysses*, vii, 11, 70, 81,
    149

Kant, Immanuel, 16–17, 21, 30, 65n4, 121,
    131n26
Kieran, Matthew, 137, 143, 149n2
Kivy, Peter, 18, 47, 49, 58–65, 65n4,
    67n68, 68n69, 68n73, 89, 93, 94
Korsgaard, Christine, 8, 9, 10, 15

Lamarque, Peter, xi, 21, 23, 47, 58, 69, 89,
    91n35, 93, 98–99, 108n7, 115, 130n3,
    132n34, 134, 135, 148; aboutness, 95,
    96, 107, 110n47, 137; form-content
    inseparability, 51, 52, 57, 62–63,

64–65, 118; narrative opacity, 75,
    77–78; work identity, 11, 12, 78, 79
Larkin, Philip, 100, 102
Lavender, William, 115, 131n7
Leavis, F.R., 24, 83, 110n40, 143
Leighton, Angela, 54
Levinson, Jerrold, 10, 80, 91n55, 123
literary cognitivism, 18
literary moralism, 20
literary thickness, 95, 117
Lynn, David H., 84

Magnell, Thomas, 8
Mill, John Stuart, 9
Milton, John, 20, 51–52, 53, 70
Mole, Christopher, 100, 109n28

Nabokov, Vladimir, 20, 82, 83, 141
Narrative Thickness, 78
Nussbaum, Martha C., viii, ix, 24, 25, 29,
    37–40, 41–44, 45n27, 45n29, 46n45,
    103, 133, 142–146, 147–148

Olsen, Stein Haugom, 11, 12, 16, 17, 21,
    80, 91n35, 95, 96, 98–99, 101, 103,
    107, 108n7, 110n47, 115, 121, 135,
    137, 147

Pater, Walter, 21, 47–48
Pittock, Malcolm, 138–139
Plato, 9, 16, 24, 48, 63, 65n4, 83, 84
poetic thickness, 58
Posner, Richard A., 21, 37, 41, 46n45,
    92n72, 147
principle of functionality, 115

Quine, W.V.O., 75

Rabinowicz, Wlodec, 9, 10
Reisz, Matthew, 148
Repp, Charles, 83, 142
Ribeiro, Anna Christina, 54, 67n53, 70
Richards, I.A., 21, 47, 48, 49, 53–54,
    55–56, 56, 57, 59, 65, 67n53, 142
Ricks, Christopher, 101, 102–100, 103,
    109n22
Riffaterre, Michael, 21, 93, 95, 96–97, 98,
    104–105, 105, 106, 107, 108, 113, 128
Rønnow-Rasmussen, Toni, 9, 10

Rowe, M.W., 99, 100, 101, 101–103, 134
Ryle, Gilbert, 94, 98

Scruton, Roger, 21, 24, 116
Searle, John R., 93, 105, 140
Sidgwick, Henry, 16
Sidney, Sir Philip, 16, 24, 27n40, 83
Smuts, Aaron, 83
Stang, Nicholas F., 123–125, 126
substantive axis, 107
Suppes, Patrick, 54

Thomson-Jones, Katherine, 18, 24, 50, 51,
    97, 145

Todorov, Tzvetan, 22, 71, 114–115

Weitz, Morris, 18, 47, 48–50, 65n2, 66n19,
    67n53
White, Hayden, 71–72, 90n17
Wiggins, David, 73
Wilde, Oscar, 21, 21–22
Williams, Bernard, 94
Wilson, Catherine, 18, 19, 24, 98, 134, 147
Wordsworth, William, 131n26; "Yew
    Trees", 96–97, 98, 105, 108n9, 122,
    140

About the Author

Rafe McGregor is Associate Lecturer at the University of York's Centre for Lifelong Learning. He specialises in aesthetics and ethics, synthesising both analytic and critical approaches. His publications include papers in the *Australasian Journal of Philosophy*, *British Journal of Aesthetics*, and *Orbis Litterarum*.